EAST ASIA BEFORE THE WEST

Contemporary Asia in the World

Contemporary Asia in the World

David C. Kang and Victor D. Cha, Editors

This series aims to address a gap in the public-policy and scholarly discussion of Asia. It seeks to promote books and studies that are on the cutting edge of their respective disciplines or in the promotion of multidisciplinary or interdisciplinary research but that are also accessible to a wider readership. The editors seek to showcase the best scholarly and public-policy arguments on Asia from any field, including politics, history, economics, and cultural studies.

Beyond the Final Score: The Politics of Sport in Asia, Victor D. Cha, 2008
The Power of the Internet in China: Citizen Activism Online, Guobin Yang, 2009
China and India: Prospects for Peace, Jonathan Holslag, 2010
India, Pakistan, and the Bomb: Debating Nuclear Stability in South Asia, Šumit Ganguly and
     S. Paul Kapur, 2010
Living with the Dragon: How the American Public Views the Rise of China, Benjamin I. Page and
     Tao Xie, 2010
Harmony and War: Confucian Culture and Chinese Power Politics, Yuan-Kang Wang, 2011
Strong Society, Smart State: The Rise of Public Opinion in China's Japan Policy, James Reilly,
     2012
Asia's Space Race: National Motivations, Regional Rivalries, and International Risks, James Clay
     Moltz, 2012
Never Forget National Humiliation: Historical Memory in Chinese Politics and Foreign Relations,
     Zheng Wang, 2012

EAST ASIA
BEFORE THE WEST

Five Centuries of Trade and Tribute

DAVID C. KANG

COLUMBIA UNIVERSITY PRESS   *New York*

COLUMBIA UNIVERSITY PRESS
Publishers Since 1893
NEW YORK   CHICHESTER, WEST SUSSEX

Library of Congress Cataloging-in-Publication Data
    Kang, David C. (David Chan-oong), 1965–
      East Asia before the west : five centuries of trade and tribute / David C. Kang.
        p. cm. — (Contemporary Asia in the world)
      Includes bibliographical references and index.
        ISBN 978-0-231-15318-8 (cloth : alk. paper)—ISBN 978-0-231-15319-5 (pbk. : alk. paper)—
ISBN 978-0-231-52674-6 (e-book)
        1. East Asia—Commerce—History.   2. East Asia—Foreign relations.   3. East Asia—
      Politics and government .   I. Title.   II. Series.

      HF3820.5.K36 2010
      327.5009'03—dc22

                                                                              2010008583

⊗

Cover image: ©istockphoto

References to Internet Web sites (URLs) were accurate at the time of writing. Neither the author nor Columbia University Press is responsible for URLs that may have expired or changed since the manuscript was prepared.

For Emily Yejin Kang

CONTENTS

ILLUSTRATIONS AND TABLES

PREFACE

THIS IS A BOOK of political science, not history. The key element of historical research is the use of primary documents, and aside from an occasional visit to the library, I did not spend years in dusty archives in Hanoi, Tokyo, Beijing, and Seoul. Rather, I relied upon a careful reading of the most recent and important secondary historical literature about East Asian international relations, trade, and domestic politics. My aim was to utilize these historical works to inform our knowledge about East Asia and our theories of international relations, with the aim of answering one seemingly simple question: how did international relations function in East Asia from the fourteenth to the nineteenth centuries?

This interest grew out of my increasing frustration with the types of theories that we use to explain international relations and the types of empirical cases that international-relations scholars use to test those theories. Overwhelmingly, these theories and cases come from European history, and my own research on contemporary East Asia led me to conclude that many of those theories performed poorly in explaining the current relations in East Asia. The result was a book, *China Rising*, that could be considered the first part of my attempt to make sense of East Asian international relations. I focused on explaining why contemporary East Asia is more stable than many scholars had predicted and emphasized that the goals, beliefs, and national identities of East Asian states were more important to explaining their relations than was the balance of power or their level of economic interdependence.

This book could be considered the second part of this research project, although it was conceived independently of *China Rising*. Having explored contemporary East Asia, I began to look more carefully at how East Asia developed and what its historical international relations had been like. In both my undergraduate and graduate education, I had learned about the Spanish Armada, the Holy Roman Empire, Napoleon, and the European experience with war, state formation, economic development, and cultural achievement. In contrast, until I started this research, I had never been exposed to any scholarship about the Chinese tributary system or Japanese foreign relations in the Tokugawa era, and indeed I had never even heard.of the Imjin War. Especially mortifying is that I am considered a scholar of East Asia, yet I knew almost nothing earlier than its twentieth-century politics. I began to rectify my lack of knowledge about East Asian history, and the more I read, the more fascinated I became.

Furthermore, as I read the historiography of the region, I came to notice two broad trends in the literature. First, almost all the research conducted on this time period consisted of either single-country case studies or bilateral case studies, such as books that explore China-Mongol relations or Korea-Japan relations. There was almost no research that looked at the region as a whole and attempted to discern broad patterns, similarities, and differences. The second trend I saw was a marked sense of nationalist historiography with a clear political purpose. All history, and indeed all writing, is of course aimed at some purpose. But the twentieth century—with the arrival of the West and its norms, institutions, and ideas—created an enormous challenge to the existing worldviews of East Asian nations. In their struggle to create or maintain cultural, political, and ideological stability, East Asian writers, politicians, and governments engaged in a project of nationalist history writing aimed overall at elevating their countries using the standards set by the West. Writers and historians claimed in particular the equality and sovereignty of their own countries, wrote glorious histories that emphasized martial and military exploits, and projected backward a coherence that was only loosely related to the reality of their histories. These trends led me further and further into the past, in an attempt to take as seriously as possible the relations at the time and to probe for ways to provide a coherent view of the region.

This book is the result of that research. In this book, I explore how the four main states of historical East Asia—Korea, Vietnam, Japan, and China—conducted their foreign diplomatic, economic, and cultural relations with one another. I also contrast the experience of these Sinicized states with their relations with the nomadic tribes of the northern and western frontiers, arguing that cultural explanations account for the remarkable stability of the East Asian international order just as much as military or economic explanations do.

In this way, I hope this book also contributes to viewing East Asia actually as a region, with many different states, and begins to move our conceptualization of the region past the tired contrast of "China" and "the West." As such, this research is more focused on the experience of the states surrounding China than on China itself. The historical and current centrality of China in East Asia is simply a fact of life neither to be welcomed nor feared. Rather, I am much more interested in how the smaller East Asian states react to and deal with the imposing presence of China in the region, and the bulk of my work has always focused on the smaller states, such as Korea, Japan, the Philippines, Vietnam, or Malaysia.

This research has germinated over almost a decade, and it will be impossible to thank everyone whose comments or insights over the years helped form and shape the arguments in this book. However, a number of people generously gave of their time and intellectual energy to read part of this book, and I would like to thank them here. Particularly important has been my friendship with Victor Cha, whose comments, support, and encouragement ever since I first began this project have woven themselves into many of my own writings. As a colleague and friend he is a rare combination of energy, vision, and intellect. Special thanks are also due to Gari Ledyard and Bruce Cumings, for generously providing extensive insights on numerous occasions and for helping to significantly add nuance and subtlety to my understanding of East Asian history. Liam Kelley and James Anderson read many chapters and significantly shaped my view of Vietnam in particular and the tribute system in general. My wonderful editor, Anne Routon, continues to set a high standard for me. Anne's intellectual contributions about how to shape the argument and present this book over numerous drafts were essential to my thinking and writing.

Peter Katzenstein's energy in putting together a wonderful series of panels at APSA and ultimately an edited book concerning civilizational politics allowed me to hone my ideas with many other talented people working on the same subject, including Patrick Jackson, James Kurth, Susanne Rudolph, and Bruce Lawrence. Other scholars who commented on parts of this manuscript, and whose unselfish sharing of their intellectual capital has doubtless strengthened this book, include Rawi Abdelal, Bruce Batten, Stephen Brooks,

Ian Clark, Bridget Coggins, Pamela Crossley, Gang Deng, John Duncan, Evelyn Goh, Ian Hurd, Iain Johnston, Kirk Larsen, Richard Ned Lebow, Dave Leheny, Jiyoung Lee, Sebastian Mainville, Dan Nexon, Gregory Noble, Nicholas Onuf, T. V. Paul, Eugene Y. Park, John Ravenhill, Richard Samuels, Allan Stam, Kenneth Swope, Ming Wan, Alexander Wendt, John E. Wills, William Wohlforth, Brantly Womack, Gang Zhao, and the Dartmouth IR working group. Earlier versions of the argument in this book were presented at McGill, Georgetown, and Princeton Universities, the Harvard Business School, the Woodrow Wilson Center, Claremont College, and the 2008 annual convention of the International Studies Association.

EAST ASIA BEFORE THE WEST

1 THE PUZZLE

War and Peace in East Asian History

Outside are insignia, shown in state;
But here are sweet incense-clouds, quietly ours.
. . . Suzhou is famed as a center of letters;
And all you writers, coming here,
Prove that the name of a great land
Is made by better things than wealth.
— WEI YINGWU (C. 737–791)

Introduction

In 1592, the Japanese general Hideyoshi invaded Korea, transporting over 160,000 troops on approximately seven hundred ships. He eventually mobilized a half million troops, intending to continue on to conquer China.[1] Over sixty thousand Korean soldiers, eventually supported by over one hundred thousand Ming Chinese forces, defended the Korean peninsula. After six years of war, the Japanese retreated, and Hideyoshi died, having failed spectacularly in his quest.

The Imjin War "easily dwarfed those of their European contemporaries" and involved men and material five to ten times the scale of the Spanish Armada of 1588, which has been described as the "greatest military force ever assembled" in Renaissance Europe.[2] That in itself should be sufficient cause for international-relations scholars to explore the war's causes and consequences. Yet even more important for the study of international relations is that Hideyoshi's invasion of Korea marked the *only* military conflict between Japan, Korea, and China for over six centuries. For three hundred years both before and after the Imjin War, Japan was a part of the Chinese world. That the three major powers in East Asia—and indeed, much of the rest of the system—could peacefully coexist for such an extended span of time, despite having the military and technological capability to wage war on a massive scale, raises the question of why stability was the norm in East Asian international relations.

In fact, from 1368 to 1841—from the founding of the Ming dynasty to the Opium wars between Britain and China—there were only two wars between China, Korea, Vietnam, and Japan: China's invasion of Vietnam (1407–1428) and Japan's invasion of Korea (1592–1598). Apart from those two episodes, these four major territorial and centralized states developed and maintained peaceful and long-lasting relations with one another, and the more powerful these states became, the more stable were their relations. China was clearly the dominant military, cultural, and economic power in the system, but its goals did not include expansion against its established neighboring states. By the fourteenth century, these Sinicized states had evolved a set of international rules and institutions known as the "tribute system," with China clearly the hegemon and operating under a presumption of inequality, which resulted in a clear hierarchy and lasting peace.[3] These smaller Sinicized states of the region emulated Chinese practices and to varying degrees accepted Chinese centrality. Cultural, diplomatic, and economic relations between the states in the region were both extensive and intensive.[4]

Built on a mix of legitimate authority and material power, the tribute system provided a normative social order that also contained credible commitments by China not to exploit secondary states that accepted its authority. This order was explicit and formally unequal, but it was also informally equal: secondary states were not allowed to call themselves nor did they believe themselves equal with China, yet they had substantial latitude in their actual behavior. China stood at the top of the hierarchy, and there was no intellectual challenge to the rules of the game until the late nineteenth century and the arrival of the Western powers. Korean, Vietnamese, and even Japanese elites consciously copied Chinese institutional and discursive practices in part to craft stable relations with China, not to challenge them.

The East Asian historical experience was markedly different from the European historical experience, both in its fundamental rules and in the level of conflict among the major actors. The European "Westphalian" system emphasized a formal equality between states and balance-of-power politics; it was also marked by incessant interstate conflict. The East Asian "tribute system" emphasized formal inequality between states and a clear hierarchy, and it was marked by centuries of stability among the core participants. Although there has been a tendency to view the European experience as universal, studying the East Asian historical experience as an international system both allows us to ask new questions about East Asia and gives us a new perspective on our own contemporary geopolitical system. Much of world history has involved hegemons building hierarchies and establishing order, and studying these relations in different historical contexts promises to provide new insights into contemporary issues.

Although anarchy—the absence of an overarching government—is a constant in international life, international-relations scholars are increasingly aware that "every international system or society has a set of rules or norms that define actors and appropriate behavior,"[5] which Christopher Reus-Smit calls the "elementary rules of practice that states formulate to solve the coordination and collaboration problems associated with coexistence under anarchy."[6] Although scholars have expended considerable effort in studying early modern East Asian history, rarely have they explored it from the perspective of an international system.

Indeed, we tend to take for granted the current set of rules, ideas, and institutions as the natural or inevitable way that countries interact with one another: passports that define citizenship, nation-states as the only legitimate political actor allowed to conducted diplomatic relations, borders between nation-states that are measured to the inch, and, perhaps most centrally, the idea of balance-of-power politics as the basic and enduring pattern of international relations. After all, this characterizes much of contemporary international relations.

Yet this current international system is actually a recent phenomenon in the scope of world history. These international rules and norms arose among European powers only beginning in the seventeenth century. In 1648, the great powers of Europe signed a series of treaties creating a set of rules governing international relations that became known as the "peace of Westphalia." Over the next few centuries, the European powers gradually regularized, ritualized, and institutionalized these Westphalian definitions of sovereignty, diplomacy, nationality, and commercial exchange. For example, although diplomats and merchants occasionally carried various types of identifying credentials before the nineteenth century, it was not until 1856 that the U.S. Congress passed a law giving the Department of State the sole power to issue an official documentation of citizenship, and only after World War I did passports become commonplace.[7]

One outgrowth of this particular Western system of international relations is that equality is taken for granted both as a normative goal and as an underlying and enduring reality of international politics. In this current system, all nation-states are considered equal and are granted identical rights no matter how large the disparity in wealth or size. In fact, the notion of equality is deeply woven into our modern thinking about domestic rights, international rights, and individual "rights of man," from rationalist French philosophy to the U.S. Declaration of Independence, which "holds these truths to be self-evident . . . that all men are created equal."

In international relations, the idea of equality is most clearly expressed in the belief that the balance of power is a fundamental process: too powerful a state will threaten other states and cause them to band together to oppose the powerful state. This idea—that international relations are most stable when states are roughly equal—conditions much of our thinking about how international politics functions. In this way, the European experience, in which a number of similarly sized states engaged in centuries of incessant interstate conflict, is now presumed to be the universal norm. Thus, Kenneth Waltz's confident assertion that "hegemony leads to balance" and has done so "through all of the centuries we can contemplate" is perhaps the default proposition in international relations.[8]

But these patterns, ideas, and institutions are actually specific ideas from a specific time and place, an Enlightenment notion from the eighteenth century, and there is as much inequality as equality in international relations, both now and in the past. In fact, there are actually two enduring patterns to international relations, not just the balance of power: the opposite idea—that inequality can be stable—also exists. Known as "hegemony," the idea is that under certain conditions, a dominant state can stabilize the system by providing leadership. Both equality and inequality could be stable under certain conditions and unstable under other conditions. Important for us is to realize that even "anarchic" systems differ, and different anarchic systems develop different rules, norms, and institutions that help structure and guide behavior.

Because the European system of the past few centuries eventually developed into a set of rules, institutions, and norms now used by all countries around the world, we have tended to assume both that this was natural and inevitable and that all international systems behave the same way. With the increasing importance and presence of East Asian states in the world, it has been common to apply ideas and models based on the European experience in order to explain Asia. For example, Aaron Friedberg's famous 1994 article compared modern Asia to the past five hundred years of European history, concluding that "for better or for worse, Europe's past could be Asia's future."[9] As Susanne Rudolph has observed, "there appeared to be one race, and the West had strung the tape at the finish line for others to break."[10] Few scholars have taken East Asia on its own terms and not as a reflection of Europe, and few have crafted theories that can explain East Asia as it actually was.[11]

What History Can Tell Us About Today

We care about the research presented in this book both for how it might broaden our understanding of the past and for what it might mean for contemporary issues in East Asia. Knowing East Asian history helps us contextualize and make sense of the region's economic dynamism and interconnected relations of the past half century. Today's East Asian system is often discussed as if it emerged fully formed, like Athena from the head of Zeus, in the post–World War II and postcolonial era. However, as this book will show, if anything, many East Asian countries have been deeply economically integrated and interconnected, geographically defined, and centrally administered political units for much longer than those of Europe. To explain East Asian international relations in the twenty-first century, we might begin by exploring how the region got to where it is today.

The question of history's effect on the present comes in two ways: does history, either forward or backward, affect contemporary issues today? History "forward" is the typical way we think about history: time moves linearly from past to present, and what came before affects what comes after. In this way, we might ask what are the historical roots of the contemporary relations in East Asia: do the history, culture, beliefs, or goals of East Asian states reflect to any degree their evolution and formation over time?

However, although history moves forward, we also learn about history "backward," looking over our shoulder. And this backward view of history can be consequential for relations today. For a myriad of reasons, states, peoples, and leaders emphasize and glorify certain historical events, ignore or denigrate other events, and craft stories about their past. Unsurprisingly, contemporary nation-states also often disagree with one another over these stories about their shared pasts. Crafting a glorious history is central to modern national life, and disputes between countries over how history is remembered and taught is really a dispute over *whose side of the story gets told*. Put this way, we might also ask whether contemporary East Asian states care about and deal with one another in ways that privilege certain historical interpretations over others.

History forward will explore whether there are any roots that help us understand today's East Asian states and what they care about. That is, the historical countries studied in this book are recognizably the same major powers in East Asia today. And, as the twenty-first century begins, there is immense interest and concern about whether China and Japan can develop a stable relationship, whether a "rising China" will destabilize the region, and whether the Korean peninsula can finally find a peaceful solution to its division. Thus, understanding and explaining past stability may be a critical step both in explaining why East Asia is stable today and for predicting how the region will evolve.

Furthermore, many Western views reveal a striking ambiguity about East Asia. On the one hand, many of our international-relations theories, and indeed popular perception, see East Asians as essentially identical to Westerners in goals, attitudes, and beliefs. Some argue that the homogenizing influence of globalization and modernization has made us all the same and has rendered geography, history, and culture essentially irrelevant, an argument perhaps best popularized by Thomas Friedman's book *The World Is Flat*. Indeed, a basic starting point of much social-science theorizing is the universal applicability of models derived from the European historical experience.

On the other hand, our perceptions of East Asia are ambiguous, and it is certainly worth asking whether the Westphalian ideas have completely replaced older ideas in East Asia. Some scholars see a unique Chinese strategic culture; others wonder whether China can truly be a responsible member of the international community. Whether East Asian countries actually share the same basic worldviews as do Western countries is not just a diplomatic issue—for example, the rapid economic emergence of first Japan and then the other East Asian economies spawned an intense debate over the causes and consequences of that growth, and two decades ago influential books such as *The Enigma of Japanese Power* argued that Japan's economic success was fundamentally different from that of the West.[12] Today, the plethora of business-school textbooks claiming to teach how to do business in Japan or China reveals that many continue think that those societies and economies operate in different ways than do Western ones. There exists a strong undercurrent of belief that East Asian life, society, and business is fundamentally different than its Western counterparts.

If we are all the same now, and all states and peoples act and perceive the same whether they are East Asian or European, there is probably little to be gained from studying history. However, if how we got to where we are is important, then an ahistorical view of modern East Asia, one that merely looks at current capabilities and ignores the evolution of these states, is likely to be misleading. Although much has changed since the fourteenth century, it is worth asking whether and how states' and peoples' interests and beliefs have changed and how they inform their goals and beliefs today.[13] Whether the past has any bearing on the present is an open question, to be sure, but as this book will show, we ignore history at the risk of not truly understanding why the region operates today in the way that it does.

What about history backward? East Asia today is more stable, prosperous, and peaceful than at any time since the arrival of the Western colonial powers in the late nineteenth century. Few states fear for their survival, and most states have experienced rapid economic and social modernization. Yet the East Asian region is not as stable as is Europe, and some enduring and vexing disputes remain between countries in the region. Indeed, the most enduring East Asian disputes are largely about various versions of how history is remembered and characterized in the present. What Taiwan's status is, disputes between Japan and all of its neighbors over maritime borders, and other maritime issues such as the ownership of the Spratly Islands continue to plague East Asia, and these are often presented in the popular press, by governments, and even by scholars as historical disputes.[14] But they are actually current political disputes, not historical issues.[15]

That is, many of these disputes over uninhabited rocks and maritime boundaries are a result of the modern, Westphalian system that all states now unquestioningly accept—after all, five hundred years ago, nobody cared about the uninhabited rocks in the middle of the ocean except the fishermen who tried to avoid wrecking upon them. Thus, working backward into time to see what ancient kings thought of these islands is useless, because they did not think anything about them at the time. The rulers of historical states in East Asia were concerned with other territorial and border issues, to be sure, as this book will show. But the contemporary preoccupation in many East Asian countries over historical issues is really a modern political matter, as leaders and peoples attempt to craft a glorious identity that celebrates and elevates their particular country. This book helps provide a better historical context for these putatively historical disputes and places the cause and solution for their enduring disputation squarely in the contemporary era.

It is as important to explain how the past affects the present as it is to realize that we in the present create myths and folktales about the past. Much of the historiography about the region needs to be taken in context. "Nationalist" writings and histories in many of these countries during the twentieth century sought to emphasize or elevate the glory or equality of their own particular country's origins, often in response to colonialism and independence.[16] To the extent that history has become a captive of the modern nation-state, we should be wary of accepting too easily these nationalist histories about a wonderful imagined past, and we should be aware that the solution to historical disputes is in the present, not the past. What this book attempts to do is view history without nationalist lenses, to explore how relations worked at the time.

Themes in This Book

This book explains the historical East Asian international system and contains three overarching themes. First, almost all the actors in East Asia accepted a set of unquestioned rules and institutions about the basic ways in which international relations worked. Known as the *tribute system*, and involving in particular a hierarchic rank ordering based on status, these rules were taken for granted as the way in which political actors interacted with one another. Largely derived from Chinese ideas over the centuries, by the fourteenth century these ideas and institutions had become the rules of the game. This does not mean, however, that the tribute system was identically and consistently applied by every state in every situation—far from it. Like the basic rules and institutions of the Westphalian system today, different states modified, abandoned, and used these ideas in a flexible manner depending on situation and circumstance.[17] The tribute system did, however, form the core organizing principles of the system, and these principles endured for centuries as the basis for international interaction throughout East Asia.

Within this system, cultural achievement in the form of status was as important a goal as was military or economic power. The status hierarchy and rank order were key components of this system, and ranking did not necessarily derive from political, economic, or military power. China was the hegemon, and its status derived from its cultural achievements and social recognition by other political actors, not from its raw size or its military or economic power. All the political units in the system played by these rules. Even political units that rejected Confucian notions of cultural achievement—such as the nomads—accepted the larger rules of the game, the way hierarchy was defined, and the manner in which international relations was conducted, and they defined their own ideals and cultures in opposition to the dominant ideas and institutions of the time.[18] Movement up and down the hierarchy occurred within the rules, and it was not until the arrival of Western powers in the nineteenth century that there appeared an alternative set of rules for how to conduct international relations.

Second, within this larger set of rules and institutions existed a smaller *Confucian society* made up of China, Korea, Vietnam, and Japan. I use the term "society" to mean a self-conscious political grouping where shared ideas, norms, and interests determine membership in the group. Their interests may not be identical, and indeed the goals of the group members can often conflict, but they share the same basic understandings about what the criteria for membership in the group are, the values and norms of the group, and how status is measured. These four states accepted Chinese ideas and were culturally similar, and although many other political units existed in the system and used the larger rules of the game, it was essentially these four states that formed an inner circle based largely on Confucian ideas.

Within this Confucian society, Japan was the liminal—or boundary—case. In fact, Japan sat at the edge of the society of Sinicized states, was the most hesitant about accepting Chinese ideas and Chinese dominance, and was the most interested in finding alternative means of situating itself in relation to the other states. Although deriving many of their domestic ideas, innovations, system of writing, and cultural knowledge from China, the Japanese were always skeptical of China's central position. Indeed, Japanese scholars and officials often made a distinction between Chinese civilization, which they revered, and the Chinese state, which they often held in contempt. Yet even while the Japanese were hesitant and skeptical about viewing themselves as a Confucian, Sinicized state, it remained far more Confucianized than other political units in the region such as Siam or the Mongols, and, notably, Japan militarily challenged the existing order only once in five hundred years.

Finally, these rules and norms were consequential for diplomacy, war, trade, and cultural exchange between political units in East Asia. Far more than a thin veneer of meaningless social lubricants, the tribute system and its ideas and institutions formed the basis for relations between states. The tribute system, with its inherent notions of inequality and its many rules and responsibilities for managing relations among unequals, provided a set of tools for resolving conflicting goals and interests short of resorting to war.

In fact, although there has recently been a great deal of historiography about the early modern East Asian era, little scholarship has focused directly on war, and there is also almost no work that puts nomads and East Asian states in a comparative context, leading to a view of China as an "empire without neighbors."[19] In this way, the research presented in this book extends Iain Johnston's pioneering work about the sources of Chinese grand strategy, where he identifies two deeply enduring Chinese worldviews that encompass central paradigmatic assumptions about the nature of conflict, the inevitability of violence, and the enemy. Calling one "Confucian" and the other "parabellum," he argues that China and nomads operated in a parabellum strategic culture that considers that "the best way of dealing with security threats is to eliminate them through the use of force."[20]

Yet important as Johnston's work is, he does not address a key issue: why those threats arose mainly from nomads on China's northern and western frontiers instead of arising from the powerful states to the east and south such as Korea, Japan, and Vietnam. These Sinic states, which shared China's "Confucian" worldviews, had far more stable and peaceful relations with China. Early modern East Asia, like nineteenth-century Europe, operated in two very different international societies and was based on two different sets of rules: one that included the Sinicized states and one that regulated relations with the "uncivilized" nomadic world.[21]

Indeed, my central claim of East Asian stability does not imply that violence was rare in East Asia. There was plenty of violence, but it tended to occur between China and the seminomadic peoples on its northern and western borders, not between China and the other Sinicized states. This violence occurred in the form of border skirmishes, piracy, and the slow expansion and frontier consolidation of some states (such as China) at the expense of nonstate units. Although the nomads were generally more of a nuisance than a threat to China, when they managed to form statelike structures, they could become powerful and dangerous to the Sinic states. These nomads had vastly different worldviews, political structures, and cultures than the Sinicized states, and although they accepted the more fundamental aspects of the tribute system, they resisted Confucian cultural ideas, and thus crafting enduring or stable relations with them was difficult and troublesome.

The nomads and the East Asian states both operated within a unipolar system: China was the unquestioned and only superpower.[22] Yet China's relations with the nomads were characterized by war and instability, whereas its relations with the Sinicized states were characterized by peace and stability. The simple fact of Chinese military and economic predominance cannot account for both of these outcomes. Furthermore, although the states accepted Chinese authority, the nomads did not.[23] What this book demonstrates is that there was a hierarchical relationship in place in the context of China and the East Asian states that was generated by a common culture defined by a Confucian worldview. These Sinic states possessed a shared sense of legitimacy that presupposes, in the context of Confucianism, that relations operate within an accepted hierarchy. This book helps clarify the distinction between an international system based only on material power and an international society based on culture.

Perhaps most important is to ask why China had endemic conflicts with some groups such as the nomads but almost none with other states such as Vietnam and Korea. Most scholarship on war in historical East Asia has—naturally enough—focused on where the fighting was; that is, it has focused on China-nomad relations. From the popular imagination, as reflected in movies such as *Mongol*, to much more serious academic works, such as Iain Johnston's superb book, we find the overwhelming attention to war in East Asia emphasizing nomads and their relations to China. But we should also ask why some states did *not* fight—and, in fact, why war between the Sinic states was so unlikely as to be almost unthinkable is just as important a question as why war with the nomads was a constant possibility.

The Tribute System and Its Critics

This book's overarching argument about the stabilizing role of the tribute system, Chinese hegemony, and the hierarchy of early modern East Asia stands in contrast to three main ways in which scholars have generally viewed the tribute system. From the time of John Fairbank onward, scholars have generally viewed the tribute system as either functional or symbolic, or they have dismissed outright the idea of a tribute system. Yet although there was no eternal and unchanging tribute system that functioned the same way everywhere, the tribute system certainly existed and is worth taking seriously as an overarching set of rules that governed international relations at the time.

The functionalist view sees the tribute system as a set of arbitrary and somewhat comical rules that were merely a means by which states could trade with one another. That is, they view the institutions and beliefs of the early modern East Asian international system as merely a set of rationalizing conventions or rules that allow actors to coordinate or pursue their interests. A modern example of this is the agreement that all cars drive on the right side of the road: as long as some type of coordination occurs, the substance of the rules is relatively unimportant, and it is just as likely that everyone could agree that all cars should drive on the left side of the road. Viewing the tribute system as essentially functional, John Fairbank first popularized the notion that "tribute was a cloak for trade."[24] Arguing that tribute was "not exactly what it seemed," Fairbank saw the tribute system as an "ingenious vehicle" for the creation of trade between states.[25] James Hevia concludes: "Virtually all those who followed Fairbank [and Teng] faithfully reproduced what was an insistence upon seeing the tribute system as dualistic in nature."[26]

Other scholars view the tribute system as merely symbolic, as a substance-free set of acts that masked the underlying "real" international politics based on military power and commerce. This view sees the tribute system as unimportant to explaining the power politics that was "really" motivating East Asian states. In this view, secondary states engaging in the outward acts of hierarchy, emulation, and deference were at heart merely engaging in a rational cost-benefit calculation. This symbolic view of the tribute system sees the smaller states surrounding China as not powerful enough to actually deter or defeat China by the force of arms, and so rather than defy China and risk invasion and conquest, these smaller states chose the path of placating China culturally while inwardly seething with resentment and wishing they had the power to challenge their much larger neighbor.

For example, Keith Taylor has argued that "for several centuries, [Vietnam] was an independent kingdom posing as a tributary of the Chinese empire," and John Wills identifies the "appearances of the ceremonial supremacy of the Son of Heaven in the capital," thus emphasizing the distinction between the appearance and the reality of the tribute system.[27] In his review of this literature, Liam Kelley points out that some scholars have a hard time understanding unequal relationships, at least normatively, and thus attempt to "look beyond the 'rhetoric' of the tribute system in the hope of finding an understandable 'reality.' Surely there had to be a logical reason why foreign kingdoms accepted a position of inferiority in this relationship."[28]

Finally, a number of prominent scholars have challenged the tribute system's very existence. These scholars generally make two points. First, the tribute system was applied in so many different ways at different times that generalizing beyond any particular case makes a caricature of the actual history of the time. Second, they argue that projecting modern concepts backward into East Asian history makes no sense, and that the tribute system, states, and even the notion of a "Korea" or a "China" are meaningless in their proper historical context. For example, James Hevia warns that using ideas such as "China" or the "tribute system" results in "modernist models of behavior and institutional forms such as the state [that] are projected onto the past."[29] In his careful study of Vietnamese envoy writings, Liam Kelley avoids using "China" or "Vietnam," because those terms did not exist in antiquity, noting that "the names Vietnam and China are now laden with nationalistic concepts that evoke a world of ethnic boundaries and distinct cultures [which did not exist at the time]."[30] That is, Kelley argues that the cultural and ethnic boundaries that we see today were not there in the past, even though he agrees that political boundaries were definitely there.

These arguments are important, and we should take them seriously. However, one problem with the first two arguments—that the tribute system was either functional or symbolic—is that it asks us to dismiss and ignore quite a bit of what officials, scholars, and governments actually did and said at the time. And both these arguments have a number of logical problems. First, these arguments posit literally centuries of self-delusion on the part of Chinese officials. As James Hevia puts it, an emphasis on the tribute system as merely symbolic leads to a view of Chinese bureaucrats thus: "caught up in illusion, unable to rationalize beyond a certain point, China's bureaucrats can only distinguish between appearances and reality when the two mesh . . . when [they do not], Qing officials could do little more than respond defensively and cling to the illusions fostered by ceremonialism, while even the most clearheaded drifted unawares."[31]

Why would so much energy, time, thought, and money be expended on the tribute system if it were purely symbolic and believed in by no one, neither the Chinese nor the foreigners? Were Ming and Qing officials so blinded by their own ceremonial delusions that they could not see Vietnamese, Korean, Japanese, Mongolian, Siamese, and other envoys smirking at them as they went through these rituals? As this book will show, there is ample evidence that Korean, Vietnamese, and other envoys believed in what they were doing. Furthermore, rulers in secondary states such as Korea, Vietnam, and Japan used the basic institutional and discursive forms of the tribute system in their relations with one another. If the tribute system was merely a means of placating China, why would they have done so? In the case of relations between smaller states in the system, there was no need for the supposed symbolic deference to China. Perhaps most consequentially for these arguments, we are still left with the question of why there was so much stability in the system, particularly between the Sinic states. That is, the functionalist and symbolic views of the tribute system overlook one significant fact: these rules and rites were intimately involved with ordering diplomatic, cultural, economic, and political relations among a number of actors.

Perhaps more important is to ask whether the tribute system existed at all and whether we can usefully apply modern concepts such as states or institutions back into East Asian history. Indeed, as I will argue in this book, some of the contemporary disputes in East Asia over historical borders are truly ahistorical, because we have no evidence that rulers thought or cared about demarcating maritime borders until the twentieth century. So I am greatly in sympathy with being careful about projecting backward from the present.

However, other concepts, such as the tribute system, certainly existed and were used for centuries, and this book will show that one can reasonably make an argument that China, Korea, Vietnam, and even Japan were states as we think of them today—that is, as governments defined over territory with a monopoly over domestic violence. Furthermore, while political identities and notions of what it meant to be Korean or Vietnamese have certainly changed substantially over the years, and while much else has also changed in the past six hundred years, these political units conducted formal diplomatic relations with one another using a set of agreed-upon rules and institutions, and it is difficult to call this anything other than international relations. In fact, more nuanced studies and new interpretations actually only serve to underscore the centrality of the system for its participants. That is to say, we can easily acknowledge that they all saw and utilized the system in their own culturally specific ways, but that does not mean that they rejected the legitimacy of the system. As a result, we have no choice but to attempt to provide some type of general explanation and categorization for how relations worked at the time. At the same time, we should be careful to note that differences and exceptions occurred.

In sum, what few scholars have done is take the tribute system as a set of international rules and ideas in the same way that we explore the Westphalian international system that orders our contemporary world. If we do this, and if we ask what were the principles and institutions that guided international relations in historical East Asia and how did this affect the behavior of the units, we might take more seriously the norms, rules, and institutions embodied in the tribute system. In this way, I am concerned with explaining why the system worked the way that it did and showing how this affected relations among the states in the system. From this perspective, the tribute system was far more than just a simple choice between "war or tribute," and it ordered the way officials and scholars in smaller states, and in the Sinic states in particular, thought about and acted in their relations with the Chinese hegemon.

The Scope of This Study

When studying East Asia, it is sometimes seductive to claim that behavior is immutable, permanent, and unchanging from the ancient mists of time up to the present era. Yet East Asia has changed as much as any other part of the world: some traits have historical roots, others do not, and all are constantly evolving depending on the circumstance, situation, institutional constraints, political and economic exigencies, and a host of other factors. We should avoid making sweeping claims that present either an unbroken chronological continuity or an encompassing geographic component.

Chronologically, I focus on the era of the Ming and Qing Chinese dynasties up to the Opium wars between the United Kingdom and China (1368–1841)—early modern East Asia—because it represents the culmination of centuries of state building in East Asia, and at that point the East Asian international system was at its most complete and developed. The ideas and institutions in the international system developed over centuries in an uneven manner, and many of these ideas originally appeared over one thousand years earlier.

Perhaps the greatest contrast to this early modern era were the three centuries preceding it, which witnessed the breakdown of central control in China, the Mongol Yuan invasions, and widespread instability throughout the region.[32] Yet at the same time, the Yuan set the stage for the subsequent five centuries by reestablishing "centralized, unified rule in China, laying the foundation for the provinces of modern China . . . and restoring a single tax and legal system on the country."[33] Each era merits study in its own right, but it is important to explore one epoch carefully before beginning comparisons and to avoid careless conclusions and dubious claims: what was true in the seventeenth century may not have been true a millennium earlier. The Mongols invaded everybody from China and Japan to Persia and Poland and arose outside of the state system that I describe here.[34]

The geographical domain of East Asian international relations studied in this book focuses mainly on the four Sinicized states of China, Korea, Vietnam, Japan. These countries were the major actors in the system, and they constituted an international society that clearly understood the requirements for membership, how status is evaluated, and the rules of the game. The entire early modern East Asian region began with Manchuria in the north, the Pacific to the east, the mountains of Tibet to the west, and the nations of Thailand, Malaysia, and Indonesia to the south. Other political units that were sufficiently involved in the system to warrant discussion include the nomadic peoples to the north and west of China, Siam, Burma, the Philippines, the Ryukyu Islands, and Malaysia.

This book will trace and identify the contours of East Asia's international system from 1368 to 1841. I will concentrate on the four most consequential actors: China, Korea, Japan, and Vietnam, but I will also discuss the variety of other political units in the system, particularly the nomads to the north and west of China. The book first discusses the key concepts of hierarchy, hegemony, and status, as a way of clarifying the ideas that inform the rest of the book. Chapter 3 explores the nature of these Confucian states; chapter 4 discusses the diplomacy of the tribute system itself. Chapter 5 is concerned with war in East Asia; chapter 6 describes the extent of economic relations in the region. Chapter 7 compares these Confucianized East Asian states with the seminomadic peoples of the northern steppe, and chapter 8 concludes the book with some implications for the contemporary era.

2 IDEAS

Hierarchy, Status, and Hegemony

I love the name of honor more than I fear death.
— JULIUS CAESAR

THE THREE CONCEPTS that guide this book are *hierarchy*, *status*, and *hegemony*. Because they form the intellectual basis of the explanation for how early modern East Asian international relations functioned, we will spend some time discussing them. All three of these concepts are different aspects of the inequality in human life, and all three provide us insight into how inequality is expressed and maintained and into the ramifications of inequality for international life.

Hierarchy as an Organizing Principle

Following Richard Ned Lebow and William Wohlforth, among others, I define hierarchy as a *rank order* based on a particular attribute. Thus, a hierarchy is an ordinal measure from highest to lowest and "refers to some kind of arrangement or rank, among people, groups, or institutions."[1] Crucial to this definition is the social nature of hierarchy. For one actor to be at the top of a hierarchy necessarily implies that others must be below. Just as important, then, as exploring the top of the hierarchy is exploring secondary states and their views and attitudes toward hierarchy. Hierarchy itself can be imposed, or it can be accepted. That is, it can be seen as legitimate or not by actors.

There are numerous definitions for "hierarchy" in international relations and numerous other types of hierarchy. My definition is not meant to be definitive or exclusive but is merely one common type of hierarchy that we find in international relations. Perhaps the most common alternative definition of hierarchy in international relations comes from Kenneth Waltz's generation-old juxtaposition of hierarchy and anarchy as diametrical opposites.[2] Still others define hierarchy contractually, as an external restriction on a state's sovereignty, or what David Lake calls "a bargain between the ruler and the ruled premised on the former's provision of a social order of value sufficient to offset the latter's loss of freedom."[3] Max Weber defines hierarchy as a set of offices with a chain of command linking them together.[4] That is, one state cedes to another state the right, or control, over an action.[5] Each of these definitions captures one element or aspect of hierarchy, and none need be the exclusive definition. I emphasize rank because rigidly rationalist definitions of hierarchy ignores questions of standing, legitimacy, and social order, which were prime motivating factors in early modern East Asia.

Indeed, although the Westphalian system is composed of formally equal units, we see substantial hierarchy even today. For example, any mention of "leadership" in international relations is an implicit discussion of hierarchy.[6] After all, leadership necessarily implies that there are followers, and it also implies that there is a rank order that places leaders above followers. The two are not equal in voice, responsibility, standing, or influence. Leadership implies more responsibility than does following, and it also implies that the leader has more right or ability to set the course of action for the future than do followers. The most fitting term for this is hierarchy. Thus, debate about the future of "U.S. leadership" or questions about Japanese or European leadership imply a hierarchy of states, with some more influential and respected than others. Purely equal states would not have leadership; they would all simultaneously decide what to do.

Hierarchy can only emerge if there is consensus on what the hierarchy is, how it is measured, and who gets to compete. That is, hierarchy is inherently a social phenomenon. Although much of the intellectual focus is on the study of the leading states or the great powers of a system, it is probably more useful to study hierarchy by looking at all of the actors in the system. Whether and why secondary states accept hierarchy is as important as why great powers contend for the top position. Thus, questions of hierarchy also exist among smaller states, not just the great powers. Developing countries want to be rich, but they also want to be seen as culturally vibrant, modern, and sophisticated. As Andrew Hurrell notes, "policymakers in emerging states are acutely aware of the importance of hierarchy, especially of the social categories, the clubs, the memberships, and the criteria for admission through which hierarchy in international relations operates."[7]

Status as an International Motive

Given the social nature of hierarchy, two key questions are what is measured and where one fits in the hierarchy. To that end, numerous scholars have identified three enduring motivations for human behavior: wealth, power, and status.[8] As Nicholas Onuf noted two decades ago, "standing, security, and wealth are the controlling interests of humanity. We recognize them everywhere."[9] Following Iain Johnston, William Wohlforth, and others, I define status as "an individual's standing in the hierarchy of a group based on criteria such as prestige, honor, and deference," where status is an inherently relational concept and manifests itself hierarchically.[10]

Status and hierarchy are intimately linked, because status is inherently social and inherently rank ordered. Richard Ned Lebow calls status hierarchies "honor systems," which are inherently relational in nature, arguing that "honor is inseparable from hierarchy . . . the higher the status, the greater the honor and privileges, but also the more demanding the role and its rules."[11]

While it may be intuitively plausible that states value material gains such as economic wealth or military power, it is just as plausible that states and individuals value their social standing and desire social recognition and prestige. James Fearon notes that is also reasonable to assume that states pursue and satisfy a number of other goals in addition to material power as measured relative to other states.[12] One nonmaterial goal that most states are likely to value is status. Indeed, there is a fair amount of research showing that status is as important a motive as is material power. As Max Weber wrote: "A nation will forgive damage to its interests, but not injury to its honor, and certainly not when this is done in a spirit of priggish self-righteousness," and John Harsanyi has written that "apart from economic payoffs, social status seems to be the most important incentive and motivating force of social behavior."[13] States may value both material power and prestige, although the relative importance will depend on the particular international system.

Status is different than military power or economic wealth because it must be given by other states. As Lebow notes, "honor is a gift, bestowed upon actors by other actors . . . it has no meaning until it is acknowledged."[14] In this way, status is inherently relational and inherently social. Indeed, even more than wealth or power, status is relational, and one can only have status if one is a member of a group and if that group recognizes and awards status. A state has far more control over its military and economic activities than it does over its own status. Critical to this definition of status is the agreement upon what constitutes status, consensus upon how it is achieved, and agreement upon who is allowed to gain status and who is not. Status must be acknowledged for it to have meaning, and, in this way, it is inherently social.

There are a number of different types of status: some are defined by the international society and the norms and values inherent in that particular society. Status may be also formal or informal: formal status hierarchies determine restrictions and status—that is, membership in selective groups and the rights contained therein, while informal status arises from respect and influence. As Andrew Hurrell notes, "[some] status is centrally about the legal or political standing of a state as determined by its membership in some class, category, or grouping . . . this led to a concern with the principles and criteria by which states were able to enter international society and be accepted as sovereign members of the 'society of states.'"[15]

Even in the modern world there are numerous widely accepted aspects to status. Formal status involves membership in various international clubs, the most basic status being recognized as a legitimate nation-state and engaging in diplomatic and normalized relations with other states. Ranked higher than recognition as a legitimate state is membership in formal international bodies such as the United Nations, the World Bank, the OECD, G20, and G8. Formal status also manifests itself in leadership positions within these various organizations and is also an element of status: leadership or chairmanship of the IMF or World Bank, UN Security Council membership, and so on. Informal status is given in the various rankings that pervade modern life: corruption indices, human-rights indices, and rankings of economic development. More informal status is whether a state is a "responsible stakeholder," a developed or developing state, a middle power, and so on. Adhering to global norms, or being the type of state valued by international society, can also be an aspect of status—and, notably, those states that deviate are labeled "rogue."

Other status traits may be local or regional and of importance to only a few countries. In addition, some status is conditional. That is, any number of countries can be granted status as recognized nation-states in the international system. This is conditional upon a state meeting certain formal and informal criteria; chief among them being diplomatic recognition by a significant majority of states already in the system.[16] Yet another type of status is zero-sum, and what one state gains, another loses. Recognition as a world leader can be enjoyed by only one state, for example.

Status is decided by the rules of the game and the norms valued by international society, and it may or may not involve elements of material power.[17] To quote Ian Hurd, "the relation of coercion, self-interest, and status to each other is complex, and each is rarely found in anything like its pure, isolated form . . . the difficulties attending to an attempt to prove that a rule is or is not accepted by an actor as legitimate are real, but they do not justify either abandoning the study . . . or assuming ex ante that it does not exist."[18]

One critical question is whether or not status is merely a reflection of material capabilities. Do states value status independent of their material benefits? Furthermore, if status considerations conflict with material considerations, do states ever take actions that demonstrably privilege their status interests at the expense of their material self-interests? Status-seeking behavior coexists with the goals of material power, and status and material power may often work together as motivations. However, although we may grant that status-seeking behavior exists, when material and status motivations are positively correlated, it will be extremely difficult to theoretically or empirically judge which motivation is prior. Yet there are also times when material and status motivations are at odds with each other, and these instances are potentially the most interesting. When states must choose between competing exigencies that would lead to different or even opposing behaviors, we are able to see whether and to what extent status motivations are present.

There are political actors not even granted the most basic of status within the international society, that of the status of a nation-state with diplomatic recognition by other nation-states. Both Taiwan and North Korea have all the basic material requirements for gaining status as a recognized nation-state: they are clearly stable, centralized governments defined over territory; have their own political, economic, and social systems; and control their borders and interact with other countries on a regular basis. Indeed, both Taiwan and North Korea are more powerful than many recognized states, for example Sudan or Ethiopia. Yet neither Taiwan nor North Korea exists as a nation-state, and both see diplomatic recognition as one of their most central and enduring goals. Similarly, the G8 membership is not composed of the eight largest economies (Canada and Italy are the thirteenth and tenth largest economies in the world, respectively, and nonmembers India and China have economies larger than France, Germany, Russia, and the United Kingdom), and there was serious discussion within the United States about whether Russia should be "allowed" to be a member of the G8 due to its actions.[19] Indeed, decisions about membership involved much more than a mere aggregation of material-power capabilities.

Hegemony in International Relations

Closely related to hierarchy and status is the idea of hegemony. There is much discussion in the contemporary world about the nature of U.S. hegemony and, relatedly, about whether the status of the United States as the lone superpower constitutes hegemony. The simple fact of material preponderance by one state connotes only primacy, or unipolarity, and I distinguish between merely being the largest country and being the country that is expected to lead. "Hegemony" is a form of hierarchy, arising as it does from the acceptance by some states of the leadership and greater responsibility, influence, and roles of another state.[20]

Hegemony involves more than mere size. It is the influence and authority of one state over other states, where one actor has the "power to shape the rules of international politics according to its own interests."[21] Critically, however, hegemony is different from pure domination. Although realists often equate primacy with hegemony, an alternative formulation of hegemony emphasize "the social, or *recognized*, status of hegemony."[22] In this view, hegemony is not merely based on the dominant coercive capabilities of a state but involves consensual acceptance of a leading state's legitimate authority. For example, Ikenberry and Kupchan note that although material incentives are one way that hegemons assert control over other nations, "the exercise of power—and hence the mechanism through which compliance is achieved—involves the projection by the hegemon of a set of norms and their embrace by leaders in other nations."[23] Jonathan Joseph observes that "the concept of hegemony is normally understood as emphasizing consent in contrast to reliance on the use of force."[24]

Distinct from the mere preponderance of material capabilities, stable hegemony thus requires both a social order that legitimizes the system and also a credible commitment on the part of the dominant state not to exploit the secondary states if they accept the dominant state's authority.[25] That is, crafting a set of norms and rules that are viewed as legitimate by secondary states is an integral task for the dominant state. As Mastanduno notes, "the most durable order is one in which there exists a meaningful consensus on the right of the hegemonic state to lead, as well as the social purposes it projects."[26]

This consensual view of hegemony focuses on why secondary states would defer to the hegemon rather than on the position of the hegemon itself.[27]

Consensus on the right of one state to lead—that is, hegemony—is itself a form of power. It derives from the values or norms that a state projects and not necessarily merely from its military might and economic wealth. As David Lake argues, "pure coercive commands—of the form 'do this, or die'—are not authoritative. Authority relations must contain some measure of legitimacy . . . and an obligation, understood by both parties, for B to comply with the wishes of A."[28] That is, hegemony is a form of status, and it must be socially recognized in order to exist.

In addition to a social purpose, hegemony is stable when secondary states receive believable assurances from the dominant state that it will not abuse its position and exploit smaller states. There has been extensive research on the problem of crafting credible commitments in international relations, but I focus here on one key task—setting mutually recognized borders.[29] Clear boundaries between states are a good indicator of their orientation toward each other. In this way, borders are the "political divides [that are] the result of state building," and they are a useful indicator of a state's acceptance of the status quo.[30] Yet borders are not mere functionally rationalist institutions designed to communicate preferences. They also inherently assume the existence of two parties that recognize each other's legitimate right to existence. Demarcation of a boundary is thus a costly signal that a state intends stable relations with a neighbor.

Dominant states, like individual leaders, lead through a combination of bullying, bribing, and inspiring.[31] Although coercion can substitute for legitimacy in certain instances and for a short while, they are both intertwined, as well. Legitimacy is stronger when backed by coercive capacity, and coercion seen as legitimate is also more effective.[32] As Lake notes, "despite their clear analytic differences, political authority and coercion are hard to distinguish in practice . . . there is no 'bright line' separating these two analytic concepts, and I offer none here."[33]

In Sum

Hierarchy is a rank ordering of units from high to low. Primacy and hegemony are different forms of preponderance: one is derived purely from material power; the other involves legitimation and consensus. Hegemony is a form of hierarchy that involves more than material power. It also involves a set of norms—a social order—that secondary states find legitimate. Hegemony is thus a social system. Legitimacy itself is distinct from material power, and although the two are intertwined, legitimacy grows out of the social purpose that a state projects. These distinctions are important in helping us categorize and explain the different patterns of international relations found in early modern East Asia. States value status—social recognition by other states—as much as they value material power.

Although defining international systems as hierarchic instead of purely anarchic may seem a departure from accepted practice, this theoretical lens focuses us on important questions. What are the rules of the game (that is, upon what do we measure the status hierarchy)? Are states satisfied with their place in the hierarchy (status quo or revisionist)? How do states change their standings? And finally, when is conflict most likely to occur?

3 STATES

The Confucian Society

Now think upon this Dai Viet land of ours;
Truly it is a cultured nation [*bang*].
As mountains and rivers make for various lands,
So our Southern ways must differ from the North.
— NGUYEN TRAI, chief minister of Le Loi, 1428

EAST ASIA has perhaps the longest history of centralized territorial rule in the world, defined as states that established political control over defined territory. China as hegemon—and its main philosophy, Confucianism—had a powerful effect on the rest of East Asian domestic and international politics, even while what it meant to be Chinese and how best to organize society and government was continually modified and debated within China itself. Chinese civilization in the region was inescapable, and most states and societies were forced to deal with China in one way or another. Domestically, China influenced state formation and societal practices, from language and religion to political institutions and economic activity.

China lacked a messianic vision of transforming the world, yet it managed to craft remarkably stable relations with many—but not all—of its surrounding neighbors. That is, China had little interest in actively exporting its own ideals and values, preferring instead to focus on the practice of foreign relations. This allowed the surrounding peoples and polities to contest, modify, and adapt Chinese ideas to their own ends. Some states, such as Korea and Vietnam, closely copied China in a range of practices. Others, such as Japan, experimented with some but not all Chinese ideas. Still other societies—such as the diverse seminomadic peoples of the northern and western frontiers—resisted almost all of China's cultural and political ideas, but they still interacted with China, occasionally using Chinese practices and ideas in their foreign relations.

This chapter focuses on the main, enduring states of East Asia and makes two central arguments: first, there is no eternal, unchanging China, and there have been multiple strands and an ever-changing notion of what is civilization, as much invented in the present as inherited from the past at any point in time. Second, the main secondary states of East Asia chose Confucianism and Chinese ideas more for their own reasons than from Chinese pressure. In Korea, Vietnam, and Japan, the debate about how to organize government and society occurred between warriors and scholars, with the Confucian literati winning in Korea and Vietnam and the warriors ultimately winning in Japan. Although Chinese ideas were deeply embedded from the founding of these states, just as significantly, Chinese ideas were grafted onto vibrant indigenous cultures, and the two coexisted—sometimes uncomfortably—resulting in only partial Sinicization.

Were early modern East Asian political units actually states? Max Weber's famous definition of a state provides a starting point: states represent a social community and territory, with a monopoly of legitimate violence within that territory.[1] By this definition, early modern China, Korea, Japan, and Vietnam were indeed states, and they emerged far earlier than did their European counterparts. These four political units were centrally organized, bureaucratically administered systems defined over a geographic area that conducted formal diplomatic relations with one another. The crucial institutional innovation in East Asia that represented Confucian ideas about proper relationships was the emergence of a civil service based on merit, not hereditary aristocracy: "embryonic bureaucracies, based upon clear rules, whose personnel were obtained independently of hereditary social claims, through meritocratic civil service examinations."[2] Over the centuries, these states attempted to implement consistent tax policy, land reform, and nascent welfare states for famine relief.

The states of China, Korea, Vietnam, and Japan emerged over one thousand years ago as centralized political units, territorial states with internal control that conducted formal, legal international relations with one another, and for whom international recognition as a legitimate nation was an important component of their existence. Vietnam emerged three centuries later than the others, in the tenth century a.d. As John Wills writes, "Chinese hopes that their 'civilizing influence' might spread to foreign peoples . . . bore fruit among peoples of the most varied cultural and geographic backgrounds . . . these included Korea, Japan and the Ryukyu islands, and the area that become modern Vietnam."[3] This creation of distinct and enduring political identities was a central aspect to the stability of the system. These states constituted the inner core of the Chinese-dominated regional system, where Chinese cultural, economic, and political influence was direct and pervasive. Karen Wigan notes:

> Compared to most countries in the late twentieth century ... China, Korea, and Japan are among the most venerable nations in the world; although their boundaries have shifted over time, and the style of their imagining has been continually debated, the notion of nationhood has resonated long and deeply with the majority of each country's inhabitants ... this sense of region is quite different from what might be encountered elsewhere in Eurasia or Africa, where national space is often complicated ... by cross-cutting affiliations from a colonial or precolonial past.[4]

Not all the political units in early modern East Asia were states—the early modern East Asian system included a wide array of political units, some of which were more centrally organized than others. In addition to the four major states that are the focus of this book, there were numerous kingdoms in Southeast Asia, among them Siam, Burma, and Java. There were also various tribes, clans, and seminomadic peoples in the northern and western steppes; we will focus on these nomads in chapter 7. Finally, there were pirates (*wakō*) who infested the seas and were a constant threat to trade. The main violence in the system—for example, endemic frontier raids along the Manchurian border—occurred between states and these other political actors, not between the states themselves. Figure 3.1 outlines the political geography of the major East Asian states in 1600.

That states coexisted with other actors is not surprising. After all, the well-developed hierarchy that holds nation-states as the dominant political actor in international relations only came into being in Europe in the eighteenth century, at the earliest. Even as late as the nineteenth century, there remained numerous political entities powerful enough to affect the behavior of nation-states. For example, upon independence, the United States originally decided not to build a navy and to avoid competing with established European naval powers in a bid for control of the seas.[5] However, the Barbary Coast pirates of northern Africa, located mainly in Tripoli and other cities, were so powerful and such a menace to trade that the United States was forced to build its first warship, the USS *Constitution*, in 1797, and send it, along with the original detachment of U.S. marines, to fight the pirates. Ultimately these and

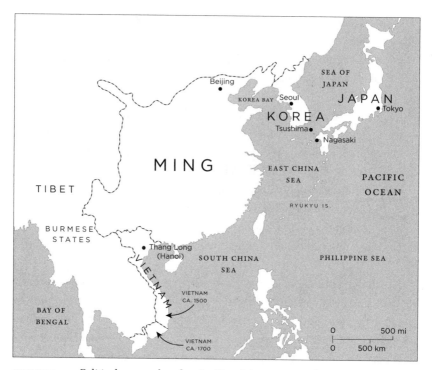

FIGURE 3.1 Political geography of major East Asian states in 1600

other smaller political units—pirate clans, Catalan separatists, principalities, and minor dukedoms—were gradually relegated to a marginal role in international relations, and much of the current scholarship tends to ignore or overlook their existence.[6] That is, that pirate clans powerful enough to force the United States to build a navy existed alongside European states well into the nineteenth century has not stopped scholars from focusing only on European states when considering important political actors. This book will avoid that overly narrow focus, and although I will view China, Korea, Japan, and Vietnam as the most consequential and powerful states in early East Asia, it is important to bear in mind the existence of other influential nonstate actors.

Modern conceptions of national identity were certainly not in existence fifteen hundred years ago, and there was no eternal and unchanging concept of "China" or "Japan." However, it is also important not to swing too far the other way and assume that there is no link between the past and the present. The nationalist cultural and ethnic boundaries that we see today were not there in the past, but some set of political boundaries definitely were. These states, and the people within them, clearly had some notion of a shared political identity and culture and differentiated themselves from the other states and actors in the system.

Civilization and the Idea of China

Civilization and state formation were intertwined in East Asia. Yet the two were distinct both conceptually and in practice. The core principles of Confucianism involved kingdoms that relied upon a set of ideas based on ancient Chinese classic philosophical texts about the proper ways in which government and society were to be organized. "The term 'Confucian monarchies' hardly conveys the breadth of the civilization that these countries shared," Woodside notes, pointing out that "all three societies [China, Korea, and Vietnam] were governed by a scholar elite with a particular type of historical consciousness."[7]

The East Asian experiment with governance began quite early, with the emergence of China and its main philosophy of Confucianism during the Axial age (800–200 b.c.). China had been unified by 221 b.c., and a nascent notion of Hua-Hsia (or Chinese) community existed during the Warring States period. Nicola Di Cosmo quotes the *Hsun-tzu*: "All the states of Hsia share the same territorial zones and the same customs: Man, Yi, Jung, and Ti share the same territorial zones, but have different institutions."[8] Over the centuries, these ideas evolved and became more full and complete, and a central government ruled much of what is China today for almost two millennia. China has expanded and contracted, depending on local conditions and the strength of the political center, and as Mark Edward Lewis notes, "China owes its ability to endure across time, and to re-form itself again and again after periods of disunity, to a fundamental reshaping of Chinese culture by the earliest dynasties, the Qin and the Han."[9] Naomi Standen notes that "we should not doubt, however, that many people in the tenth century did have a clear sense of belonging within a particular cultural nexus."[10]

Certainly, a long-standing question within China itself was over what constituted "civilization" and what constituted the "barbarian." People within what is today known as China used the term "civilization" as early as two thousand years ago, and as Charles Keyes notes, "from Han times on . . . those who lived on the frontiers of the empire were considered to be barbarians . . . that is, they had not yet accepted the order presided over by the emperor or the authority of a literature written in Chinese."[11] Throughout the next two millennia, the concepts of "Chinese" and "barbarian" were subject to debate and interpretation, and a fixed definition was never established.[12] But the ideas have been present throughout Chinese history, and Mark Strange notes that

> running through the periods (and surviving even to the present day) are a core set of defining concepts: that China is a unified sovereign state; that the Chinese polity draws legitimacy from a dominant cultural tradition, which founds itself on the value system of a core canon of authoritative texts; and that this cultural and moral tradition has close associations with an ethnic identity.[13]

However, the word *wenming* (文明), which is now what Chinese, Koreans, Japanese, and Vietnamese understand as "civilization," is a neologism that was introduced in the late nineteenth century through Japanese translations of Western works (K: *munmyŏng*; V: *văn minh*; J: *bunmei*). Thus, as with the concept of hegemony, in this book I use the term "civilization" anachronistically, as a modern term to describe the past. What was true historically was that educated Chinese saw themselves as distinct from people who followed different rituals, wore different clothing, did not read and write Chinese, and who did not base their ideas and social practices on the Confucian classics. Liam Kelley prefers the term "manifest civility" to distinguish the older Chinese concept of civilization from the modern Western concept of civilization, and he writes:

> To state that a kingdom was such a domain [of manifest civility] indicated that it belonged to a category where it shared certain governmental, ritual, educational, literary, intellectual, and social practices with other members of this category, the proof of which could be found in the existence of a body of "institutional records" that recorded such practices, as well as the presence of "wise men" who maintained these records. Furthermore . . . there was a discernible inequality in this respect, especially between Vietnam and China.[14]

Chinese civilization as it evolved consisted of both institutional and discursive practices, and although discussion of civilization tends to focus on the latter, the former practices were arguably a more present and direct means of extending Chinese ideas to various parts of East Asia. Scholars continually debated and revised ideas about the role of government, the organization of society, proper relations between groups and peoples, and the role of religion in public and private life. Literature, art, and culture were also an important aspect of this larger process of civilization, although it is not our focus here. As John Wills notes:

> a great many of the most heroic figures in the very rich Chinese stories of their own past are not rulers but selfless ministers, defending the realm against invaders, protesting against corruption and abuse of the common people, risking their own lives to give unwanted advice to unworthy rulers . . . the importance of this theme in political culture for the enduring Chinese tendency to unify a very large continental area is immense.[15]

It was arguably the Tang dynasty (a.d. 618–907) that made perhaps the most direct advances in governance, introducing a key institutional experiment that reflected these Confucian ideas: a government run by talent, not heredity, with civil servants selected through a public competition assessing candidates' qualification, open (in theory) to all males and held at regular, fixed intervals. As Alexander Woodside notes:

> The eighth century, indeed, would make a good choice as the first century in world history of the politically "early modern." It was in this century that the Chinese court first gained what it thought was a capacity to impose massive, consolidating, central tax reforms from the top down, which few European monarchies would have thought possible before the French revolution, given their privileged towns, provinces, nobles, and clergy.[16]

This was an important innovation—most of the world has governed using an aristocracy that chose rulers on the basis of hereditary ties. The examinations themselves were held in public spaces, and some sites, such as the one in Jjiangnan, held up to sixteen thousand candidates in brick huts. During the Qing dynasty, when the emperor Qianlong realized that Mongol and Manchu nobles on his frontiers could not read court edicts, he "tried to restore communications with his Mongol nobles by ordering a 'back to basics' reform of examination-system writing."[17] There was even affirmative action—in 1777, the central government allowed border students a special amnesty of thirty years in which to learn the "Central Domain" speech tones necessary for poetry examinations.

In addition to the civil examinations, bureaucratic administration in China involved a complex system of administration and governance. Chinese central administration was composed of six major ministries: personnel and appointments, finance and taxes, rites and education, war, justice and punishment, and public works. Ming-era China was also centrally organized into administrative districts down to the province level, with appointments made from the capital for most tax, commercial, and judicial posts.[18] China also introduced land reform as early as the Tang dynasty, in an attempt to create more landholding farmers. A national tax system in China had emerged before the Tang dynasty, with the ideal tax rate of 10 percent. Yang Yang (727–781) authored China's famous "two tax" law of 780, which consolidated taxes into two semiannual payments and shifted the focus away from people to property size.[19] William McNeill argues that this eighth-century reform was a "pioneering shift" from a command economy into a market-based economy.[20] By the time of the Manchu Qing dynasty one thousand years later, China had again developed a centralized process by which the government attempted to react to food shortages. R. Bin Wong notes that these "[state-sponsored] granaries represented official commitments to material welfare beyond anything imaginable, let alone achieved, in Europe. . . . To think of state concerns for popular welfare as a very recent political practice makes sense only if we again limit ourselves to Western examples."[21]

Yet there was no dedicated, linear, and focused march toward "civilization." Writing about the tenth century, Naomi Standen points out that "during those two hundred years [after the Tang dynasty collapsed] nobody knew that a Chinese empire would ever again be the dominant power in East Asia . . . the radically different world of the late Tang and Five Dynasties (907–960) . . . saw multiple power centers within the same territory interacting on an entirely different basis."[22] In fact, the various—and numerous—foreign influences on Chinese ideas also left a profound imprint on Chinese ideas. Thus, we should be cautious of implying too direct or linear a path toward modern China or toward a Confucian civilization. Cultural ideas influenced the various states that rose and fell over time, but modification, adaptation, and debate existed at every point. As Standen reminds us, "we should not . . . foreclose the issue, by adopting terms and categories, like ethnicity, that imply the inevitability of the modern Chinese nation-state and posit a linear development toward it."[23] Indeed, some traits have historical roots, others do not, and all are constantly evolving depending on the circumstances, situation, institutional constraints, political and economic exigencies, and a host of other factors.

In short, identifying a coherent East Asian civilization is as difficult as identifying a European one. China was central to East Asian culture, however, and throughout Chinese history there has been contestation and change, adaptation and innovation. Yet at the same time, there has also been considerable continuity over many centuries, and Confucian ideas and their manifestation in the state-institutional structures and social ideas of the nineteenth century would have been recognizable to those living in the eighth century.

Sinic States: Korea, Vietnam, and Japan

The states of Korea, Vietnam, and Japan that emerged between the seventh and tenth centuries a.d. are still recognizable today as roughly the same political units. These states constituted the inner core of the regional system in which Chinese cultural, economic, and political influence was dominant, direct, and pervasive. These three East Asian states were centrally administered bureaucratic systems based on the Chinese model. They developed complex bureaucratic structures and bear more than a "family resemblance" in their organization, cultures, and outlooks. This form of government, along with the calendar, language and writing system, bureaucracy, and educational system, was derived from the Chinese experience, and the civil-service examination in these countries emphasized a knowledge of Chinese political philosophy, classics, and culture. Yet while Confucian China was a pervasive influence, there was no messianic, transformative vision from China nor little pressure on subordinate states to conform to Chinese ways. Imposition of Chinese civilization was intertwined with state formation and was a top-down affair driven by elites, and multiple traditions survived—Sinicization was never complete nor thorough.

Table 3.1 outlines the various political entities over the past six centuries in East Asia.

Voluntary Emulation

Despite the overwhelming centrality of Chinese ideas to the region, Chinese relations with other countries were not marked by transformative or interventionist attempts by China to change the basic practices of other states. Indeed, pragmatism characterized Chinese relations with its neighbors, and China was more concerned with stability on its borders. As long as stability was maintained and there was no threat to China, China was content to

TABLE 3.1 East Asian states and their dynasties, 1300–1900

	1300	1400	1500	1600	1700	1800
China	1368–1644: Ming			1644–1911: Qing		
Japan	1333–1573: Ashikaga			1600–1868: Tokugawa		
Korea	1392–1910: Chosŏn					
Vietnam	1225–1400: Tran	1400–1407: Ho	1428–1778: Le		1778–1802: Tay Son	1792–1883: Nguyen

leave its neighboring countries alone. Of course, there were variations. Korea and Vietnam were most comfortable with the Chinese-oriented system, while Japan has always been conflicted about its relationship with China: genuine cultural admiration couples with a sense of unease and even competition. However, despite Japanese reservations and sense of rivalry, the Chinese influence on Japan was in many ways transformative.

Neighboring states emulated Chinese practices for a number of reasons, two of which were as a means of domestic political and social control, as well as to manage foreign relations with China. Scholars in the smaller Sinic states often called China the "central efflorescence" or "domain of manifest civility" (*wen xian zhi bang*), because it was the most complete reflection of the Confucian practices. Literally, the phrase means "using texts to rule the country" and implies a country ruled by Confucian ideas. Korean and Vietnamese scholar-officials in particular often used China as a model, comparison, or ideal, and the historical writings from these countries are thoroughly imbued with the use of China as a reference point. To cite one of any number of examples, the Vietnamese scholar-official Le Quy Don (1726–1784) wrote: "Our kingdom calls itself [a domain of] manifest civility . . . [but] compared to writers in the Central Efflorescence, we have not produced even one-tenth of what they have. This is profoundly regrettable!"[24] The East Asian states were not feudal or organized around hereditary aristocratic power. Alexander Woodside notes that in these East Asian countries, "the monarch . . . largely governed through texts composed for them by mandarins, rather than by more personal (and perhaps more feudal) means of persuasive human contact."[25] The "presented-scholar" degree, based on examinations (C: *jinshi*; K: *chinsa*; V: *tien si*), created a set of civil servants responsible to the throne, unencumbered (mostly) of aristocratic claims.

The Chinese court (and the Korean, Vietnamese, and Japanese courts) also produced "veritable records" of government activities (C: *shilu*; K: *sillok*; V: *thuc loc*), sometimes on a daily basis. Furthermore, all four of the most Sinicized countries used the same word for "history," (C: *shi*; K: *sa*; J: *rekishi*; V: *su*), the original meaning of which implies royal secretaries who "wrote and preserved the government ordinances and princely genealogies of ancient Chinese rulers." Woodside notes that "history writing became a major form of 'boundary maintenance' by Vietnam and Korean centers and their elites against Chinese hegemony."[26] It is notable that distinctiveness between explicitly unequal states was maintained in part through literature and not force of arms and that such writing used Chinese and Confucian ideas.

Indeed, another example of the Chinese influence is in language, with the wholesale importation of Chinese script and vocabulary into these three other cultures. They employed Chinese-language cultural and political systems yet retained their own unique indigenous cultures, as well. This is best exemplified by the diglossia in their linguistic traditions: Chinese was used for writing in Korea, Vietnam, and Japan during the entire time under study, even while these countries retained their own indigenous languages and, in some cases, script.[27] For example, the Korean, Vietnamese, and Japanese word for "country" (C: *kuo*; K: *kuk*; V: *quoc*; J: *koku* or *kuni*) is the same and was derived from the same Chinese character. Thus, although Koreans used Chinese characters for writing and borrowed a large portion of their vocabulary from China, indigenous Korean writing and vocabulary continue to exist today, and often there are two words—one Chinese, one Korean.

Although Korea was occupied by the Han dynasty around 100 b.c. and was populated by numerous kingdoms after that, the Silla dynasty unified the peninsula in a.d. 668, and since that time Korea has existed separately from China.[28] Over fourteen centuries, Korea had only three dynasties: Silla (668–918), Koryŏ (918–1392), and Chosŏn (1392–1910). Although the Korean Koryŏ dynasty was Buddhist in many respects, the dynasty's founder, Wang Kŏn (T'aejo, r. 918–943), remarked: "We in the East have long admired Tang ways. In culture, ritual, and music we are entirely following its model."[29] Even though the Mongols subdued Koryŏ in 1259 and ruled through intermarriage for more than a century, "the almost one hundred years of Mongol domination of Korean affairs . . . seem to have left but a light imprint. The Mongols were admired for their military organization and prowess, but apart from some fancy fashions, they seem to have furnished little of substance for imitation."[30]

John Duncan's magisterial study of the founding of the Chosŏn dynasty has pointed out the way in which *yangban* (elite)-status families interacted with and promoted reforms to the government. Practical measures such as the "rank land law," which reformed land ownership, "harked back to Chinese antiquity," and these new officials selectively chose ideas and practices from various Chinese dynasties. Duncan notes that "proposals were based on the reformers' understandings of historical Chinese and Korean systems," including the Ch'in (249–207 b.c.), Han, and T'ang, as well as from the preceding Koryŏ dynasty.[31] With the establishment of the Chosŏn dynasty and the intensification of neo-Confucian practices, "scholar-officials . . . became directly involved in policymaking at all levels."[32]

The best evidence of this cultural borrowing comes from Korea's adoption of the examination system as a means for selecting scholar-officials as government bureaucrats. This key institution was borrowed directly from China and represented an institutional manifestation of the highest of Confucian ideals: a government run by scholars selected through a public examination (*munkwa*) based on Confucian classical texts. At the beginning of the Chosŏn dynasty, there was a corresponding military examination system (*mukwa*) that was comparable to the civil-service exam. It rapidly became marginal to the government, prompting Eugene Park to note that "the late Chosŏn period saw the total dominance of the civilian Confucian scholar-officials in politics . . . when the state finally needed the military—during the nineteenth-century conflicts—the effectiveness of its military men was minimal."[33]

The Korean examination system had been used since the eighth-century Silla dynasty, although it became fully incorporated into public life under the Chosŏn dynasty.[34] Ch'oe Ch'i-won (857–?) spent seventeen years in Tang China, passing the civil-service examination in 874, and his return to Korea was a major factor in passing Confucian ideals into the Silla dynasty. The Songgyungwan Confucian institute was founded in 992. Passing the civil-service exam was the only way to join the government, which came to be seen as the highest position a person could attain. By the beginning of the Chosŏn dynasty, in an attempt at transparency and meritocracy, an extensive system had developed to protect the candidates. To assure anonymity, candidates' names were concealed from the examiners before the test, and after completion, tests were recopied into other handwriting before examiners saw them. The exams were collected by different officers than those who recorded and read them, and they were also read by more than one examiner, to ensure fairness in grading.[35]

In some ways, Korea became more Confucian than China itself. Korea had almost ten times as many Confucian academics (*sowon*) per capita as China.[36] Korea, in fact, used a bureaucratic system borrowed wholesale from the Chinese model. Chosŏn-dynasty court dress was identical with the court dress of the Ming-dynasty officials, with the exception that the identical dress and emblems were two ranks (in the nine-rank scheme) lower in Korea. That is, the court dress of a Rank I (the highest rank) Chosŏn official was identical to that of a Rank III official at the Ming court.[37] Korea also used the same six ministries (K: *yukcho*) and a similar state council (K: *pibyŏnsa*) as in China. The six ministries covered taxation, military affairs, punishments, public works, personnel, and rites.[38]

The State Council (*uijongbu*) was the highest organ, comprising three High State Councilors, and it served as the advisory council to the king and the administrative body that directed the six ministries.[39] The country was divided into eight provinces: Kyonggi, Chungchong, Kyongsang, Cholla, Hwanghae, Kangwon, Hamgyong, and Pyongan—essentially the same provincial division that exists today. Within those provinces were various types of counties. County magistrates were not allowed to serve in the counties in which they resided, to keep their loyalties to the crown rather than to the people they governed.[40] In 1390, the Chosŏn king, Yi Songgye, introduced land reform and built village granaries to guard against famine. Yet despite emulation and borrowing, China simply did not "dominate" Korea during the two-millennia period before 1900—Korea was de facto independent, and its Sinicization was most pronounced when Korean neo-Confucians quite self-consciously imposed Confucianism as an ideology on Korea, apart from whatever the Chinese might have wanted. Korea was clearly an independent state, conducting its own internal domestic politics and independent foreign policy.

As with the Korean state, Vietnam adopted many Chinese practices in order to preserve Vietnamese autonomy and independence by presenting itself to China as a recognizably similar political unit, one whose accomplishments and sophistication made it worthy of treatment as a state. The Vietnamese centralization of authority also was not a cause or effect of war; indeed, emergence as a state had more to do with domestic ideas about how best to govern. Victor Lieberman's long survey of Southeast Asia concludes: "Interaction with China was probably more important in shaping Vietnamese self-identity than warfare with Chams, Khmers, or Thais."[41] Moreover, in terms of religious expression and social organization, after the neo-Confucian revolution,

"Vietnam, especially though not exclusively at the elite level, became more notionally Chinese."[42]

The Chinese Han empire conquered northern Vietnam in 208 b.c., establishing it initially as an independent state and later incorporating Nam Viet into China as the province Giao Chi.[43] The Chinese introduced administrative districts and built roads, ports, canals, dikes, and dams. Chinese immigrants also introduced Chinese-style schools, marriage rites, social customs, agriculture, and laws. In the ninth century, a Tang governor established a Confucian academy. This Confucianism was as specific as to dictate economic and family organization at the village level, patrilineal inheritance, and even dress. The peoples at the time retained their indigenous language for unofficial uses and indigenous social and religious customs, chief among them Buddhism. Some of these Chinese-imported political institutions and cultural norms would survive into the twentieth century. The bureaucratic-examination system, for example, was used by Vietnam under the Han, and when the French arrived in the nineteenth century, success in the civil-service examination still required the use of Chinese characters and a knowledge of Confucian classics.

Over the centuries, these peoples also occasionally rebelled, with two major insurrections, one in a.d. 40, the other in a.d. 248. Seven centuries later, in 938, the local inhabitants were successful in their rebellion, and in 967, Dinh Bo Linh became first ruler of Dai Co Viet.[44] After defeating the Chinese in battle, he won acceptance for independence by entering into a tributary relationship with China, a relationship that would essentially continue until the nineteenth century.[45] This is the beginning of the political organization of what came later to be known as Vietnam.

The initial Ly dynasty (1009–1225) was nominally Chinese in its organization but remained at its base more indigenous than Chinese. The literati had not yet developed into a powerful Confucian bureaucracy but instead, during this initial period of the dynasty, were servants of the king, while the ruling class was a feudal, landed nobility.[46] Even this early, however, elements of what are considered a state appeared, and the way in which people ruled over what was to become "Vietnam" at this point was the same as the way over which much of China in that period was ruled—through reliance on controlling spirits and mediating between gods and humans.[47] Over time, political control became more centralized and institutionalized, and Phan Huy Chu, a Vietnamese scholar writing in the early 1800s, traced the Vietnamese national tax system to the year 1013. However, it was the Tran dynasty (1225–

1400) that set up Chinese-style "population registers for each village, the better to improve tax collections, the military draft, and river diking."[48] In 1253, the Tran established a "National College (*Quoc Hoc Vien/Quoc Tu Vien*) . . . scholars were ordered to focus on the classical Chinese texts."[49]

The Tran dynasty also saw the writing of the first dynastic history: in 1272, Le Van Huu completed his *Dai Viet Su Ky* (Historical Annals of the Great Viet Kingdom). Like Korea, this was an attempt to separate Vietnam from China and create legitimate political space for Vietnam in Chinese eyes. As Brantly Womack observes, "[Le Van Huu's] task was to establish a record of autonomy from China. Without such a record, autonomy gained under the Song was up for renegotiation with the Yuan and other succeeding dynasties." Womack quotes the modern Vietnamese historian Nguyen The Anh: "The concern was to affirm the equality of North and South, according to the political and cultural criteria already used by China to proclaim its superiority over other peoples."[50] The poem at the beginning of this chapter is another good example of this emphasis on both difference and similarity. It was written upon the withdrawal of the Ming occupying forces in 1428 and is often thought of as a "declaration of independence" by the Vietnamese. Yet the poem, written in the classical Chinese genre *phu*, accepts the Confucian criterion for being a civilized nation (*bang*) and uses China ("the North") as the basis for defining Vietnam ("the South"). Woven through Vietnamese conceptions of themselves and their country were these larger Confucian ideas about what defines status and what countries were ranked highly.[51] This concern with similarity and difference was to continue throughout the centuries. Between 1663 and 1695, Confucian scholars compiled a history of the Le dynasty, and although it was not an official dynastic history — which were normally written to legitimize a regime — it did emphasize the dominant position of the bureaucracy in the state.[52]

The Chinese influence on Vietnam was thorough. The civil service–examination system in Vietnam grew directly from the Chinese experience, and by the eleventh century, three-stage regional examinations were held on successive weeks of the seventh lunar month, there were word limits (for example, three hundred words for policy questions at the regional level), and winners were publicly announced in order of excellence. Like the Chinese and Korean systems, attempts to keep the process as fair and transparent as possible included measures such as prohibitions against examiners meeting with each other privately, and special care was taken to ensure that families of candidates — fathers, sons, and uncles, for example — were not colluding while taking the test. By the fifteenth century, as many as thirty thousand men took the regional examinations each year, and by the sixteenth century some seventy thousand men were eligible for the first level of examination.[53] Yet between 1426 and 1643, only 1,694 scholars in total passed the examination, an average of eight per year.[54]

These literati formed the core of Vietnam's Confucian leaders. These scholars, such as Dao Cong Soan, Nguyen Cu Dao, and Nguyen Ba Ky, were key figures in guiding the fifteenth-century Vietnamese state to incorporate Chinese ideas in the governance of Vietnam. They pushed for "modern examinations every three years, bureaucratic administration, and the moral Neo-Confucian orthodoxy."[55] As John Whitmore concludes, the Thang-tong emperor (r. 1460–1497) "was crossing a line and moving Dai Viet from a position of separation from the Sinic world to one of explicit participation in it."[56]

The Vietnamese, like the Koreans, adopted Chinese practices as both genuine emulation and as a means of diplomacy. As for emulation, cultural borrowing from the most advanced state in the region is not surprising. The complexity of emulation and difference is reflected in famous Vietnamese nationalist poems from the eleventh and fifteenth centuries. These poems celebrated victories over China—but they were written in Chinese using a Chinese literary style and used China as a basis for defining what was Vietnam.[57]

Of the four major states in early modern East Asia, Japan had the most conflicted relations with China. The Chinese influence—although constant and powerful—was mitigated and had less of an effect in Japan than in either Korea or Vietnam. The Japanese state that developed over the centuries was in many ways influenced by China, which has always loomed large as both myth and reality for Japan. David Pollack observes that "until modern times the Chinese rarely troubled themselves about Japan; the Japanese, however, were preoccupied with China from the beginning of their recorded history until the opening of the West in the last century."[58] Chinese influence was not just political; it was cultural, as well, and Keene writes: "The central factor of Japanese literature—if not the entire traditional culture—was the love for and the rejection of Chinese influence."[59] Pollack further notes that "for the Japanese, what was 'Japanese' had always to be considered in relation to what was thought to be 'Chinese.'"[60]

Early in its history, Japan experimented with Chinese-style governance. With the promulgation of the Taiho Code in 701, Japan introduced a bureaucratic system that relied heavily on imported Tang-dynasty institutions, norms, and practices.[61] John Wills notes that "the real story of the 600s was a great flow of Japanese students of Buddhism and of Chinese traditions and political practices to China."[62] In fact, a scholarly consensus has developed over the past twenty years that "premodern 'Japan' is not a figment of the essentializing modern imagination: it was a real country with real boundaries, yet it was never isolated from the world around it."[63]

The Nara state (710–794) developed concepts of the inner lands (*kenai*) and outer lands (*kegai*), the inner lands being under direct administrative control and the outer lands being outside direct administration but still within the Japanese "world." The Nara state defined its northern provinces of Dewa and Mutsu as extending all the way to the end of the island of Honshu. However, Kudo Masaki notes that second-level administrative units (districts) within these two northern provinces revealed decreasing control, from districts that were entirely administered and under Japanese control, to "frontier districts" populated by colonist-soldiers, to "Emishi districts" ruled by native Emishi chiefs who were progovernment, to Emishi territory entirely outside Japanese authority.[64] As Batten concludes: "During the Nara period . . . the establishment of a strong, centralized state was associated with the emergence of an imperial ideology, the recognition of a clear distinction between incorporated 'inner lands' and unincorporated 'outer lands,' and an ongoing attempt to convert the latter into the former through territorial expansion."[65] The Heian state (794–1185) continued this process, incorporating the entire island of Honshu within its control by the end of its reign.

By the eleventh century, Japan's university system was based on a curriculum that studied the Chinese classics. Its bureaucracy continued to be organized on Chinese lines, and the capital city of Kyoto was modeled after the Tang-dynasty capital of Chang'an in China.[66] The Kamakura and Ashikaga bakufu also oversaw a transition from a barter economy to a monetized economy and from serfdom to a society of smallholders. In his classic book *Government and Local Power in Japan, 500–1700*, John Hall argues convincingly that Japan was not a feudal system and that "feudalism as a historical concept applied to the analysis of Japan's past caused historians to make facile comparisons of European and Japanese history."[67] Kenneth Grossberg argues that it was the Ashikaga (Muromachi) shoguns that transformed themselves from chieftains into monarchs:

> The Ashikaga shoguns of the first half-century of the dynasty constructed a political synthesis which embraced aristocratic elements from the imperial court, feudal elements from their own samurai heritage, and bureau-

cratic elements which they adopted from the Kamakura Bakufu (1185–1333) and the Heian state. These various sources of legitimate authority had always overlapped, but the Ashikaga Bakufu was the first government in Japanese history to combine them successfully in one regime.[68]

The Chinese example as a normative precedent remained very important even for the Tokugawa Japanese. Japan and China continued to trade informally, with up to ninety Chinese ships visiting Japan each year during the seventeenth and eighteenth centuries, and Japan imported over one thousand Chinese books each year.[69] When Tokugawa shoguns were looking for legal and institutional models for how to structure their own government and society, "they were usually Chinese in origin," such as the "Six Maxims" first issued by the Ming dynasty's founder, T'ai-tsu, in 1398, as well as Qing and even Tang and Song legal and administrative codes.[70] Indeed, the *Tokugawa jikki* (the official annals of the Tokugawa era) contains numerous references to Japanese legal scholars consulting with Chinese and Korean scholars as they attempted to interpret various Chinese laws and precedents and modify them for Tokugawa use.

By the time of Tokugawa Japan, "educational institutions at every level across the nation followed a similar curriculum of Japanese and Chinese texts ... the *Tangshixuan* collection of Chinese poetry was a required text, where it was regarded as a canonical work." Chinese literature was so in demand that between 1727 and 1814, one publisher, Suwaraya Shinbei, put out twenty-seven editions of the *Tangshixuan*.[71] During the Tokugawa era, there were Chinatowns peopled with up to five thousand Chinese, including numerous artists, scholars, religious leaders, and other artisans, living in Japan, not only in Nagasaki but also Edo, Kyoto, and other cities. For example, the abbots at Mampukuji temple in Uji (near Kyoto) were Chinese from the Fujian "parent temple," from its founding in 1661 until 1740; after that, the abbots alternated with their Japanese counterparts until 1800.[72]

Although the Japanese studied Chinese institutions in all periods, they did not import the names and terminology but rather the *ideas* that those institutions reflected. There were no "six ministries" in Japan. In this respect, the Japanese were much less slavish than their East Asian state counterparts. Yet the Chinese influence was real and in many ways so thorough as to be indistinguishable from indigenous aspects of Japanese culture. The mixing, borrowing, and adaptation that occurred in Japan thus has as many similarities to the rest of the states in East Asia as it has differences.

Civilization and State Formation: Imposition from Above

Chinese ideas tended to be imposed top-down by states as they attempted to centralize authority and extend control over their territories. In domestic politics, smaller states would borrow from China because it was a model that offered solutions to practical problems faced by elites. Relations with China also offered legitimacy at home and access to trade abroad. In Korea, Vietnam, and Japan, the process of importation was essentially a conflict between warriors and scholars. In the case of Korea and Vietnam, the neo-Confucian revolution of the fifteenth century came about as these states actively consolidated their rules. This conflict between state and society and between scholar and warrior marked all three of the Sinicized East Asian states. In Japan, the scholars lost out. In Korea and Vietnam, they triumphed.

Expanded Vietnamese centralization and state control using Chinese models was crucial for the royal house to expand its control over the seven thousand villages that composed traditional Vietnam. Rationalizing taxation and land use expanded state revenues and gave the capital an increased ability to reward supporters and eliminate opposition. At the subprovincial level, royal appointments oversaw thirty to seventy villages, where they gathered data, standardized weights and measures, and encouraged better agricultural practices.[73] In contrast to Korea, the Vietnamese state dramatically expanded its geographical scope over time. The great "southward advance" occurred in the 1300s and 1400s, as Vietnam eventually crushed the Champa kingdom over the course of a series of wars. Vietnam thus had a greater ethnic makeup than did Korea or Japan, and in that respect it was more like China.

The Le dynasty (1428–1788) lasted three and a half centuries and oversaw intensified Confucianization of Vietnam. The Le dynasty's power was occasionally less than complete, however. From 1627 to 1673, two rival clans fought for power, the Trinh in the north and the Nguyen in the south. Yet even though the Le kings held little power during this time, both the Trinh and the Nguyen factions retained superficial loyalty to the Le dynasty, largely because without firm control of the entire country neither warring faction could claim the legitimacy needed to found a new dynasty. Furthermore, as Keith Taylor notes, "preservation of the Le dynasty lessened the possibility of Chinese intervention," as the Chinese had recognized "the Le as legitimate rulers of Vietnam."[74] In fact, neither the Trinh nor the Nguyen challenged the concept of unified political rule over what is today Vietnam, nor did they reject the increasing

Confucianism that the Le dynasty had begun. Both factions intended to be the legitimate rulers of all Vietnam "and retained a strong sense of themselves as ethnic Vietnamese."[75] As Liam Kelley has pointed out, just as the Japanese daimyō did not challenge the idea of Japan, this was also the case in Vietnam.[76] Beyond modern nationalist interpretations, we have very little evidence that the rationale at the time was to prevent Chinese intervention. That is, the Nguyen in the south did not hope or attempt to establish a separate state but rather sought to overthrow the Le. We also have no evidence that the Chinese would have intervened or that the Chinese court was engaged in discussions about a military solution to the domestic troubles facing the Le dynasty.

In fact, the centralization and Confucianization of Vietnam continued apace throughout this period. King Ho Quy Ly attempted a land reform in 1397 and built local granaries for famine relief, as part of a nascent welfare strategy.[77] After a two-decade Ming Chinese interregnum, state building continued when Le Loi founded the Le dynasty (1427–1788) and began a series of neo-Confucian reforms, including a Le law code that regulated land sales, debt interest, and relief for peasants.[78] Of particular note was the protection of peasant rights to communal land, the only land subject to taxation at the time. Although the Ming occupation was relatively short, it had a lasting effect on Vietnam, hastening the centralization and organization of the state. Whitmore notes that "while the Vietnamese violently rejected Ming political control, these literati equated Ming models with modernity."[79]

The Le-dynasty Vietnamese political structure of the fourteenth and fifteenth centuries more clearly modeled its political organization along Confucian lines. This era is often called the "neo-Confucian revolution," because the Chinese influence became much more thoroughly integrated into Vietnamese political and cultural life. Lieberman notes:

> Although Confucian influence in Vietnam fluctuated after c. 1460 and although in practice patron-client ties remained crucial to the operation of the state, Chinese bureaucratic norms, first institutionalized during the so-called Neo-Confucian revolution of the fifteenth century, tended to encourage in that country a more impersonal, territorially uniform, and locally interventionist system than was found in Indianized polities to the west.[80]

There were six ministries to make policy, identical to the six Chinese ministries. Below them were thirteen provincial headquarters, which in turn administered district offices and the village level, with inspectors traveling the country to monitor the civil service, as was the case in China.[81] This rationalized system of governance covered almost ten thousand villages organized into a "Chinese-style grid," composed of circuits (*dao*), prefectures (*phu*), and districts (*chau*), and it was "exceptionally penetrating by Southeast Asian standards."[82] There was also a standing army of up to two hundred thousand troops, a census every three years, and civil-service examinations.[83] Indeed, after driving out Ming forces in the fifteenth century, the Sinicization of Vietnam actually increased. Those who passed the exam and became mandarins were given privileges such as land and special attire, but they were not allowed to own larger estates with serfs, nor were they allowed to retain their own military militias or armed forces.[84]

The Japanese Ashikaga shoguns of the fourteenth century encouraged the growth of Kyoto and commercial, economic, diplomatic, cultural, and Zen monastic ties with China. The bakufu also developed a civil service and employed bureaucrats, although not on the scale of China and Korea. Known as *bugyonin*, the Muromachi bakufu used the bureaucrats to administrate public finance and tax collection, adjudicate lawsuits brought to the bakufu, and process land claims and other shogunal decrees.[85] Although those at the lowest rungs of society were often subject to personalistic rule by local magistrates, "if you were a civil, military, or ecclesiastical landlord, or a steward of such a person, then the system looked reliable, even modern . . . 'law' was a salient feature of the Japanese medieval era: groups had rights and litigation was not yet suppressed, legal experts flourished both in the bakufu and the imperial system."[86] However, in comparison to the centralized control achieved by Korea, China, and Vietnam, Japan was clearly less statist in its organization. Indeed, "Koryŏ and Chosŏn court officials were acutely aware that the shogun and the Muromachi bakufu could neither prevent piracy nor regulate trade, much less govern areas far from Kyoto."[87]

After Hideyoshi's 1588 prohibition against private warfare, the daimyō had no realistic recourse to military action in order to enlarge their lands. Economic advancement was the only avenue, and "rapid growth of state power was reflected in a recentralization of authority."[88] The period of 1570–1630 was a "great transformation," the "decisive turning point in the start of Japan's 'modernity.' Unification, urbanization, the creation of distribution and marketing networks, and the commercialization of attitudes were all a part of this Japanese leap."[89] Indeed, upon Tokugawa authority, the daimyō were regularly moved around the country and spent half of each year in residence in Edo.

The daimyō complied with Tokugawa dictates to conduct annual censuses. The bakufu changed the national maps to representations based on provinces and districts rather than on the daimyō domains.[90] Even the larger domains of Satsuma and Tosa were subject to these regulations, and they complied. Bruce Batten highlights the range of instruments under state control and the centralization of power in Ashikaga and Tokugawa Japan, which, rather than being an isolated island nation, was connected by the sea to the world around it.[91]

Each of these states had a sizeable permanent military and long military traditions. So if they were not fighting each other, what were these armies doing? Putting down rebellions, guarding the central government, and maintaining essential systems. In Korea, the units of the army that were the best trained and most dependable were always in Seoul to protect the palace and the bureaucracy. Each province had at least two major towns with military garrisons, and naval units were stationed in the important southern provinces. The military ran the land and sea transport for grain taxes and other government logistics and managed communication (including the fire towers for overnight links to the capital—weather permitting!) and postal facilities, which were almost entirely for official use. Every commoner was in the reserves up to the age of sixty, and his household had to pay the cloth tax that supported the military.[92] The military handled these routine duties quite well but sadly proved worthless against foreign invasions.

Here, too, Japan was the exception. In the shogunal system, military resources were under the separate and individual control of many daimyō in addition to the shogun. Mobilizing them was a mere extension of politics (it could be easy, difficult, or risky, depending). But since the participation of the daimyō was essential, he had a political stake in its success, and since this factor provided for a special bond between commander and troops, military effectiveness could be enhanced. Heroism could be locally recognized and the rewards locally applicable to life's opportunities.[93]

Multiple Traditions

Despite the obvious Chinese influence in all aspects of government and society, none of these countries were exact replicas of China. Their political and cultural systems were mixed: rationalized attempts at centralized and national governance coincided and coexisted with traditional elements, such as hereditary monarchies and slaveholding. Confucianism and Buddhism coexisted with indigenous shamanistic religions in all the countries of the region, and Confucian ideals about social, educational, literary, and family structure melded onto existing structures to create new forms of social organization.

Confucianism was grafted onto quite different social and cultural patterns in these other countries. During the first millennium A.D., a rough division had obtained, with Confucian ideas influencing governance and Buddhist ideas influencing social norms. Yet Confucianism slowly began to influence and transform both state *and* society. This process was largely carried out by elites and accelerated in the fifteenth century, with the neo-Confucian revolution in Korea and Vietnam. However, although Confucianism seeped deeply into the social fabric of society, it never fully eradicated Buddhism or the indigenous social practices in any of the societies. This transformation was neither quick nor complete, and even today there are elements of indigenous culture and Buddhist ideas that coexist with Chinese ideas about family life and social structure, the proper role of societal actors, and their relationship to the state. This hybridization was also occurring in China itself, and all of these countries existed within a cultural context that had both local and more general influences; we should be wary about overemphasizing the distinctiveness of these places.

Although Korea was deeply influenced by Chinese culture and ideas, this Chinese influence was laid over an indigenous culture and society, and the two coexisted without truly synthesizing. As mentioned above, Koreans used Chinese characters in writing, and often there are both Korean and Chinese words for the same thing. Similarly, culture and society borrowed many Chinese customs while retaining many uniquely Korean customs. As Martina Deuchler comments, "[Korean] Confucian scholar-officials emerged from the old aristocratic matrix and carried over some distinct elements of this heritage, notably an acute consciousness of status and descent."[94] The Chosŏn king Sejong (r. 1418–1450) believed that local society should not be completely overwhelmed by Chinese rites, arguing, "how can we be bound by what the people of the past did?"[95] Even the examination system was not above controversy. As one critic wrote in 1775:

> Why do we use the civil service examination to identify potential civil servants, anyway? These days those examinations test candidates on their ability to write according to the currently accepted essay format. . . . People study the essay format from childhood and finally pass the examination

when they are old and gray. The examination system thus selects men who are useless, and it does so on the basis of useless writing.[96]

The creation of a Vietnamese state involved the interweaving of Chinese ideas with indigenous Vietnamese ideas. As in Korea, a tension existed between the military and court men, who viewed kinship, Buddhism, and aristocratic ties as important for Vietnamese order, and the scholars, who emphasized Confucianism, education, and impersonal state institutions as the bases of leadership. Numerous scholars have noted the flexible, syncretic nature of Vietnamese social and political institutions, and Mahayana Buddhism was the prevailing religion well into the Le dynasty. Although the Tran and Le dynasties used strict patrilineage for royal succession, primogeniture did not become deeply rooted until the neo-Confucian reforms of the fifteenth century.[97]

However, Vietnam was more deeply influenced by China than was the rest of Southeast Asia. As Victor Lieberman concludes, "if Sinic influences varied by class and locale, in terms of social structure, administration, law, and religion, such influences increasingly did distinguish the eastern lowlands as a whole from the rest of Southeast Asia."[98] He notes that the "Chinese model probably appealed to the literati and to their royal patrons because it promised a variety of practical benefits: Chinese bureaucratic techniques offered to curb regionalism in an unfavorable geographic environment, [and] to strengthen central control over local units."[99]

The domestic process of expanding centralized political control occurred in Japan just as it did in other countries in the region. And, like all countries, Japan saw a waxing and waning of state power over the centuries and competing centripetal and centrifugal forces. Martin Collcutt notes that "for much of the Muromachi period the Kanto and large tracts of Tohoku and Kyushu were outside the pale of Bakufu authority."[100] Yet it did gain financial control over the central provinces. Hall notes that although the centralized bureaucratic structures of the previous governments had weakened, they were also not replaced by the fully patrimonial delegation of lord to vassal. Instead, as Jeffrey Mass argues, family organization was the key building block of Japanese society, "providing the basic framework through which authority was exercised."[101] But we should note that the form of Japanese state organization, although it shared some similarities with feudal Europe, was also unique, and any strict equation with a European system is misleading. Politically, Tokugawa Japan was strong, stable, and exerted central control across much of what is now modern Japan.

Although central control broke down during the Warring States era (*sengoku*: 1467–1568), "the idea of 'Japan' as a single country remained fairly strong."[102] Tellingly, at no time did any of the potential daimyō attempt to create an independent state. Indeed, they all remained explicitly committed to the emperor as ruler of Japan—the only issue being who would be the most powerful actor, not who would reign—"shogun," not emperor. While various powerful political leaders often contended for the power to rule Japan, none attempted to overthrow the institution of the emperor. Hideyoshi conducted a national land survey and implemented a national system of taxation in the late sixteenth century. The Tokugawa bakufu continued the centralizing trend. Although there remained important exceptions to centralized power, the Tokugawa bakufu had complete authority in foreign affairs, military matters, control of the currency and national highway system, and complete control over the religious life of Japan. Land registers and maps, and a national census, were implemented continuously from 1716 onward.[103] Because of the national currency, products could be marketed throughout the whole of Japan.

By the time of the Tokugawa shogunate, the civil service had become much smaller, a samurai warrior caste had developed, and the Chinese influence became increasingly indirect. Yet even "indigenous" Japanese practices such as Shinto were codified and centralized in response to the arrival of Buddhism and Confucianism in Japan. Even a quintessentially Japanese product such as the *Tale of Genji*—a Heian masterpiece—is "everywhere underlaid by a structure of Chinese archetype."[104] During the Tokugawa era, "Chinese books, rigorously checked to make sure they contained no mention of Christianity, [and] found many readers among ambitious, peace-bound samurai."[105] David Pollack concludes that in language, culture, arts, government, and economics, China either as model or as context still "exerted a powerful pressure on every act of culture."[106]

Other Political Units: Southeast Asian States

In addition to the main political units that conducted international relations, there were other significant political or military actors in the region. Of these, the two most consequential were the various peoples that lived in the north, an area now known as Manchuria, and the pirates that infested the inner sea, at times causing havoc as they raided up and down the coasts of Japan, Korea, China, and Vietnam. These other political units were not as enduring, centralized, or institutionalized as the major states of East Asia (table 3.2). As a result, these other political units also tended to have more difficulty interacting with the major states. I deal directly with the "nomads" and the *wakō* in chapter 7; here I will deal with other types of political units. In sum, there were many other types of political organizations neighboring on and interacting with the major states of early modern East Asia.

As a general rule, the other states in the system were less organized and less influenced by China. Southeast Asian continental states were more Indianized than Sinicized, "polities whose codified religious, literary, and political traditions derived primarily from India in the first and second early millennia CE."[107] From 900 to 1350, four major polities dominated mainland Southeast Asia: Pagan (upper Burma), Angkor (the Mekong basin), Champa (the southeastern coast), and Dai Viet. By the fourteenth century, it was possible to find at least twenty-three independent kingdoms on the Southeast Asian mainland. By 1600, consolidation at the expense of these smaller

TABLE 3.2 Other East Asian political units, 1200–1900

	Northern steppe	Manchuria	Thailand	Malaya	Java
1200	1206–1368: Yuan (Mongol)	1121–1234: Jin (Jurchen)	1238–1350: Sukhothai	Thai domination	1222–1293: Singosari
1300			1350–1782: Ayuthia		1293–1520: Majapahit
1400				1402–1511: Malacca	
1500				1511–1641: Portuguese Malacca	
1600		1616–1912: Qing (Manchu)		1641–1796: Dutch Malacca	1619: Dutch colony
1700			1782: Chakri	1796: British colony	
1800					

kingdoms had resulted in the expansion of Burma, Siam, and Vietnam, although smaller kingdoms continued to exist, such as the principalities of Lao, Cambodia, and Assam.

Geographically more distant from China, states such as Siam, Java, Angkor, Champa, and Burma engaged in extensive relations and interactions with the other states, and although they followed some Chinese norms and practices in dealing with other states, they were not directly influenced by Chinese culture and politics to the same extent as were Japan, Korea, and Vietnam.[108] Although not as tightly incorporated into the Chinese system, these states were deeply incorporated into the regional trading economy. Janet Abu-Lughod writes: "From the time the southern Sung first took to the seas in the late twelfth century . . . the petty kingdoms of the [Malacca] strait . . . changed from 'gateway' to dependency . . . the Strait area must be conceptualized, at least in part and in the preceding centuries, as a dependency of China."[109]

However, with the exception of Vietnam, few of the other Southeast Asian political units had even the nascent beginnings of a state in the modern sense. Many scholars have described Southeast Asian kingdoms as borrowing their organization more from the Indian mandalas than from Chinese ideas about centralization and institutions.[110] Martin Stuart-Fox notes that "to call a Southeast Asian kingdom a *mandala* is to draw attention, metaphorically, to relations of power that connected periphery to the center. The *mandalas* of Southeast Asia were constellations of power, whose extent varied in relation to the attraction of the center. They were not states whose administrative control reached to defined frontiers."[111] Victor Lieberman writes that "Champa depended on royal personality and the most rudimentary administrative apparatus to coordinate autonomous, often mutually hostile principalities."[112]

These kingdoms overwhelmingly remained loose groupings of local families and villages connected to the center, and the kings performed religious as much as political roles. Tony Day notes the "fluid, unpredictable role of temples as outposts on the frontiers which separated masters from followers, the living from the dead."[113] Early Javanese states emphasized temple building, ancestor and family cults, and agriculture.[114] Philippine village society was organized around a "circle of indebtedness" based more on the shifting and provisional authority of the chief than on enduring lineages. As Rafael notes: "Nor did meticulously compiled genealogies establish the historical basis for the privilege of one group or family over others."[115] Siam itself, although having deep ties with China, did not implement a Chinese-style governance system. In Siam, the country was governed as most feudal kingdoms were, with noble and royal families that intermarried and controlled and occupied all the key posts. These mandalas were typically hereditary, with a high king overseeing relations from the center. Powerful local families were tied to the "high king" by family or patronage ties, and "reliable royal control in the sense of resource extraction was therefore confined to the capital zone . . . which might not exceed a sixty-mile radius."[116]

During the sixteenth and seventeenth centuries, some states such as Burma and Siam attempted to introduce administrative reforms, but they never achieved the same degree of state centralization and formal control as the Chinese-influenced states.[117] Siam, Burma, Java, and Cambodia in the seventeenth century all saw a shift toward centralized rule, "mobilization of armies, royal monopoly of trade, codification of law, and replacement of hereditary chiefs by ministries."[118]

The states of Southeast Asia experienced twin cultural influences, from India and from China. Hinduism, Islam, and ethnic flows were much more pronounced in Southeast Asia. As Ryan notes: "Throughout history Malaysia has been influenced by both India and China . . . Chinese influence was always less direct, but at certain times . . . the Chinese empire took a very keen interest in the events of South-East Asia."[119] The Malacca Malay sultanate (a.d. 1398–1511) had perhaps the closest cultural relationship with China. Malay rulers visited China numerous times, exchanging tribute. As will be discussed in more detail in chapter 4, this was in part because the Malay sought Ming investiture to protect them from Siamese pressure to the west. Ryan notes that "China was the dominant political power because she was generally a united empire. It was to the Chinese emperors that embassies and gifts were sent. . . . China was the overlord rather than India. She did not directly interfere very much in South-East Asian affairs but she was always there in the background."[120] The Ming regularly sent envoys to Southeast Asia; Zheng He himself visited Malacca seven times between 1405 and 1433.

Conclusion

Chinese civilization had an enduring and wide-ranging political, social, and cultural influence on the surrounding states and peoples. States emulated China in order to deal more effectively with the massive presence that China presented, and Chinese ideas were grafted—sometimes uncomfortably—onto and into vibrant indigenous cultures and societies. These Chinese practices also provided a range of institutional and discursive hierarchic tools that graduated and moderated notions of sovereignty, which helped mitigate and avoid conflict. Indeed, China was the key factor in the early emergence of states in East Asia, and the Chinese influence was pervasive and enduring. Korea, Vietnam, and Japan adopted Chinese practices out of genuine respect for Chinese accomplishments and as a means of consolidating their own rule and presenting themselves to China as a state worthy of treatment as such. Other political actors such as pirates, nomads, and mandalas were a part of the system, but they existed on the periphery of these four major states. Thus, national states of varying size and technological capability existed in an international system based on formal recognition and regulated by a set of norms. For well over six centuries, this system functioned in essentially the same manner.

4 DIPLOMACY

The Tribute System

Traveling in faraway places, I recall the old days wearing my Chinese-style garments and being with my beloved wife.
— ARIWARA NO NARIHIRA

CHINESE CIVILIZATION had an enduring and transformative effect on the domestic politics and societies of many surrounding states, and those most Sinicized formed a Confucian society with shared norms, values, and agreement on what constituted membership. But early modern East Asian international relations was also part of a larger international system, as well: it included all of the political actors in the region, not just the deeply Confucianized states. These more general international rules, norms, and institutions formed the basis of international relations in early modern East Asia.

This international order in East Asia encompassed a regionally shared set of formal and informal norms and institutions that guided relations and yielded substantial stability. With the main institution of the "tribute system," this international system emphasized formal hierarchy among nations while allowing considerable informal equality.[1] As long as the hierarchy was observed and China recognized as hegemon, there was little need for interstate war. Sinic states, and even many nomadic tribes, used some of its rules and institutions when interacting with one another. Status as much as power defined one's place in the hierarchy: China sat highest, and secondary states were ranked by how culturally similar they were to China—not by their relative power. This tribute system also involved restraint by China and provided benefits to the secondary states. As Liam Kelley notes: "It should be clear to the reader that the manner in which we view the world today—that is, as divided between equal nations, each of which takes pride in its own cultural uniqueness—is perhaps inappropriate for viewing the world of the East Asian past."[2]

Michael Mastanduno points out that "hegemony is unlikely to endure if it is primarily coercive, predatory, or beneficial only to the dominant state. In other words, leaders need followers."[3] Incorporation into the Chinese world left the secondary states free to pursue domestic affairs and diplomacy with one another as they saw fit and also brought economic and security benefits at a cost lower than by engaging in arms races or by attempting to develop a counterbalancing alliance against China. Yet more than this functional aspect were the ideas and norms embodied in the tribute system, and Korean and Vietnamese elites in particular accepted the values and ideas of the tribute system.

Thus, it was a mix of legitimate acceptance and rational calculation that motivated Korea and Vietnam to lend their submission to China. They understood China's goals and worked within an overarching set of largely Chinese norms and practices, not against them. The legitimacy of this order played an important role in stabilizing relations between actors. The explicit acceptance of China as hegemon and as the source of civilization and the norms embodied in the various institutions were central to the conception of these states' emerging identities as influential and legitimate political entities.

However, while this underlying set of norms and institutions were the basic building blocks of international relations, by no means were these rules identically and consistently applied by all states in the region. In fact, it is best to view the tribute system as the starting point for international relations, and all the states modified, changed, and sometimes ignored these basic ideas as circumstances dictated. There was no intellectual challenge to the ideas of status, hierarchy, and Chinese civilizational centrality, but what was open for modification were the myriad of ways in which secondary states chose to deal with China, one another, and themselves. As noted in the previous chapter, while some states chose to move closer to China and emulate Confucian practices, others, such as Japan, remained on the edge—a part of, but never wholly embracing, the Confucian society. Still others, such as the various nomadic tribes, used the rules and ideas of the tribute system but explicitly rejected any notions of cultural assimilation along Confucian lines.

Diplomacy

The core of the tribute system was a set of institutions and norms that regulated diplomatic and political contact, cultural and economic relations, and in particular explicitly stated a relationship between two political units. In contrast to the modern Westphalian ideal of equality among nation-states, the tribute system emphasized the "asymmetry and interdependence of the superior/inferior relationship," and inequality was the basis for all relations between two units.[4] The tribute system was formalized in two key institutions: recognition by the superior state, known as "investiture," and the sending of embassy envoys to the superior state. Investiture involved the explicit acceptance of subordinate tributary status and was a diplomatic protocol by which a state recognized the legitimate sovereignty of another political unit and the status of the king in that tributary state as the legitimate ruler.[5] Tribute embassies served a number of purposes: they stabilized the political and diplomatic relationship between the two sides, provided information about important events and news, formalized rules for trade, and allowed intellectual and cultural exchange among scholars. Missions themselves, composed of scholar-officials, interpreters, physicians, alternates, messengers, and assistants, could consist of hundreds people.

For example, when the Chinese emperor established a tributary relationship with another country or community, that established the sovereignty of that country in Chinese eyes and entitled the recipient to rights of entry into China. The *Da Qing tongli* (Comprehensive Rites of the Great Qing) begins the section on receiving envoys with reference to the ancient Zhou dynasty (1027–481 b.c.): "In the *Rites of Zhou* the Grand Conductors of Affairs (*Daxingren*) handled the rites and ceremonies of the guest. Kingdoms external to the nine provinces were called foreign kingdoms (*fanguo*)."[6] As in the modern Westphalian system, this mutual recognition of legitimacy and sovereignty was the key diplomatic aspect of the tribute system. Classifying foreign kingdoms as *guo* (country) shows both difference and similarity: *guo* was the designation for Qing itself, and thus foreign kingdoms were viewed as similar, although unequal, units.

The tributary was expected to use the Chinese calendar in all communication to the emperor, send diplomatic missions or embassies to China at regular intervals, and present documents or "tallies" that allowed access to China's borders. However, different regulations and rites applied to different categories of visitors, according to their status. For example, more exalted diplomats were excused from kowtowing and were also allowed to trade privately; these were benefits denied to lower-status officials.[7] As James Hevia notes, "the superior/inferior relationship is signified as such in several ways . . . superiors initiate, set affairs in motion, are a source; but inferiors bring affairs to completion."[8]

Yet beyond these measures, China exercised little authority over other states: "When envoys bowed before the Chinese emperor, they were in effect acknowledging the *cultural* superiority of the Chinese emperor, not his *political* authority over their states."[9] Relations with China did not involve much loss of independence, as these states were largely free to run their domestic affairs as they saw fit and could also conduct foreign policy independently from China.[10] As Liam Kelley writes, "Vietnamese envoys passionately believed that they participated in what we would now call the Sinitic or East Asian cultural world, and that they accepted their kingdom's vassal status in that world."[11]

The Status Hierarchy

A key element of the tribute system was the explicitly unequal nature of the relationship. In early modern East Asia, although states were largely free to do as they pleased, perhaps most significant was the explicit recognition that China was at the top of the hierarchy. Other states were not allowed to call themselves the equal of China, although this had little effect on their domestic politics. This hierarchy was rank ordered, based in part on how culturally similar these states were to China. Rank on the hierarchy was explicit and brought with it different rights, chief among them access to China. James Hevia notes that "it is not, therefore, simply a matter of proposing hierarchy as an organizing principle in 'traditional' China. Rather, the notion of hierarchy to which the *Comprehensive Rites* appears to refer is materialized via a logic of inclusion or encompassment which simultaneously maintains difference."[12]

Korea and Vietnam were no stronger than Japan, but they were ranked more highly by virtue of their relations to China and their more thorough adoption of Chinese ideas. Korea in particular was seen as a "model" tributary[13] and was unquestionably near the top of the hierarchy. Indeed, Korea ranked first in the Ming hierarchy of tributary states, a distinction of pride for Koreans, and they "saw their relationship to China as more than a political arrangement; it was a confirmation of their membership in Confucian civilization."[14] Chosŏn-Ming relations were quite close, with Korea annually dispatching three embassies to China during the fifteenth century, and Korean elites "eagerly import[ed] Chinese books and ideas."[15] Ki-baek Lee concludes that the Chosŏn "relationship with Ming China on the whole proceeded satisfactorily."[16] This stable relationship continued under the Qing, and Hevia notes that "Korea emerges in Qing court records as the loyal domain par excellence. In the *Comprehensive Rites*, Korea appears first among the other domains, and imperial envoys dispatched to the Korean court are always of a higher rank."[17]

Vietnam, like Korea, was "widely recognized as [one of] the premier domains of manifest civility after the Middle Kingdom," and during the 15th and 16th centuries sent missions to Beijing almost every year. [18] Vietnam first entered into a tributary relationship with China upon its independence in the tenth century, and from that time on, "Song [Chinese] rulers unquestionably placed the Vietnamese kingdom at the top of a hierarchical system of relationships with leaders along the southern frontier."[19] The Le Dynasty (1427–1787) was considered one of the "most loyal" tributaries of China, and tribute missions and cultural imports and learning were regular and comprehensive.[20] Indeed, we consistently find writings such as that by the eighteenth-century Vietnamese scholar-official Nguyen Vinh, who wrote of his service as an envoy to China that:

> The only literatus who can expand his capacity to the greatest degree, have his prestige praised at court, and his name honored for all ages in other lands is the envoy. Only someone who has the skill to govern . . . [is] always aware of what is most important. . . . During the years of the Song dynasty [960–1279] . . . the great talents all emerged in the south. It was at this time we came to be called a domain of manifest civility. Now to be able to see with one's own eyes [China] all that one has read in books, is that not the great joy in one's life?[21]

What Nguyen Vinh described was a process where all of the things that today we would label "traditional Chinese culture" gradually spread southward from the Yellow River valley. Later, when the Vietnamese Nguyen Anh completed his overthrow of the old Le dynasty in 1802 and sought investiture from the Qing, the question came up of what to call the new country. Previously it had been "Annam," but the Annamese now called themselves the Nam Viet.

> This was completely unacceptable to the Qing court, since these characters (Chinese reading nan yue) were the name of an old state that had been centered in what was now Guangdong and Guanxi. Several exasperated exchanges produced no solution. Then someone in the imperial court suggested simply reversing the two syllables. Nguyen Anh agreed to call his kingdom Viet Nam. . . . Thus, one of the most passionately cherished national names of our times . . . was invented within the red walls of the Forbidden City of Beijing.[22]

Japan, the Ryukyus, Siam, the Burmese kingdoms, and the other political units that engaged in tribute relations with China were ranked lower than Korea and Vietnam. These kingdoms were allowed to trade and interact with China, but they received fewer benefits and had less access to China than did those ranked more highly. Japan, for example, was technically restricted to one mission every ten years, although it sent tribute missions slightly more frequently.[23]

Tribute Missions

The Ming and Qing "established specific regulations per contact regarding the frequency of tribute missions and the number of people who could attend each mission."[24] For example, sixteenth-century Chosŏn Korea was allowed annual missions and during the Chosŏn dynasty sent an average of three to seven tribute missions to China every year.[25] Vietnam was initially allowed annual missions in the fifteenth century, which eventually became one every three years; Japan was allowed one mission every ten years.[26] Thus, between 1637 and 1881, Korea sent 435 special embassies to the Qing court, or an average of almost 1.5 embassies per year. In practice, however, this was flexible, and some states managed to avoid or modify the number of missions they were allowed to send.[27]

By the fifteenth century, Vietnam was sending embassies to Beijing "every year or two," where the new regime

sought recognition, offered tribute, congratulations, and condolences, and explained events that were occurring on the southern border. . . . Besides the standard role of political subordination and contact that these tributary missions undertook, they increasingly brought Vietnamese literati, those scholars committed to the beliefs of the Chinese classical and Neo-Confucian texts, in touch with the Sinic literati world as it actually existed and functioned. This included both administrative and social roles, as well as the literary.[28]

The Vietnamese official Ho Si-Dong (1739–1785) wrote of his time as an envoy on a tribute mission:

I was transferred to take up the post as surveillance commissioner of Hai Duong. Later I received orders to serve as an envoy to the North [China].

I recalled when I was studying in the capital the Master [Nguyen Tong Khue] was living in seclusion in his home. I always regretted that I could not study under him. Now I was fortunate to be able to follow in his footsteps and view the [moral] radiance of the Esteemed Kingdom [China]. . . . This was truly a meeting of the minds.[29]

Japanese ambivalence toward China was more powerful than in Korea. However, the Japanese have traditionally described the world as *ka-i no sekai*, or "the world of China and the barbarians," and Kazui notes that "from the time of Queen Himiko's rule over the ancient state of Yamatai [a.d. 183 to 248] to that of the Ashikaga shoguns during the Muromachi period, it was essentially these same international rules that Japan followed."[30] Japan had stopped sending envoys to China in 890 and did not resume them until the Ashikaga shogunate of the mid-fourteenth century, and even then it was only a formal tributary of China for 150 years. For example, in 1370 Prince Kaneyoshi of Japan presented a *hyosen* (*piao-chien*, a foreign-policy document presented to the Chinese emperor) in which he referred to himself as "subject," and Yoshimitsu's acceptance of Chinese suzerainty became a powerful legitimizing tool for his government.[31] Writing about the fifteenth century, Key-huik Kim adds:

In 1404—a year after the ruler of Yi Korea received formal Ming investiture for the first time—Yoshimitsu, the third Ashikaga shogun, received Ming investiture as "King of Japan." The identical status assigned to the rulers of Yi Korea and Ashikaga Japan under the Ming tribute system seems to have facilitated the establishment of formal relations between the two neighbors on the basis of "equality" within the "restored" Confucian world order in East Asia.[32]

During the one and a half centuries that Ashikaga Japan was a formal tributary of the Ming, the Shogun sent a total of 20 embassies with accompanying personnel numbering in the hundreds. The Shogunal representatives were staffed by an official ambassador of the Shogun, and included other court officials as well as the occasional domain representative. The missions engaged in tally trade, returned captured pirates, and exchanged news about each country.[33] Yet the Japanese had a visceral resistance to the subordinating rituals required by the formal tributary conditions that China laid down, and internal criticism along those lines forced the Ashikaga shoguns to discontinue tribute relations after 150 years. John Wills notes that Ashikaga Yoshimitsu's investiture by the Chinese court "has been reviled by *Tenno*-traditionalists ever since."[34]

Although in theory the number of people allowed on a mission was restricted, this number was also often exceeded. The tribute missions entered China at the border, conducted rituals there, and were eventually escorted to the capital for a series of rituals that took place over several weeks. This included the exchange of tribute gifts and letters. Accompanying personnel would interact with their counterparts, and official trade would occur. Trade also occurred at the border between envoys left there to trade.

The Vietnamese court would begin the process of sending an embassy by instructing the Ministry of Revenue and the Imperial Household Department to draft an official request for approval to cross the border on a given day. This request would be delivered to the border, and a delegation of "awaiters of orders" would be dispatched to the border to await a response [from China]." The Vietnamese court would also select envoys and other members of the actual entourage. "A chief envoy journeying to the North to request investiture for the Southern king would have to be an official of at least second rank, while the first and second assistant envoys had to be of the third or fourth rank."[35]

Serving on a mission was an immense honor, as is reflected in the following poem composed by the scholar-official Nguyen Co Phu for the Vietnamese king in the fourteenth century:

To this distant domain which desires to be transformed official word has
    come . . .
I will sincerely report our fief's efforts when I visit the Celestial Court
The benevolence we bathe in is as if from a golden goblet brimming to
    the rim
Already the radiance seems so close as I set off to receive his moral
    blessings
In this distant wilderness we will joyfully maintain this enterprise for
    ages to come

Liam Kelley notes that the poem "describes the South's relationship with the North in strikingly unequal terms . . . why [would] a Southern official describe the relationship in this manner to his own monarch? Could it be that the Southern elite actually believed in this characterization of their relationship with the North?"[36] It is important to take seriously the beliefs of the actors at the time. Viewing the world as unequal was not strange; instead, it seemed self-evident to the people of the time. Thus, that rules and norms developed around an unequal, hierarchic international order rather than being based on principles of equality is also not a surprise. Vietnamese tribute sent to the Song in 1156 reveals the character of the relationship:

> The tribute is extremely rich and all the characters in the letter were written with gold. There were 1,200 *taels* of gold wares, half of them decorated with pearls or valuables; 100 pearls contained in gold vases, of which three were as big as eggplants, six as big as the cores of jackfruit, 24 as big as peach pits, 17 as big as palm hearts, and 50 as big as date pits, making a total of 100; there were 1,000 catties of aloewood, 50 kingfisher feathers, 850 bolts of gold brocade decorated with dragons, six imperial horses complete with saddles, plus the regular tribute of eight horses and five elephants. The envoys were quite proud of being able to bring so rich a tribute.[37]

Liam Kelley ends his extensive research on the writings of the Vietnamese scholar-officials by concluding that

> this way of viewing the world as consisting of unequal domains of manifest civility [Confucian] which partook in a common cultural tradition, and this sense of anxiety that some Southern scholars felt at their land's inability to live up to the standard of such a domain, are important to keep in mind. . . . For while the existing scholarship has accustomed us to think of Southern [Vietnamese] envoys as proud believers in their own (cultural) importance who only "posed" as tribute bearers, in fact . . . their minds may have been filled with quite contrary thoughts. Rather than seeking to demonstrate that "Vietnam" was "civilized" so that the "Chinese" would not invade, Southern envoys may have harbored other thoughts and intentions when they journeyed to the North.[38]

Commitment Not to Exploit

A key aspect of legitimate hierarchy is a credible commitment on the part of the dominant state not to exploit the subordinate states. The tributary system provided a range of flexible institutional and discursive tools with which to resolve conflicts without recourse to war, and a good indicator of the stability in the system is that the borders between Korea, Japan, Vietnam, and China were relatively fixed and did not significantly change during the five centuries under review. Beth Simmons writes: "When they are mutually accepted, [borders] drastically reduce external challenges to a government's legitimate authority . . . and clarify and stabilize transnational actors' property rights."[39] As Wendt and Friedheim note: "Recognizing the sovereignty of subordinate states imposes certain restraints on dominant states."[40]

By the eleventh century, Korea had established the Yalu river as its northern border, and it was the affirmation of this border and the Korean acceptance of tributary status in the fourteenth century that precluded a war between the new Ming Chinese and Chosŏn Korean dynasties. Near the beginning of the Ming dynasty, in 1389, the Ming notified Koryŏ that it considered the area of northeastern Korea that had been under direct Mongol control (the Ssangsŏng commandery) to be part of its territory. Koryŏ decided to fight the Ming over the demarcation of the border, and it was this campaign, and General Yi Sŏnggye's unwillingness to fight it (preferring negotiation), that led to the fall of Koryŏ and, three years later, the creation of a new dynasty, the Chosŏn.[41] Yi immediately opened negotiations with China, and the Ming did indeed settle for Chosŏn's tributary status. Significantly, in exchange for entering into tribute status with China, Chosŏn Korea retained all territory previously held by Koryŏ, and the subsequent relations between China and Korea remained close and stable for two hundred and fifty years, with the two sides exchanging numerous envoys and regularly trading.

The late Koryŏ-dynasty era in Korea was turbulent: the Mongols had attacked and subjugated the dynasty in the thirteenth century; *wakō* pirates attacked and plundered along the southern coast 378 times between 1375 and 1388; Jurchens continually raided Koryŏ's northern border; and, most importantly, a resurgent and militarily powerful Ming China in the fourteenth century was a potential military threat to the new Chosŏn dynasty's survival.[42] One obvious response to these security threats could have been a full militarization of the new Chosŏn dynasty and a resort to force. Yet the opposite occurred: the founding of the Korean Chosŏn dynasty in 1392 heralded an intensification of Confucian practices, and "scholar-officials . . . became directly involved in policymaking at all levels."[43] Deuchler notes: "To the social architects of early Chosŏn, the adoption of ancient Chinese institutions was not an arbitrary measure to restore law and order, but the revitalization of a link with the past in which Korea itself had a prominent part."[44] Indeed, the

Chosŏn dynasty's founder, Yi Song-gye, looked to Ming China for legitimacy with his own aristocracy, who were skeptical of Yi's humble origins, and in the Chosŏn "Founding Edict" he explicitly used the Chinese calendar, and its initial memorials made explicit reference to Chinese dynasties of the past.[45]

This intensification of Confucian practices has been called the "neo-Confucian revolution," during which scholars imposed their ideas about proper government and society over the objections of the military class. The founders of the new Chosŏn dynasty were not outsiders rebelling against an established order—in fact, they came from the educated elite—and their dissatisfaction was driven by a desire to intensify neo-Confucian practices, not overturn them.[46] For example, in his "Admonition to the New King," the Inspector-General wrote:

> The reason for the falls of Kings Chieh and Chou is that they lost virtue and ruled by force. . . . King Yu of Hsia demonstrated his virtue by building his palace low. . . . Emperor Wen of Han displayed his exemplary attitude by being thrifty . . . how much less should the sovereign be careless in his expenditure in Korea, whose land is squeezed between the mountains and the sea and whose population and taxes are not numerous![47]

The Chosŏn founder, Yi Song-gye, looked to Ming China for legitimacy with his own aristocracy, who were skeptical of Yi's humble origins. In this case, investiture from Ming China not only stabilized their border and territory, but diplomatic recognition also provided the Chosŏn king with domestic legitimacy. Thus, the Chosŏn "Founding Edict" explicitly used the Chinese calendar, and the initial memorials also made explicit reference to Chinese dynasties of the past.[48]

By the fifteenth century, Korea's long northern border—along both the Yalu and Tumen rivers—was essentially secure and peaceful; these two rivers have formed the border between China and Korea ever since. The Changbaishan/Paektusan area was negotiated in 1713.[49] Chŏng Yagyong, a Korean scholar-official writing in the eighteenth century, noted that

> the southern slopes of Mount Changbaek, where both the Tumen and Yalu rivers have their headwaters, lay within our territory, but the winding ridges and layers of peaks make the exact location of the border unclear. However, [Qing] Emperor Kang-hsi ordered Area Commander Wu-la Muk'eteng to delineate the border and erect a stone boundary marker. As a result, the border between those two rivers is clear as well.[50]

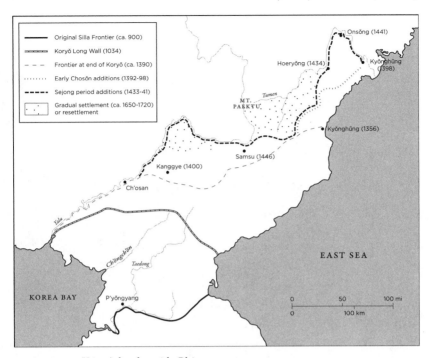

Legend:
- Original Silla Frontier (ca. 900)
- Koryŏ Long Wall (1034)
- Frontier at end of Koryŏ (ca. 1390)
- Early Chosŏn additions (1392-98)
- Sejong period additions (1433-41)
- Gradual settlement (ca. 1650-1720) or resettlement

Onsŏng (1441)
Hoeryŏng (1434)
Kyŏnghŭng (1398)
MT. PAEKTU
Tumen
Kyŏnghŭng (1356)
Samsu (1446)
Kanggye (1400)
Ch'osan
Yalu
EAST SEA
Ch'ŏngch'ŏn
Taedong
KOREA BAY
P'yŏngyang

0   50   100 mi
0   100 km

FIGURE 4.1 Korea's border with China, 900–1999

In the late 1880s, the Chinese reopened the issue of the border. Over the course of these negotiations, the Koreans presented documents and maps from the 1710–1713 negotiations with which to document their case. Rather than risk losing, the Chinese abandoned the negotiation and never returned to the table, and the Korean status quo stood (figure 4.1).[51]

Gari Ledyard notes:

> While the Koreans had to play the hand they were dealt, they repeatedly prevailed in diplomacy and argument . . . and convinced China to retreat from an aggressive position. In other words, the tributary system did provide for effective communication, and Chinese and Korean officialdom spoke from a common Confucian vocabulary. In that front, the relationship was equal, if not at times actually in Korea's favor.[52]

The Vietnam-China border was also clearly drawn. Vietnam and China demarcated their border in 1079, "which has remained essentially unchanged to the present day."[53] The Vietnamese and Chinese had agreed that "the Quan Nguyen and Guihua prefectures [were] two sides of a 'fixed border' (*qiangjie*)

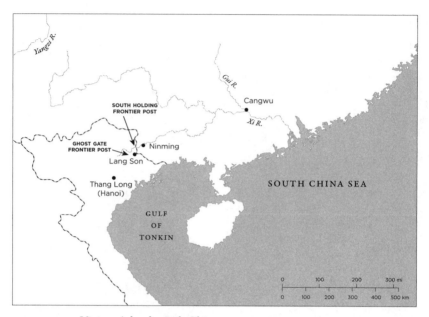

FIGURE 4.2 Vietnam's border with China, 1079–1999

region between the two states."[54] A fifteenth-century Vietnamese map shows the "official [route] for Vietnamese embassies traveling to the Chinese capital of Beijing. Going north from the capital, the map . . . moves past the walled city of Lang-son to the great gate on the Chinese border leading into Guanxi Province."[55] When China and Vietnam signed their modern treaty in 1999, they agreed upon essentially this same border (figure 4.2).

Recognition of the border and the stability it represented is woven through the writings of government officials of the time. The Tran Nam/Zhennan Frontier Post, or "South Holding Frontier Post," was located at the border of Guangxi province and Lang Son defense command. For centuries it was "the main border post between the two domains."[56] As the scholar-official Nguyen Du (1765–1820) wrote in 1813:

> The old affairs of Ly and Tran are distant and hard to find
> The two kingdoms evenly divide at this lone rampart
> But it is close to the Celestial, so one can finally understand the depth of
>   the benevolence we receive
> From the [Qing] emperor's palace looking down, this place is as if be-
>   yond the scattered clouds
> Yet by my ears I can still make out a bit of the imperial tune.[57]

The Vietnam-China border, especially the western areas, were especially difficult to define and patrol, given that the frontier was jungle mountains populated by hill tribes and that "the Qing had regular procedures for the extradition of criminals to Annam. . . . Qing authorities knew they had all they could do to control territory on their side of the border as it filled up with miners and frontier farmers, frequently encroaching on and clashing with the hill peoples."[58] For example, in 1725, Vietnam moved the border 120 *li* northward (about forty miles) into Yunnan, toward promising copper mines. Given the difficulties in dealing with the border, Ertai, an official and confidant of the Yongzheng emperor, argued: "If we get the land we won't be able to defend it; if we get the people we won't be able to make any use of them." The emperor agreed to let Annam keep eighty *li*; forty *li* returned to Qing. "The King of Annam sent officials to greet with great ceremony the emperor's edict conceding the territory," and the matter was settled.[59]

Rulers often relied on diplomatic recognition by China to stabilize their own domestic rule, to ensure Chinese acceptance of their rule, and prevent Chinese intervention to stabilize Chinese borders.[60] Japanese historians such as Ishii Masatoshi, Murai Shosuke, and Tanaka Takeo explicitly acknowledged Japan's subordination to China in the Heian and Muromachi eras—Murai emphasizing that the adoption of investiture was a means of securing legitimacy of rule domestically and securing a monopoly of trade with China.[61] Ashikaga Yoshimitsu received Ming envoys in 1402, along with a letter from the emperor and the Chinese calendar (which "indicated respectful subordination to China"), by offering incense and kneeling "reverently" in order to read it.[62]

Even some Southeast Asian kingdoms benefitted from tribute relations. For example, in 1767, Siam was in chaos due to Burmese incursions that managed to capture the capital city of Ayutthaya. After the Burmese had been pushed back, a Siamese provincial governor, Taksin, sought investiture from the Qing as ruler of Siam. The Qing responded that he should first try to find a ruler from the previous ruling house and sent three envoys to Siam to investigate the situation. When the Qing concluded that Taksin was the best alternative, they recognized him—not formally as king but as "lord of the country."[63] When Taksin was deposed in 1782, a general emerged in Siam—Rama I—the first king of the Chakkri dynasty, which rules to this day. In appealing to the Qing for recognition, he wrote in Chinese to the Qing court that his "father" Taksin had "exhorted me to rule with care, not to change the old order, to have care for our own sovereign land and to honor the Heavenly Dynasty."[64]

China's strength also allowed it to provide security benefits to lesser states that agreed to play by the system's rules. Parameswara Iskandar Shah, the sultan of Malacca from 1394 to 1414, entered into a tributary relationship with China in order to protect himself from Siamese influence in 1403. Ryan notes that "the Chinese were not averse, therefore, to accepting Parameswara's request for protection. In 1403 a Chinese fleet led by an admiral named Yin Ching arrived in Malacca confirming Parameswara as the ruler of the settlement. In return further envoys were sent to China in the same year and again in 1407."[65] Siam sent seventy-eight tribute missions to China between 1371 and 1503.

Arrighi, Hui, Hung, and Selden note that "the China-centered tributary-trade system can often mediate inter-state relations and articulate hierarchies with minimal recourse to war. Japan and Vietnam, being peripheral members of this system, seemed more content to replicate this hierarchical relationship within their own sub-systems than vie directly against China in the larger order."[66] Thus, even though Japan only sporadically accepted tributary status, the system as a whole was stable because Japan accepted Chinese political, economic, and cultural centrality in the system, and it also benefited from international trade and the general stability the system brought.

Systemic stability seems to have been good for the political regimes in each of these Sinicized East Asian countries, which, in comparative perspective, were remarkably long lived. Tellingly, this was the case even more for the weaker states. The East Asian experience may be the pacific obverse of "imperial overstretch." Rather than being foolish for relying on bandwagoning and regional diplomatic order instead of constant self-strengthening and displays of resolve and commitment, in retrospect these states appear quite canny.[67] Pamela Crossley noted that "this set of institutional and discursive practices provided a wide range of tools with which to mediate conflict in East Asia."[68]

Legitimacy

The best evidence that secondary states saw China and Confucianism as legitimate are the voluntarily adoption of Chinese and Confucian ideas and institutions; the absence of evidence that Koreans, Vietnamese, or Japanese were smirking at Chinese behind their backs; and the use of the tribute system by secondary states in their dealings with one another. There is extensive discussion in the historical records of Korea, Japan, and other Sinic states about Confucianism, civilization, and their states' and societies' roles. There is also little evidence that such discussion was merely a façade designed to fool Chinese diplomats. One good example of the explicit acceptance of Confucian ideas about civilization came in the wake of the Manchu (Qing) conquest of China in 1644. The Qing conquest caused intense debate within China and also in the surrounding states about whether the new dynasty was legitimate and whether it was Confucian. For example, in a 1786 memorial to the Korean king Chongjo (1776–1800), Pak Chega, a noted official, wrote:

> Our country served the Ming as a tributary subject for more than two hundred years . . . even though the Qing have now ruled the world for more than one hundred years, the descendants of the Chinese and their etiquette still prevail . . . thus, it is quite incorrect to rashly call these people [Manchu] "barbarians." . . . If we want to revere China, there is no greater reverence than to put the Chinese ways into practice.[69]

Significantly, even the Japanese accepted notions of Confucian civilization, although they grimaced at China's centrality in the system. Perhaps most interesting was a Tokugawa report from the 1730s. Edited by Hayashi Shunsai, it was titled *Ka'i hentai*, or "the Chinese-Barbarian Transformation." The book's title comes from the Qing's conquest of China; the author saw the Manchu conquest as transforming Ming China from civilized to barbarian.[70] As Mizuno notes, "the perception of the Manchus as barbarians seemed to remain among the Japanese throughout the Tokugawa era."[71] That the Japanese retained Confucian ideas about what comprised status, cultural achievement, and the larger hierarchic and tributary order is significant. Implicit in both the Korean and Japanese debates about the Qing is both the idea and the acceptance of what constituted Confucian civilization and what constituted the rightful rule of China.

Indeed, Liam Kelley reports: "I have found no evidence of mockery or belittling of the tributary relationship in any of the poetry that Southern [Vietnamese] envoys composed. One finds instead that this relationship and the concepts on which it was based were part and parcel of these envoys' understandings of the world and the way it worked."[72] Thus it was a mix of legitimate acceptance and rational calculation that motivated states such as Korea and Vietnam to lend their submission to China.

Although dominant or hegemonic states might exploit secondary states, what China appears to have wanted was legitimacy and recognition from secondary states, not necessarily material benefits such as wealth or power. Extensive trade relations did not necessarily favor China and, as we will see in chapter 6, was sometimes a net loss.[73] Militarily, China was content to coexist with the Sinic states as long as they were not troublesome. Yet recognition of China as dominant was important, and a challenge to legitimate authority was a key factor in the cause and resolution of the one war between China and Vietnam during this time. As a hegemon, the Chinese tributary relationship could be costly for the Chinese government. Gregory Smits notes: "China, in effect, purchased the participation of surrounding states by offering them incentives."[74]

Alliance behavior existed as well, yet states worked with China, not against it. Other states bought into the Chinese role as system manager. In 1592, for example, King Naresuan of Siam learned of Japan's invasion of Korea and sent a mission to China in October of that year, offering to send the Siamese fleet against Japan. Wyatt emphasizes: "This was no empty gesture. Naresuan understood the interconnectedness of international relations, and he wanted to maintain a balance of power favorable to open international commerce and to China's dominance in an orderly Asian state system."[75]

Even John Wills, a critic of the concept of the tribute system, concludes that

it is crucial to my critique of the tribute system as a master concept that important parts of Qing foreign relations had little or no relation to the institution of the tribute embassy. But the relations with Siam and with Annam were very much within the tribute system . . . relations with Siam were managed with far better information about the foreign polity and far more realistic policy making than in most cases.[76]

Vietnam fell into domestic disorder in the 1500s, as the Trinh (north) and Nguyen (south) fought for legitimacy, and in 1644 the Qing accepted the restored Le dynasty under Trinh hegemony. Wills notes that "the Le kings sent regular tribute embassies, were meticulous in the use of seals and terminology, and prepared their own tribute memorials and accompanying documents in quite respectable literary Chinese."[77]

This type of diplomacy reveals the way in which international relations had a formative influence on states throughout the region. Although China was clearly the center, and maintaining stable relations with it was paramount, these states sought information about each other, interacted with each other, and had a set of norms and practices that were recognized and accepted that communicated information about each other's preferences, interests, and goals. As noted above, being able to read and write in sophisticated Chinese was central to presenting the state in a positive light to China. "Looking at the stability of their tribute relations with stable and effective states in Vietnam and with Siam in the early nineteenth century, the Qing rulers had every reason to believe that their inherited practices were working very well . . . a multiplicity of sources of information increased the possibility that the emperor could demonstrate his mastery of the situation."[78] In sum, states engaged in diplomacy with one another on a consistent basis. Far from being isolated and autarkic, the early modern East Asian system developed rules and norms governing trade, diplomacy, and international migration.

Hierarchy and Relations Between Secondary States

Further reflecting the acceptance of the tributary system as legitimate is the fact that Korea, Japan, Vietnam, and other states used the institutions of the tribute system and also replicated these rank orders in their own relations with other political units. Indeed, the emphasis on status and hierarchy pervaded not just states' relations to China but extended to all foreign relations of the time. The tribute system was the regionwide political framework that allowed for diplomacy, travel, and official and private trade between all the states in the region. Secondary states also replicated these rank orders in their own relations with other political units. These states conducted formal diplomatic relations with each other, with elaborate protocols, ranks, and systems of interaction. When other states interacted with each other, the rules were still hierarchic and within the tributary system—Korea and Japan each looked down on the other as less advanced, and Koreans looked down on Jurchens and Japanese as being lower than Vietnamese, because of their less Confucian ways. Status in the hierarchy was a function of cultural achievement, not economic wealth or military power.

The tribute system ordered relations regarding the management of borders, dealing with crises, and regulating a host of other interactions. International diplomacy was not merely a functional set of rules to allow trade, either: in general, the tribute system was the political framework that allowed for diplomacy, travel, and official and private trade between all the states in the region. By the early fifteenth century, the Korean Chosŏn court had divided foreign contacts—such as envoys from Japan, the Ryukyus, and Jurchens—into four grades, with several statuses within these grades. These grades corresponded not only to different diplomatic statuses and rights but also entailed different trading and commercial rights, regulated Japanese and Jurchen contact, and covered issues such as the repatriation of traders and sailors who had been shipwrecked in Japan. Korea, for example, explicitly ranked its relations with other countries: various Mongol tribes were rank 4, the Ryukyus rank 5.[79]

Japan also maintained tribute relations with other states, most notably with Korea and the Ryukyus. The Japanese also devised an elaborate set of rights and regulations—to be discussed in detail in chapter 6—that covered economic relations. For example, in 1601, Tokugawa Ieyasu wrote to the Vietnamese lord Nguyen Hoang, stating: "In the future, ships visiting your country from our country are to be certified by the seal shown on this letter, and ships not carrying the seal should not be deemed lawful."[80] These shipping licenses granted by the shogun were called *shuinsen* (朱印船) and were similar to Chinese tallies, although without as extensive a political or diplomatic relationship attached to the trade.

As for Korea, Kenneth Robinson concludes that the Chosŏn Korean court "borrowed, adapted, and expanded upon rights and policies of the sinocentric tribute system," developing "a tribute system designed over time in part to organize interactions with a broad collection of Japanese elites and separate them into a multi-level hierarchy for reception and ritual purposes."[81] Ha Ubong argues that Chosŏn relations with the shogun were conducted on the basis of equality, but Chosŏn relations with Tsushima and Japanese traders were hierarchical.[82] Kenneth Swope notes that "when addressing states such as Ryukyu they [Korea] considered to be inferior in status within the Chinese tributary system, they implied . . . paramountcy. Japan they regarded as an equal or as an inferior depending upon the occasion."[83]

Different rank led to different rights: the highest-grade Japanese officials, for example, were allowed to outfit up to three ships for trade with Korea "and also move an unlimited amount of that cargo . . . but Korean officials severely restricted the volumes of official trade permitted contacts in the two lower grades."[84] Entry into Korea was governed by an official seal, and Japanese officials occasionally attempted to forge diplomatic seals in order to gain better trading benefits. By the fifteenth century, Korea and Japan had developed elaborate rules governing the recognized Japanese envoys to Korea and their status for the purpose of reception, where envoys and traders could land in Korea and where they could travel, the number of trading ships allowed to visit the country, the manner in which trade was to be conducted, and who would actually be allowed to trade. For example, by 1418 copper seals were required to distinguish authorized Japanese traders from pirates, and a treaty in 1443 limited the number of Japanese ships to fifty per year and required them to receive credentials from the lord of Tsushima to be presented in one of three Korean ports: Pusan-po, Chae-po, and Yon-po.[85] Trade between Korea and Japan was so extensive that by 1494 over three thousand Japanese were permanently residing around Pusan. After the Imjin War, Korea restricted Japanese traders and diplomats to only the port of Pusan.

The key diplomatic institutions concerning Korea-Japan relations were the Korean *waegwan*, or "Japan houses," that were built as early as 1419. Originally designed to house official envoys and separate them from Japanese living in Korea, by the seventeenth century the Pusan *waegwan* had become a series of buildings within a compound and was the sole legal place for Japanese envoys and traders to stay while they were in Korea. Official permission was required to leave the *waegwan*. In existence until 1876, the *waegwan* housed over one thousand Japanese and had operated continuously except for the interruption of the Imjin War.

There is a great deal of evidence that both Korea and Japan regarded each other as inferiors. States without the cultural or civilizational influence of China had far less claim to superior status relative to other secondary states. As a result, states down the hierarchy had trouble dealing with each other and with determining their own hierarchic ranking. Kenneth Robinson concludes about the fifteenth century:

> Japanese went through the motions of obeisance, used the right words, such as "tribute" . . . and sought entry as frequently as possible. They did not assume this posture so that they could first and foremost display their respect to the King of Chosŏn and his officials. They wanted entry to Chosŏn for the grains, cloths, Buddhist sutras, and other items of value in Japan and among Jurchens.[86]

The Japanese followed the same procedure. During the Muromachi bakufu of the fifteenth and sixteenth centuries, Japan sent twenty delegations to China, "but during the same period, hundreds of groups . . . traveled to

Korea."[87] Japan-Korea interactions occurred on multiple levels—not only the central governments but also regional and local governments as well as common people traded and traveled between the two countries.[88] The Japanese, of course, regarded the Koreans as inferior. During the fifteenth and sixteenth centuries, relations between the two had been distant but relatively stable. Mizuno notes that Hideyoshi "described traditional Japanese-Korean relations as "*gyuji no mei* (an alliance of cow ears)." The term came from a Chinese classic, *Chun qiu Zuoshiizhuan* (Spring and Autumn Annals and Zuo Commentary), and meant hierarchical bonds or a partnership between two parties.[89]

The Imjin Wars of the 1590s (to be discussed in chapter 5) severed relations between Korea and Japan. Given the domestic politics of the subsequent Tokugawa regime (1600–1868) and its need for legitimacy, the Tokugawa shoguns preferred to see Korea as a subjugated state after the Imjin War, despite the overwhelming evidence that Japan had lost the war. Internationally, the Japanese leaders needed to find a way to interact with the other states, and the Korean restrictions on Japanese travel provided them with a convenient excuse. As Mizuno points out, "the bakufu were neither ignorant of the implications of diplomatic protocols nor self-flatteringly imbued with a belief in Japan's superiority over Korea. It was obviously aware of the discrepancy between its own ideal vision of relations with Korea and the actual state spelled out through diplomatic protocols."[90]

Quite illuminating as to how both Japanese and Korean elites viewed each other and the international system of the time is the diplomatic wrangling that took place between Japan and Korea over reestablishing diplomatic ties, which took place nine years after the conclusion of the Imjin War. Particularly, the trading families that had been most affected by the war sought to repair relations between the two sides. Thus, the So family of Tsushima worked to repatriate captives and "ingratiate themselves" to the Koreans as early as 1599. Much of the disagreement between the two states, however, had to do with the explicit positioning of the two states on the status hierarchy. The Japanese shogun Ieyasu began negotiations in 1602, opening communications through the Tsushima domain of So Yoshishige. Ieyasu told So that "I had no personal grudge against Korea. Hence I will grant peace if the country wishes it. However, an overture of peace must not be a matter for Japan to propose first."[91]

Eventually, the Korean king sent two emissaries to Kyoto in 1605, and in 1606 the Korean court agreed to consider normalizing relations, as long as it was Japan, not Korea, that made the first move. Hence the Korean court would wait for "Ieyasu [to] ask for peace by submitting a letter."[92] Doubting Ieyasu's sincerity, the Korean court wanted a *kukso* (J: *kokusho*), an official "document of state." At this point the history becomes unclear: numerous scholars have suggested that the intermediaries between the two courts— particularly the So Yoshishige house on Tsushima—forged letters, seals, and documents to make both the Korean and Japanese courts feel that they had achieved what they wanted.

What is known is that the first letter that Ieyasu sent, on July 4, 1607, was found to be unbearably insulting to the Korean court, and they demanded revisions before they would accept the letter. The Japanese tone of this first letter was that of victor to supplicant. Ieyasu had written to the Koreans: "Your country requests restoration of its previous association [with Japan]. Why would my country decline it?"[93] Worse than the tone were the title and the era name; neither the title of the Korean king nor the Chinese era name, *Wangli*, was in the shogunal letter. The shogunal letters instead used the Japanese era name, *keicho*. Refusal to use equivalent titles of "king"—*Ilbon Kukwang* or *Chosŏn kokuo*—implied subordination. Sharing the same honorific implied parity between the two rulers. Confucian honorifics in diplomacy had specific hierarchies: the highest title was "majesty" (C: *bixia*; J: *heika*; K: *p'yeha*), followed by "highness" (C: *dianxia*; J: *denka*; K: *jonha*), and then "excellency" (C: *gexia*; J: *kakka*; K: *gakha*). Although Ieyasu first used *gakha* in referring to the Korean king, eventually the Tokugawa shoguns and the Korean kings settled on referring to each other as "highness" in letters written to a peer, to "avoid trouble."[94] This was not mere diplomatic wrangling about a relationship that would surely have come about another way. Rather, this negotiation over status was central to the diplomatic relations of the two states. The ability to situate oneself on a ranking was critical to the hierarchical order; without it, relations were impossible to normalize. The reflection of status and hierarchy was central to the international relations of the time.

After a semblance of diplomatic recognition had been achieved between Korea and Japan, Chosŏn Korea did not permit Japanese envoys to travel to the capital, restricting them to the port city of Pusan. For its part, Korea sent twelve envoy missions to Tokugawa Japan between 1607 and 1871. Although the Koreans were clear that these envoys were explicitly *not* tribute missions, the corresponding prohibition on Japanese diplomatic missions to Korea allowed the Japanese to act as if the Korean envoys actually were tribute missions from a supplicant Korea dispatched to Tokugawa. Given the lack of Japanese diplomatic access to the Korean capital and the amount of trade that occurred, the ambiguity of the Korea-Japan relationship remained over the years, allowing both sides to view the situation in their own preferred manner. "The *bakufu* attempted to exploit the presence of the foreign missions on Japanese soil as a political tool to vindicate the legitimacy and authority of its own regime."[95]

For its part, Japanese tribute missions (considered a "humiliation" by the Tokugawa bakufu but maintained nonetheless) consisted of an envoy offering a letter (*sogye*) from the lord of Tsushima addressed to the Korean Third Minister (Sr. 3) in the Board of Rites. A return letter consisting of gifts was delivered a few days later. Japanese tribute (the Tokugawa bakufu used the term *pongjin*, "special gifts") was typically pepper, alum, sappan wood, gold or silver lacquerware, ink-stone cases, figured paper, and sometimes other goods from Southeast Asia. Korean return gifts were usually ginseng, leopard and tiger skins, dogs, hawks, linen, white silk thread, oil paper, brushes, ink, inkstones, swords, bamboo saddlebags, fans, combs, oil, honey, starch, juniper seeds, chestnuts, and dates. Following this exchange of letters and tribute trade was a "tea ceremony," or banquet.[96] After this, the real trading began between the two sides. Until the 1876 Kanghwa treaty, which began the modern era of relations between the two countries, tribute relations were the diplomatic protocol that governed economic relations between Japan and Korea. However, by delegating responsibility for Korean relations to Tsushima, the bakufu was able to hedge their relationship with Korea, and this allowed the Koreans to pretend that the shogun was actually engaging in tribute with the Korean king, while the shogun could pretend that such actions had nothing to do with the central government but were rather the actions of the local Tsushima lord.

Korea and Vietnam did not have as intense or frequent interactions as did Korea and Japan, but there was some indirect (and direct) contact and trade between the two sides. When emissaries from Korea and Vietnam met in the Chinese capital, for example, they could communicate through their knowledge of Chinese and Confucian classics. For example, the Vietnamese scholar-official Li Bancun wrote in 1748 that:

> Chosŏn [Korea] and the Secure South [Vietnam] are especially considered as domains which have established the proper institutions. In the past I perused the *August Dynasty's collections of Pearl and Jade* and the

Record of Collected Airs from Dongxing. From these I saw that poetry in Chosŏn is deeply imbued with the ways of the Efflorescence [Confucianism]. My only regret is that I have never seen such a poetry collection from the Secure South.[97]

Le Quy Don, writing in the eighteenth century, noted:

The people of Chosŏn are gentle and respectful. Envoys from our Viet kingdom who journey to Beijing to present tribute often meet with their envoys. . . . The Eastern Kingdom [Chosŏn] is a kingdom of exemplary men who take pleasure in upholding trust and propriety and following [the teachings in the *Classic of*] *Poetry* and the *Venerated Documents.* This all inspires respectful admiration among others.[98]

Tokugawa Japan's Foreign Relations

The role of Japan is perhaps the most important to discuss, because for centuries Japan was the second-largest country in East Asia. Did the system really encompass Japan? Japan is the liminal, or borderline, case of the Confucian society. That is, Japan was heavily influenced by Chinese and Confucian ideas in both its domestic politics and international relations, and it unquestioningly accepted the larger diplomatic rules of the tribute system and both the hierarchic nature of the institutions and the way in which status within that society was determined. However, Japan was the most skeptical of and uncomfortable with China's dominance within the Confucian system. Indeed, over the centuries Japanese rulers and scholars have distinguished between Confucian ideas and Chinese civilization—which they accepted virtually completely—and China itself as a state—about which they were far less impressed, to say the least.

Even this sense of Japanese skepticism was dormant and muted until the seventeenth century. In the centuries before the Tokugawa shogunate (1600–1868), Japan followed essentially the same rules as other Sinicized states. The question of Japan's status and place in the international hierarchy came into sharp focus with their defeat in the Imjin War. The new regime that arose after Japan's defeat, the Tokugawa, thus faced a decision about how to conduct its foreign relations. Should it return to the Chinese system, and, if so, how should it fit into it? Their retreat from both the tribute system and from active maritime trade was an "epochal change: a maritime East Asia with an active Japan would have been a very different place."[99]

Numerous scholars have disagreed about whether or not Tokugawa originally considered accepting tributary status with China. Ronald Toby argues that "the Tokugawa bakufu had had ambivalent feelings about participating in the Ming world order from the very beginning,"[100] while in contrast Mizuno "does not find any concrete evidence that the bakufu sought to obtain the specific status of an equal with China . . . ambiguity remained in the Japanese views and attitudes over a status relationship with China even after it came under the control of the 'barbaric' Manchu Qing."[101] What is clear is that by the mid-seventeenth century, explicit tributary relations between China and Japan no longer existed.

The evidence from the seventeenth century is illuminating yet inconclusive. On the one hand, the Tokugawa shogun Ieyasu sent a letter to the Ming in 1600 in which he expressed his wish to reopen relations with China and to resume the "tally trade" that had governed China-Japan relations until the mid-sixteenth century. The tally trade was part of the tribute-system institutions and was a process by which Ming China allowed vassal states—such as Thailand and Japan—a set number of seals ("tallies") that distinguished approved traders from pirates. The tally trade put control of trade with the Chinese, and Ashikaga shoguns had previously accepted investiture and a lower hierarchical position from the Ming, in return for which they were allowed tally trade. As Mizuno notes, "since 1404 [lasting until 1551], Japan had been a participant in the Chinese tributary system and received one hundred sets of tallies upon the accession of each new Ming emperor."[102] However, there is growing suspicion that this letter in 1600 did not indicate Ieyasu's desire to resume tributary status with China but rather merely that he wished to reopen trade with China, but this time that it would be Japan—not China—that was the grantor of trade and hence be in the dominant position.

The Chinese ignored this letter, and in 1611 Ieyasu approached Ming China indirectly, though the Ryukyus. The 1611 letter did not include the customary honorific *biao* to the Chinese emperor, yet at the same time, "the Japanese seemed to be historically aware that they would need to give way to the Chinese to a certain degree."[103] In Tokugawa Japan's indecisiveness about how to interact with China we see reflected two enduring themes: the Japanese acceptance and recognition of China's position as a cultural and economic center and a Japanese ranking of status and respect based not on size but on culture. As Mizuno notes:

The Japanese had, on the other hand, continued to revere China and had drawn extensively from its civilization since antiquity. Even claims and discourses on Japanese superiority had depended on Chinese rhetoric, consciously or unconsciously. . . . Japanese, fascinated, adoring, envying and yearning after the Chinese civilization, had tried to preserve their independence and individuality by fostering a sense of rivalry . . . the Japanese also refused to accept the disparity in size as a rationale for China's superiority.[104]

Perhaps most central to the question of Japanese Tokugawa status was the issue of its overall foreign policy. One common misperception in the scholarly literature is that Tokugawa-era Japan (1600–1868) was a closed and isolated nation that operated outside the East Asian international system. Although this policy is sometimes referred to as *sakoku*, the reality was that trade with China and the rest of the world continued to be an important part of Japan's economy. Indeed, Ronald Toby has pointed out that the term *sakoku* only first appeared in a translation of a Dutch traveler's stay in Japan and that its meaning was focused more on Japan's relations with the West, not Asia.[105]

Indeed, in the last two decades, a revisionist view has become widely accepted, one which sees Tokugawa as deeply interested in, and interacting with, the rest of East Asia. There was a change in Japan's international status following its attempts in 1592 and 1598 to invade China through Korea. China essentially derecognized Japan, forcing it outside the legitimate international order of the time. The Ming in 1621 expelled Japan from the Chinese world system, making it the "outcast of East Asia."[106]

The more recent scholarship interprets *sakoku* as merely "maritime provisions" that were "simply a part of a sequential process rather than firm indications of new policy directions.[107] As noted previously, Japanese exports in the seventeenth century are estimated to have reached 10 percent of its GNP.[108] This revisionist view sees Tokugawa foreign relations more as an expansion of state power and regulation within Japan itself rather than as a policy of isolation related to other countries. China and Japan, even during Tokugawa and Qing, had extensive relations. Klein notes that "by the end of the seventeenth century the Tokugawa regime had succeeded in maneuvering Japan into the center of a regional system of international diplomacy of its own making."[109] Wray adds that "[Tokugawa] Japan had a distinctive policy for virtually every country or area with which it traded. There were far more Chinese than Dutch ships coming to Nagasaki."[110] Historians today interpret these maritime provisions more as examples of normal statecraft and the extension of Tokugawa control rather than as paranoia or cowering xenophobia. Toby argues that Japan under Tokugawa had an "active state-sponsored program of international commercial and technological intelligence . . . that enhanced domestic sovereignty and enabled the state to regulate a desired foreign trade."[111] Most significantly, the Japanese continued to see the world in hierarchic terms and used the same ideas and measures of cultural achievement as before. That is, the Japanese attempted to find a way out of explicit recognition of China, but they did not reject the larger rules and institutions of the tribute system itself.

As a result, Japan was forced to find an alternative way to conduct its foreign relations and trade. Although not fully reincorporated into the tributary system, Japan operated by essentially the same set of rules, following the function if not the explicit form of tributary relations with China. The key point is that Tokugawa Japan continued to accept the Chinese-centered system even though formal tributary relations were never fully restored. Indeed, after the Hideyoshi invasions of Korea in 1592–1598, the Tokugawa shogunate recognized China's centrality and Japanese-Korean relations as equal. Kim writes:

> The Tokugawa rulers understood and accepted the Korean position. Japan after Hideyoshi had no ambition for continental conquest or expansion. They tacitly acknowledged Chinese supremacy and cultural leadership in the East Asian world. . . . Although Tokugawa Japan maintained no formal ties with China . . . for all intents and purposes it was as much a part of the Chinese world as Ashikaga Japan had been.[112]

The Japanese called this new policy the *Taikun* (Great Prince) diplomacy, and some view this as a way for Japan to opt out of the Chinese tributary status yet remain within the larger set of diplomatic rules and institutions. It allowed the Japanese to conduct foreign policy without explicitly recognizing the Chinese emperor as superior while still not provoking too harsh a response from the Chinese by formally challenging the position of China. However, the Tokugawa rulers remained integrated into East Asia and made systematic efforts to gather information on regional affairs.[113] Trade was still conducted through Nagasaki and the Ryukyus, and indirectly through Tsushima with Korea. As John Wills notes, "there was no government-to-government connection, and the Japan-China connection was weaker than it had been at any time since before the Tang."[114]

Indeed, Tokugawa relations with the Ryukyus provides an informative window on Japan's foreign relations and their views of both China and the larger rules of the game. The Ryukyus gave tribute to both China and Japan during the seventeenth and eighteenth centuries. The two most powerful East Asian states both claimed suzerainty over the same Ryukyuan territory, but at least through the late nineteenth century they never come to blows over it. Gregory Smits notes that "in 1655, the [Japanese leadership] formally approved tribute relations between Ryukyu and Qing, again, in part to avoid giving Qing any reason for military action against Japan."[115] The Japanese pressured the Ryukyus to actually increase the rate of tribute missions to China, hoping to indirectly "increase its trade with China and thereby relieve ongoing financial woes."[116] So careful were Japanese authorities to conceal their involvement in the Ryukyus that when Chinese envoys visited the islands, Japanese officials hid in a small village outside of the capital.[117] Evidence of the ambiguous hierarchy continued—the Tokugawa bakufu accepted Ryukyu tributary status to the Qing, realizing that Ryukyuan "authority and legitimacy could not be preserved without the bestowal of the title of king [on the Ryukyus] from the Qing."[118]

Conclusion

The tribute system was not merely a symbolic set of actions that diplomats had to go through before they could get to the "real" issues such as trade and war. Rather, the tribute system was a set of institutional structures that provided an overarching framework for organizing external relations among political actors in early modern East Asia. A set of rules and institutions developed over time that regulated foreign diplomatic relations, social and economic interaction, and provided a clear sense of order to the system. Yet we cannot ignore that key elements of the early modern East Asian international system involved a clear hierarchy that was marked as much by cultural achievement as it was by purely military or economic prowess. And surrounding states, as much as China itself, acknowledged and embraced these ideas. There was rational pursuit of self-interest and a set of institutions designed to solve problems. But inherent to those solutions and woven into the institutions were basic values and ideas regarding status and hierarchy and a set of ideas about how international relations should function.

5 WAR

The Longer Peace

The post–World War II system of international relations . . . after four
decades of existence shows no perceptible signs of disintegration . . . this
great power peace has survived for so long . . . we could do much worse.
— JOHN LEWIS GADDIS, "The Long Peace"

THE PAST MILLENNIUM of European history was soaked in blood, and
that experience has affected the way we tend to view history in every
region of the world. Jeffrey Herbst describes the situation well: "[European]
Peace was the exception and long periods with no major fighting were almost unknown, as for centuries weak states were routinely defeated and populations regularly absorbed by foreign rulers."[1] States engaged in the "great
game" of the balance of power, alliances, and conquest whenever possible.
The slightest advantage was to be seized; the slightest weakness was exploited.
States constantly jockeyed with one another to survive, and survival meant
conquest. Scholars such as Thomas Hobbes saw life outside government as a
war of "all against all," where life was "nasty, brutish, and short," and a classic
work of international relations referred to a four-decade span without war as
"the long peace."[2]

Because European states were constantly under threat of attack, being bigger and more powerful enhanced a state's chances of surviving. Thus states
strove and competed to become as powerful as possible. Yet, if one state became too big, it would threaten to take over the entire system and conquer
all the other states. In response, other states tended to join together against
the strongest power, flocking to the side of the weak, in order to keep any one
state from dominating the system and conquering everyone else. This European pattern gave rise to one of the most enduring concepts in international
relations: balance of power.

However, patterns of conflict in East Asia do not correspond to European balance-of-power expectations. Balance-of-power theory is not a theory of war. Nonetheless, as a theory that explains systemic tendencies toward balance, it would predict that a system as dominated by one state as Asia was by China would be inherently unstable, owing to underlying antihegemonic systemic forces. The theory expects that a state as dominant as China will likely seek further territorial expansion at the expense of weaker neighbors. This is, after all, why balancing is supposed to be the prime directive of states' foreign policies: to prevent a dominant state from expanding at the expense of the sovereign security of other members of the system. For this reason, the theory also expects those neighbors to fight to resist Chinese dominance when possible. Neither of these expectations is borne out. The most striking feature of the system was its comparative peacefulness (table 5.1). Indeed, China did not seek to translate its dominant position into a systemwide empire by force of arms. After the Mongol invasions of the thirteenth century, China developed enduring and stable relations with its smaller Sinicized neighbors. Between 1368 and 1841, there were only two wars of conquest between China,

TABLE 5.1 Major wars in East Asia, 1368–1841 (wars between Sinicized states in italics)

Years	War	Comment
1. 1407–1428	*Chinese invasion of Vietnam*	
2. 1592–1598	*Japanese invasion of Korea*	*Imjin War*
3. 1618–1644	Manchu conquest of China	
4. 1627, 1637	Manchu invasions of Korea	*Pyongja horan*: Manchu goal was pacification, not conquest
5. 1690–1757	Chinese conquest of Xinjiang	Gradual eradication of various Mongol tribes, culminating in the destruction of the Zhungar Mongols
6. 1839–1841	Opium wars British expeditions against China for trade relations	

Sources: Compiled from author's translation of People's Liberation Army, *Zhongguo lidai zhanzheng nianbiao*; Kohn, *Dictionary of Wars*; Dupuy and Dupuy, *The Harper Encyclopedia of Military History*; Davis, *Encyclopedia of Invasions and Conquests*.

Japan, Korea, and Vietnam. In contrast, England fought directly against or with France at least forty-six times between 1300 and 1850, and even Sweden fought thirty-two wars over that time.[3] Not only were there few wars of conquest among Sinic states in East Asia, but Alexander Woodside notes that "there were no Huguenot wars . . . no large-scale holy wars, religious inquisitions, or St. Bartholomew massacres in Chinese, Vietnamese, or Korean history," and he calls the avoidance of religious wars "their greatest historical achievement."[4] Conflict tended to occur not to check rising Chinese power but rather as order within China itself was decaying. Even the nomadic tribes valued Chinese stability, and Perdue notes: "The collapse of a Chinese dynasty threatened the stability of the steppe empire. This relationship explains why, for example, the Uighurs intervened to keep the Tang dynasty alive."[5]

Furthermore, behavioral patterns in the early modern East Asian system are difficult to reconcile with balance-of-power theory. Most important, there is simply scant evidence of balancing. We do not see alliance formation against China, notwithstanding large fluctuations in Chinese capabilities that might have offered other states windows of opportunity to at least attempt to diminish Chinese dominance. To be sure, neighboring states did seek to emulate Chinese practices, but there is little evidence that the aim was to build up capabilities in order to match and rein in Chinese power. On the contrary, as we have seen, emulation actually had the opposite effect of ramifying the Chinese-dominated order. In sum, the larger behavioral pattern is precisely what balance-of-power theory does not expect: stable system dominance by a materially preponderant state.

This brings up a final major difference between Asia and contemporary Europe that suggests the existence of a different systemic logic: in Asia, major political units remained essentially the same after war. As chapter 3 discussed, the borders between Korea, Japan, Vietnam, and China were relatively fixed and did not significantly change during the six hundred years under review. In 1500, Europe had some five hundred independent units; by 1900, it had about twenty.[6] For example, as late as 1850, the Italian peninsula was composed of some eight independent states, and middle Europe still consisted of Bavaria, Prussia, and the Holy Roman Empire. In East Asia, the major countries and their boundaries have remained essentially the same since a.d. 1200.

However, the comparative "peacefulness" of early modern East Asia is a claim limited to relations among the major states. In this chapter, I am chiefly concerned with relations between the major states in East Asia. East Asian states used force in different times and in different places. As we shall see in chapter 7, there was endemic border conflict between states and nonstate actors. Border raids on China and Korea's northern frontiers occurred regularly, sometimes involving thousands of men who would breach the wall, attack a village, and plunder it, retreating back to the steppes with their booty. But we must distinguish between active conquest and raids that occur along a loosely institutionalized frontier.[7] For example, chronic raids by the nomadic Mongol tribes led to running border battles, and the Chinese at times employed five hundred thousand troops in an effort to secure their long northern border.[8] However, when, whether, or why China would use force against marginal actors on its frontiers is immaterial to explaining why the largest and most institutionalized states had exceptionally peaceful relations with one another.

I concentrate on China, Japan, Korea, and Vietnam because they were the biggest and strongest political units at the time yet also the most peaceful: this is the interesting anomaly. That China used force in other regions at other times is unrelated to explaining why the four most consolidated and powerful states had peaceful relations.[9] Posed this way, the question becomes: why did the four most powerful states not fight for such an extended period of time, despite having the capability to do so?[10] Furthermore, this is not a "cultural" argument about Chinese or East Asian peacefulness.[11] China and the other East Asian states certainly used force when it was deemed effective, and this book does not make the argument that China has a cultural, unchanging predilection for peace. My question is both larger and smaller than that: why did the major states in East Asia develop a stable and peaceful coexistence?

Measuring East Asian Wars

Was East Asia really as peaceful as I claim? After all, the United States has fought major wars, including both world wars, and it has also invaded tiny countries, such as Panama in 1989. Although both World War II and the invasion of Panama might be classified as "wars," we would surely want to differentiate between their scale and impact. In fact, even if we restrict our focus to Latin America, the U.S. military intervened *forty-three* times in Latin American countries in the twentieth century alone for other than normal peacetime purposes.[12] These U.S. military interventions in Latin America included a two-decade occupation of Nicaragua from 1912 to 1933 and the suppression of a general strike in Panama in 1925, as well as the more widely known instances, such as the pursuit of Pancho Villa into Mexico by General Pershing in 1916 and the more recent military interventions into Grenada (1983) and Haiti (1994). The same holds true for early modern East Asia: some wars were massive and consequential; others were border incidents. We need to be much more precise in how we categorize and count wars.

We begin by measuring conflict in East Asia. Some scholars, such as Iain Johnston, emphasize the violence in early modern East Asia, claiming that the Ming dynasty engaged in over three hundred wars during its existence.[13] In addition, a dominant strand of Korean identity consists of a "master narrative" depicting the Korean experience as "one of almost incessant foreign incursions."[14] However, a number such as "three hundred wars" requires more careful categorization. All anarchic systems are potentially violent, and all states use force when they deem it effective. Early modern East Asia was no exception.

Measurement of wars is no simple task, but it is central to any defensible empirical description. Kenneth Swope, for example, defines a major war as one that involves an intent for conquest. He argues that it is "misleading" to call the decades-long wars on the Korean peninsula during the mid-seventh century—wars that involved Tang China, Paekche, Silla, Koguryo, and Yamato Japan—an East Asian "world war," because "there was never any grand design for overarching conquest by any one power, even Tang China."[15] The Correlates of War project has defined war as "sustained combat between/among military contingents involving substantial casualties (with the criterion being a minimum of 1,000 battle deaths)," although such distinctions are difficult to make in premodern times.[16] Not only were there rarely any counts of battle deaths, but sharp distinctions between states and nonstate actors is difficult, and many political units such as Mongol tribes rarely had written documents, resulting in an overreliance on Chinese sources simply because they are available.

However, we do have good records and data from the four Sinicized states of China, Korea, Vietnam, and Japan during this time period. Significantly, the most striking feature of the system was the comparative peacefulness among these states (table 5.1). From the founding of the Ming dynasty to the Opium wars between Britain and China, there were only two wars between China, Korea, Vietnam, and Japan: China's invasion of Vietnam (1407–1428) and Japan's invasion of Korea (1592–1598). Scholars such as George Childs Kohn, Ernest and Trevor Dupuy, and Paul Davis arrive at a similar conclusion about the stability of the region. For example, Kohn finds only eight Chinese wars over the time period in question, including the defensive wars during Manchu invasions of China and the defense of Korea during Hideyoshi's invasion.[17]

If we wish to focus only on a Chinese use of force, there is another important source that must be noted. The most comprehensive record of Chinese use of force is the *Zhongguo lidai zhanzheng nianbiao* (中国历代战争年表, "Chronology of Wars in China Through Successive Dynasties").[18] This chronology lists 336 external Chinese uses of force between 1368 and 1841, or more than one every two years.[19] The *Zhongguo* counts incidents by year, but wars often lasted over a number of years. For example, the *Zhongguo* lists China's support of Korea during the Japanese invasion of 1592–1598 as four separate incidents.

Using the *Zhongguo* necessarily involves care in interpreting the data. For example, there are a number of conflicts listed in these volumes that did not involve Chinese dynasties but were between two nomad tribes. These are included presumably as part of a contemporary political ethnic policy regarding Chinese minority groups, because the Chinese Communist Party claims that all peoples within modern China's borders are Chinese (even non-Han peoples), and thus conflicts between nomads who eventually became part of modern China are counted in these volumes. Just as importantly, the *Zhongguo* does not provide citations for the original source material from which the chronology is derived. There are general references in the introduction, but none of the data has specific references or citations, which makes corroboration exceedingly difficult. Thus we have no way to assess whether the *Zhongguo* made any intentional or accidental omissions.

Furthermore, even if we assume the *Zhongguo* is a rigorous history that would meet scholarly standards, its source data likely came mainly from annals of the dynasties themselves, which were also highly politicized and written by court magistrates who were probably not objective historians. These magistrates had numerous reasons to emphasize or deemphasize certain events over others. This does not render this information useless, but it should be taken with great care.

However, given these caveats, the *Zhongguo* is an important starting point because it is the only consistent attempt to measure all types of Chinese use of force across the centuries. Furthermore, some scholars cite the *Zhongguo* as proof that China fought hundreds of wars without truly or directly engaging the substance of the records. Attempting to avoid those problems, I attempted to do as finely grained an analysis as is possible and ultimately created a database with over eight hundred cases.

I examined all Chinese uses of force from the founding of the Ming dynasty in 1368 to the Opium wars between the United Kingdom and China in 1841, when the changing international system resulted in the breakdown of the China-dominated East Asian order. After listing the year and a brief description of the conflict, I then coded two basic categories: which political units were involved and what type of conflict they fought. I coded for four general types of political units:

1. Conflict with "nomads," which included all the polities to the west and north of China, including Tibetan polities as well as the range of Mongol, Khitan, and other peoples on the steppe;
2. *Wakō* or pirate raids;
3. Conflict between the Sinic states of Japan, Korea, Vietnam, and China;
4. "Non-Chinese" conflicts or diplomatic initiatives, such as Zheng He's voyages.

I coded six general types of conflicts:

1. *Border skirmishes* that resulted in fewer than one thousand battle deaths or were not intended as conquest;
2. *Interstate wars* (Chinese involvement in wars of conquest or major mobilizations);
3. *Pirate raids*;
4. *Non-Chinese conflicts* that did not involve Chinese dynasties or Chinese diplomacy;
5. *Internal conflict* (farmer's riots, rebellions, mutinous provincial officials, etc.);
6. *Regime consolidation* where one dynasty was establishing control.

Following the "Correlates of War" project, I coded conflict as a "border skirmish" when there were fewer than one thousand battle deaths or when the conflict was a result of local conditions not aimed at major territorial expansion. Sometimes the data contained an actual casualty count; often there was none. In that case, a qualitative judgment was made based on the evidence at hand. For example, instances of border skirmishes include the rescue of Chinese envoys to Burma detained by a local chieftain on the border in 1405; a Chinghai tribe's theft of tribute intended for China, which resulted in a

Chinese attack in 1430; a Chinese attack on Tartars in 1546 that resulted in twenty-seven Tartar deaths; and a Tartar raid on Liaoyang in southern Manchuria in 1563, which was repulsed by the Chinese, with a loss of seventy-five Tartar lives and the capture of fifty horses.

The least consequential wars, the least threatening to the survival of states, and yet the most frequent in East Asia were skirmishes along states' frontier borders between states and nonstate actors such as tribes or clans. All states attempt to control their borders as much as possible, and all states attempt to delineate and limit the entry and exit of goods and people from their country. This type of conflict includes border raids by nonstate actors such as nomadic tribes, border groups, and pirate clans. These raids, sometimes involving thousands of warriors, would generally involve an attack on a border town or village with the aim of plunder. Rarely were these raids anything more than that, and the aim was not to gain and hold territory but rather to make a quick strike and return home. The U.S. Monroe Doctrine, extensive interventions into Latin America, and the billions spent each year by the DEA and Coast Guard to patrol U.S. borders are examples of attempts in the modern era to control and stabilize borders and periphery. The early modern East Asian system was no different.

Conflicts coded as interstate war include China's support of Korea during the Japanese invasion of 1592, by providing one hundred thousand troops; and China's decades-long total elimination of four Zunghar Mongol tribes and establishment of formal institutional control of the Ili Valley, a conflict that ended in 1757. Examples of pirate raids include a 1372 attack by *wakō* that resulted in the Chinese capture of twelve boats and 130 people and a *wakō* raid in 1552 that looted several villages in Huangyan county and escaped before Chinese troops could retaliate. Chapter 6 will discuss the causes and consequences of the *wakō* in more detail.

Some "non-Chinese" or diplomatic conflicts involved Zheng He's voyages to Southeast Asia and other skirmishes among nomadic tribes that occurred within modern China's borders. Perhaps the most humorous of these was the arrival of two Japanese tribute missions to the port of Ningbo in 1523. The two missions began to argue and eventually fight with each other over which was the genuine tribute mission, and the Chinese eventually sent them both back to Japan without letting either mission present its (dubious) credentials.

Following the "Correlates of War" project, the decision when to code conflict as "imperialism" and hence interstate war and when to call conflict "regime consolidation" and hence internal conflict also depends on a qualitative judgment as to when consolidation of control occurs. For this dataset, I have used the accepted dates for the start and end of dynasties: before the accepted date for the founding of a dynasty, I coded conflict between the old and new dynasty as interstate war. After the date of dynastic transition, I have judged the new dynasty to have effective control, and all remaining conflicts between the new and old dynasties are coded as regime consolidation. Clearly, a more finely grained categorization is possible, and certainly further research will add detail to many of the incidents only briefly analyzed in the dataset. But as a first cut with which to begin analysis, the database reveals a number of interesting findings.

Overall, the most stark distinction is the relative absence of conflict between the Sinicized states and the relative prevalence of conflict between China and nomads on its northern and western borders. Only twelve out of 336 conflicts of any type (3.57 percent) involved China, Korea, Vietnam, or Japan (table 5.2). When counting wars and not incidents, China and Japan fought one war during this time, and Vietnam and China also fought only one war.[20] In contrast, 252 conflicts of all types occurred between China and nomads (75 percent). Finally, pirate raids (sixty cases) were five times as likely as was conflict between the Sinic states.

The most prevalent type of conflict were skirmishes along states' frontier borders between states and nonstate actors such as nomads (table 5.3).[21] Over 66 percent of use of force (225 cases) were border skirmishes on China's northern and western frontiers. For example, the Ming emperor Wanli (1573–1620), who sent troops to aid Korea against the Japanese, engaged in the *Wanli san dazheng* (three great wars of the Wanli emperor). The other two "wars" were the suppression of a mutiny on the northern frontier and eradication of an aboriginal chieftain in the southwest, incidents typical of border maintenance but not approaching major interstate war and thus designated as "skirmishes." There were also occasional skirmishes along China's southern border involving Burma, Shan tribes, or other peoples, but as Frederick Mote notes, "the southern frontier truly presented no threats to the security of Ming China, but troublesome disputes among unruly peoples along that boundary often led to requests for Chinese intervention."[22] Interestingly enough, the Manchu pacification of Korea (discussed later in this chapter)— although humiliating for Korea—would not count as a war by the standards of the COW project, because fewer than one thousand battle deaths occurred.

TABLE 5.2 Chinese Opponents, 1368–1841

Type	Number	Percent
Ming dynasty		
Conflict with nomads	200	71.94
Wakō pirate raids	60	21.94
Sinic conflicts*	11	3.96
Non-Chinese/diplomatic	7	2.52
Total	278	100.00
Qing dynasty		
Conflict with nomads	52	89.66
Wakō pirate raids	0	0.00
Sinic conflicts*	1	1.72
Non-Chinese/diplomatic	5	8.62
Total	58	100.00
Total, 1368–1841		
Conflict with nomads	252	75.00
Wakō pirate raids	60	17.86
Sinic conflicts*	12	3.57
Non-Chinese/diplomatic	12	3.57
Total	336	100.00

Note: After the Opium Wars of 1839–1842, the China-dominated system broke down under the weight of Western imperialism, so even though the Qing dynasty survived until 1911, I stop counting at 1842.
* Sinicized states = Japan, Korea, Vietnam, and China.
Source: author's dataset, based mainly on author's translation of People's Liberation Army, *Zhongguo lidai zhanzheng nianbiao*; Kohn, *Dictionary of Wars*; Perdue, *China Marches West*; and Park, "War and Peace in Premodern Korea."

TABLE 5.3 Type of conflict, 1368–1841

Type	Number	Percent
Ming dynasty		
Border skirmishes	192	69.06
Interstate war	26	9.35
Pirate raids	60	21.58
Non-China or diplomacy	13	
Internal conflicts	264	
Regime transition	23	
Total noninternal use of force	278	100.00
<u>Qing dynasty</u>		
Border skirmishes	33	56.90
Interstate war	25	43.10
Pirate raids	0	0.00
Non-Chinese or diplomacy	10	
Internal conflicts	120	
Regime transition	57	
Total noninternal use of force	58	100.00
Totals, 1368–1841		
Border skirmishes	225	66.96
Interstate war	51	15.18
Pirate raids	60	17.86
Total	336	100.00

Source: author's dataset, based mainly on author's translation of People's Liberation Army, *Zhongguo lidai zhanzheng nianbiao*; Kohn, *Dictionary of Wars*; Perdue, *China Marches West*; and Park, "War and Peace in Premodern Korea."

The key points remain that major wars generally did not involve the Sinic states and that most of the conflicts come from Qing China's seven-decade expansion into the western Xinjiang area at the expense of a number of Mongol tribes, such as the Zunghars. Similar to both the American and Russian continental expansions, Perdue concludes that the "Qing project was to eliminate the ambiguous frontier zone and replace it with a clearly defined border."[23] Some former Ming tributaries in Tibet, northwestern China, and Central Asia were conquered and eventually reorganized as new provinces (for example, Qinghai and Xinjiang).[24] The Qing dynasty asserted control over Tibet in the seventeenth century and kept it to the end, and territory under direct Chinese administration prior to the seventeenth century was perhaps about half of what it claims now.

Thus, the comparative "peacefulness" of early modern East Asia was limited to relations among the major states, and even a conservative assessment of Chinese military history reveals that the large majority of conflicts were in fact border skirmishes with nomads. The contrast between the stability and relative peacefulness of Chinese, Korean, Vietnamese, and Japanese relations and the endemic conflict between China and nomads is striking. Because wars involving the Sinicized states were so rare, we turn now to discussing them in some detail.

The Imjin War (1592–1598)

In almost five centuries, Japan challenged its place in the Confucian order only once, in 1592, when Hideyoshi attempted to conquer Korea. As mentioned in chapter 1, this invasion involved a half million men and over seven hundred ships, and it was many times the scale of the Spanish Armada of 1588.[25] The Japanese had involved themselves only once previously in a war on the Asian mainland: in a.d. 663, Yamato Japan sent forces to help the Paekche kingdom in its struggle against Silla and Tang. Since that time, Japan had tended to accommodate and adjust to China, although it generally avoided an explicit and formal tributary acceptance of the Chinese world.

With the stabilization of its border with Ming China in the fourteenth century, regularization of relations with the Jurchen tribes to its north, and the waning of piracy along its coasts, Chosŏn Korea had been so peaceful for two centuries that on the eve of the Imjin War in 1592, it had fewer than one thousand soldiers in its entire army.[26] Kenneth Lee writes: "After two hundred years of peace, Korean forces were untrained in warfare and were scattered all over the country in small local garrison troops. Koreans were totally unprepared on land."[27] Ki-baek Lee describes the quality of the Korean military in 1592 as "meager and untrained."[28] In the mid-sixteenth century, the Chosŏn court had responded to instability in both China and Japan by creating the "Border Defense council," composed of both civilian and military officials, but it proved to be ineffective due to bureaucratic infighting.[29] The only adequate military preparations were by Admiral Yi Sun-shin, whose advances in naval technology and genius at strategy and tactics during the Imjin War were to make him Korea's greatest military hero.

After the Japanese initially routed the sparse Korean forces and drove north past Pyongyang, China intervened and pushed the Japanese all the way back down the peninsula, and it soon became clear to both sides that Japan could not hope to conquer Korea, much less China.[30] Japan and Korea certainly never allied together to balance China, even if at the beginning of the war China deeply suspected that possibility. It took three months of intense Korean diplomacy to convince Ming that Korea was not conniving with Japan against China.[31] It is doubtful that a balancing strategy would ever have occurred to the smaller states, because each had their own separate relationship (tributary or not) with China, and China was the only pole in the East Asian state system.

As the Japanese stormed up the peninsula, they were met with greater Korean resistance and struggled with extended supply lines, which were repeatedly cut by Admiral Yi's relentless attacks on the Japanese ships. The Chinese joined the war in 1593, meeting and defeating the Japanese at Pyongyang and pushing them back to Seoul. Japanese soldiers began to defect in large numbers; there were reports of over ten thousand Japanese having joined the Korean side. Hideyoshi was now forced to negotiate, and he demanded that Korea cede to Japan four southern provinces and that the Ming send a daughter to the Japanese court to remain as hostage. After years of fruitless negotiations in which Hideyoshi's demands were rejected, Hideyoshi launched a second invasion in 1597, which was much less effective than the first. By this time, the Korean and Ming forces were stronger and better prepared, and the Japanese forces had been weakened. Hideyoshi suddenly died in 1598, and the disorganized remnants of his forces retreated in chaos back to Japan.

Why Hideyoshi decided to invade Korea remains unclear, and Kenneth Swope argues that while Hideyoshi's motivations for invading Korea were "diverse and debatable . . . one can infer from the demands he would later present to the Ming that trade was possibly the most important goal of his enterprise . . . the means to solve some of his domestic economic problems by linking trade in Asia through Japanese ports."[32] Yet Swope also emphasizes Hideyoshi's desire for status, noting that he "craved recognition and homage from foreign rulers. This goal should not be trivialized . . . modern scholars have tended to emphasize economic and domestic political factors, downplaying Hideyoshi's desire for glory."[33] Elizabeth Berry also sees a desire for greater status, concluding that Hideyoshi "was clearly less interested in military dominion abroad than in fame."[34] Hideyoshi's own letters to various kingdoms reveal a level of hubris that is partly bluster and partly threat. In a letter to Manila in 1591, he wrote: "The Ryukyus, other distant countries, and foreign regions have submitted and I have received them. Now I desire to subjugate China . . . you should bear the banner of surrender and come to submit to me. If, creeping and crawling along, there is any delay [in your arrival], it will be necessary promptly to attack [your country]."[35] Hideyoshi himself wrote to the Korean King Sŏnjo in 1590, stating that "I plan that our forces should proceed to the country of the Great Ming and compel the people there to adopt our customs and manners. . . . Our sole desire is to have our glorious name revered in the three countries [of China, Korea, and Japan]."[36]

The Korean king, Sŏnjo, replied:

> The relation of ruler and subject has been strictly observed between the supreme state and our kingdom. . . . Our two countries have always kept each other informed of all national events and affairs. . . . This inseparable relationship between the Middle Kingdom and our kingdom is well known throughout the world . . . we shall certainly not desert our lord and father country and join with a neighboring state. . . . Moreover, to invade another state is an act which men of culture and intellectual attainments should feel ashamed.[37]

Note in particular King Sŏnjo's emphasis on Hideyoshi's common origins and lack of education. Kenneth Swope notes that "the Chinese and Koreans steadfastly rejected Hideyoshi's bombastic designs and berated him for his foolish ignorance of the proper diplomatic forms and protocols."[38]

Some historians find economic motives for the war. Gang Deng saw Hideyoshi's strategies as revealing a Japanese desire to reenter into tribute status with China, writing that "trade is also shown because of the fighting over the ability by tributary states to pay tribute. Hideyoshi invaded Korea, a Ming vassal state, to force China to allow Japan to resume a tributary relationship, and threatened that a refusal would lead to invasion of China itself."[39] Etsuko Hae-jin Kang argues that Hideyoshi saw gaining a monopoly on foreign trade (through tribute relations with the Ming) as a means of gaining control over Japan's domestic economy, and hence political consolidation. Yet Kang concludes that Hideyoshi "failed to perceive that other Asian states had a thoroughly dissimilar ideological and political makeup and, more importantly, he lacked insights into the foundations of the Chinese world order which was based on the concepts of Confucianism."[40]

If Hideyoshi's decision had been based on his views about his military power or upon his belief that Japan was materially capable of conquering China, we should see ample evidence of strategic discussion among Japanese generals and Hideyoshi about how Japan compared to China in terms of its military capacities, Ming leadership or organizational capabilities, or the strategic situation that Japan faced with respect to China. Notably absent is any Japanese assessment of the relative military capabilities of the two sides, and Berry concludes that "there is no evidence that he [Hideyoshi] systematically researched either the geographical problem or the problem of Chinese military organization."[41]

There may have been a domestic rationale for the invasion, as well. The Ashikaga shogunate had begun to crumble in the middle of the sixteenth century—its last tribute mission was sent in 1547—and by 1574, the country had dissolved into all-out civil war. Hideyoshi was able to unify the country through force, but one of the problems that occurred was that the regional daimy were inclined to attack each other in search of greater wealth with which to pay their massive armies. Naohiro writes that "independent military initiatives by the daimyo to expand their domains at one another's expense would collide directly with Hideyoshi's aim of unification."[42] In order to avoid letting the country slide into civil war yet again, Hideyoshi began to consider conquest overseas. As Ki-baek Lee notes, "having succeeded in unifying the country, Hideyoshi sought to direct the energies of his commanders outward, thereby to enhance the solidarity and tranquility of Japan itself."[43] In 1591, Hideyoshi even threatened to attack the Philippine islands.[44] Samuel Hawley suggests that continual war was a way for Hideyoshi to quell internal dissension among his followers.[45]

The Chinese would never acknowledge equality, but they did consider granting Japan investiture at a status similar to certain Mongol leaders, below

that of Korea and Vietnam.[46] Korea—and China—sent minor officials to negotiate with the Japanese, because "the Koreans valued highly the tributary
system and their place within the first rank of tributary states. As the Japanese held lower rank, the Koreans would have jeopardized their status had
they sent royalty as envoys."[47] Kenneth Swope notes that "Hideyoshi could
have extracted trade concessions had he accommodated himself to the established rules. Hideyoshi, however, in bidding for recognition as the equal of
the Ming, was trying to alter an established system; the Ming were not willing, and could not yet be forced, to agree to such changes."[48] In 1598, Japan
retreated from Korea without gaining anything.

Thus, Japan's sole revisionist attempt was a disaster. Thereafter, although
Japan remained formally outside the tribute system, it did not challenge the
system. As Alex Roland notes: "The Tokugawa shogunate turned inward and
gave up war, not the gun."[49] Swope adds, "because the Tokugawa maintained
order in Japan, piracy was not the problem it had been in the past and the two
states co-existed in relative peace until the late nineteenth century."[50] Indeed,
it was only with the arrival of Western imperial powers and the implosion of
the China-dominated system in the late nineteenth century that Japan was
able to successfully challenge China's position and begin its own expansionist
policies.

The consequences of the Imjin War would reverberate up to the present.
The Japanese plundered much of Korean civilization, bringing back count-
less national treasures, religious artifacts, and numerous craftsmen, who introduced advanced techniques into Japan. Jurgis Elisonas estimates that at least
fifty or sixty thousand Koreans were taken to Japan as captives, noting that
"some of the most famous types of Japanese ceramics—for examples, Arita
ware and Satsuma ware—owe their origins to groups of Korean artisans who
were resettled in the domains of their captors."[51] Korea was devastated, and
80 percent of the farmland in the southern Kyongsang province was destroyed. Some of Korea's greatest temples and palaces were razed. The census
registers had been destroyed, plunging the government into such chaos that it
had difficulty collecting taxes or enforcing laws.

Yet domestic and international stability soon returned to Korea, so much
so that Eugene Park notes that "the late Chosŏn state maintained an army no
bigger than what was dictated by internal security," estimating that the Korean military in the eighteenth century comprised only ten thousand "battle-
worthy men."[52] Furthermore, the Chinese military presence in Korea by 1598
was massive, with over one hundred thousand troops still on the peninsula,

and diplomatic control of relations with Japan were firmly in Chinese—not Korean—hands. Yet even though China could easily have remained in Korea and incorporated it into the Ming empire, the troops quickly left, and the Chinese exerted no more political control over Korea after the Imjin War than it had before. In fact, the possibility of incorporating Korea into China appears not to have even entered into Ming thinking at the time.

For the next two centuries, Japan avoided confronting China. For example, due to Ming loyalists, China felt compelled to conquer Taiwan in 1683 and remove to Fujian almost all of the local Han inhabitants (of course, immigration quickly resumed, despite periodic repression).[53] The Japanese Tokugawa regime was deeply involved in Taiwan—the Ming resistance leader Zheng Chenggong had been born in Japan of a Japanese mother, Japanese traders and pirates were active in Taiwan, and Taiwanese trade with Japan in the seventeenth century involved fifty ships a year. Zheng made five separate requests for Japanese assistance between 1648 and 1660, yet the Tokugawa chose not to become involved.[54]

China's Abortive Conquest of Vietnam (1408–1428)

Although dominant or hegemonic states might exploit secondary states, what China appears to have wanted from them was legitimacy and recognition, not necessarily material benefits such as wealth or power. As mentioned earlier, extensive trade relations did not necessarily favor China and indeed was sometimes a net loss for the hegemon.[55] Militarily, China was content to coexist with the Sinic states as long as they were not troublesome. Yet recognition of China as dominant was important, and the challenge to legitimate authority was a key factor in the cause and resolution of the one war between China and Vietnam during this time.

As noted previously, Vietnam had been a tributary state of China since the tenth century, and the China-Vietnam border had been clearly demarcated and stabilized by the eleventh century. The fifteenth-century occupation of Vietnam was thus an anomaly in China-Vietnam relations. In fact, China had not initially had designs on colonizing Vietnam. The preceding four centuries had seen a stable relationship between the two, and indeed the first Ming emperor, Hongwu (r. 1368–1398), explicitly listed Vietnam (along with Korea, Japan, and twelve other states) in his guidelines for future generations as "not to be invaded." However, although China had invested the Tran dynasty (1225–1400) as the rulers of Vietnam, that dynasty began to lose domestic control in the 1390s. In 1400, Le Quy-li deposed a Tran king and declared himself the founder of a new dynasty. A member of the Tran royal family appealed to China for help in overthrowing the usurper, and China initially sent troops and an envoy merely to restore a Tran as king. The party was ambushed and wiped out just over the border, at Lang-son. To avenge this humiliation, the Chinese sent a punitive force of 215,000 into Vietnam in 1406. After an easy victory, the Chinese emperor made a "disastrous decision" to incorporate Vietnam into China.[56]

The Ming ruled harshly, and large military garrisons occupied the country. Furthermore, Ming personnel sent to Vietnam were of the "weakest sort— sons of Army officers who failed their military examinations were banished to Vietnam, and . . . a regional inspector reported that most of the Chinese officials in Vietnam were inept and untrained southerners."[57] Le Loi—one of Vietnam's greatest heroes—fought a ten-year campaign against the Ming, and in 1427 he defeated one hundred thousand Ming forces at the Chi Lang pass.[58] Le Loi immediately became a tributary of China to ensure peace. In a face-saving move, the Ming emperor Xuande wrote, "I am specially sending envoys with a seal and am ordering that Le Loi temporarily take charge of the affairs of the country (guo) of Annam and govern the people of the country."[59]

Stanley Karnow notes that Le Loi "furnished the Chinese with five hundred junks and thousands of horses to carry them home, and apart from a last abortive attempt in 1788, China never again launched a full-scale assault on Vietnam."[60] "Factors external to Vietnam were critical, including Ming financial difficulties, Ming worries about their northern frontier with the Mongols."[61] The Ming realized that taking Vietnam, at best a risky proposition, would require more effort and attention than it was worth, and Ming ambitions thereafter focused on maintaining stability in the relationship, not "regaining" lost territory. As Brantly Womack notes, "Although China remained suzerain of Vietnam and occasionally interfered in its politics, it no longer aspired to its territory."[62]

This incident, and the centuries of stability between China and Vietnam that both preceded and followed it, reflect the legitimacy of the system more than the military balance between the two states. Had China wanted to conquer Vietnam but simply lacked the power to do so, we should find Chinese court debates about whether to invade Vietnam and arguments about the futility of so doing. Yet during both the Ming and Qing dynasties, the sporadic discussion in the Chinese court about Vietnam concerned "normal" events about an legitimate political counterpart, not debate about whether China could conquer Vietnam. Furthermore, if Vietnamese independence were only a function of military power, we should find evidence of Vietnamese forces fortifying their border in an effort to deter China—and Chinese troops preparing and planning for an attack on Vietnam—yet this also does not appear to be the case. For example, in the late sixteenth century, the scholar-official Phung Khac Khoan wrote about the China-Vietnam border:

> North of the Lang Chau border is the Pingxiang border
> South of Radiating Virtue Terrace is the Revering Virtue Terrace
> With the two kingdoms on good terms, nothing more to report
> So people keep coming and going, coming and going.[63]

Vietnam accepted tributary status in 1428 in exchange for Ming withdrawal, and it remained a tributary into the nineteenth century. Had Vietnam's independence been purely based on military power and an ability to deter or defeat Chinese attacks, there is no reason for Vietnam to have conducted such elaborate rituals, nor to explicitly acknowledge China as dominant, nor to continue sending scholars to study in China. Embassy missions were a vital part of the tributary relationship, and the Le dynasty (1428–1778) initially sent embassies every year, which eventually settled into a pattern of one embassy every three years.[64]

Brantly Womack observes that

> the Chinese court innovated and refined its institutions and ideology to face the challenge of preserving central order for the common good . . . [Vietnamese rulers] faced the same problem, and China provided an agenda of "best practices." . . . It should be emphasized that if China were still an active threat, then Vietnam's political task would have been military cohesion, and its intellectual task would have been one of differentiation from China [not emulation].[65]

Even when Vietnam was riven by internal factionalism, both sides retained the royal throne, which had been invested by China. Although Vietnam fought numerous wars with its Southeast Asian counterparts, China-Vietnam relations remained stable and peaceful until the twentieth century.

Instead of balancing against China and fortifying its northern border, Vietnam immediately resumed its subordinate relationship with the Ming. As the scholar-official Ho Quy Ly wrote, "I will tell you that customs are pure in Annam. The dress we follow is Tang fashion, and the rituals we practice are Han style."[66] Although the Ming were unable to defeat the Vietnamese, it was clear to Le Loi that only by establishing a relationship with China could Vietnam be left alone. The historian Khac Vien Nguyen notes that "never again would the Ming try to reconquer Dai Viet. The following time of peace between China and Dai Viet was to last for over three centuries."[67]

The point here is not that legitimacy-based hierarchy is always peaceful, as that is clearly not the case. Rather, although conflict and use of force is possible, authority considerations as much as power considerations were the cause of stability. East Asia was notable, however, in that the hierarchy was explicit and unambiguous, and this is part of the explanation for why the region was relatively stable.[68] Brantly Womack writes that "Vietnam considered itself the equal of China only in its right to autonomy, never in the relationship itself. But deference to China was not the same as submission."[69] China "learned that Vietnam, although never a threat, was impractical to subdue."[70] Vietnam defined itself in relation to China.

Subsequent China-Vietnam relations concerned typical matters, for example border disputes, especially because the border itself was mountainous and miners and other peoples lived on both sides of the border. "On several occasions China declined opportunities to split Vietnam that were presented by the petitions of separatist groups for legitimation."[71] During the mid-eighteenth century, Qing documents offer "detailed accounts of at least nine major disorders or rebellions in far northern Annam . . . none of these disorders posed an immediate threat to the stability of even border areas of the Qing, but the Qing authorities were concerned that they might develop into something larger."[72]

By 1788, the largest of those disturbances, the Tay Son rebellion, had engulfed the entire country and heralded the end of the Le dynasty. When the Tay Son took Hanoi, the Le-dynasty king Chieu Thong sought asylum at the Guanxi border and appealed to the Qing emperor, Kien-lung, for help in dealing with the rebellion. In contrast to the past centuries of noninterference in Vietnam, in 1788 the Qing responded with alacrity and, within ten days of the news reaching Beijing, began preparations for a full-scale invasion of Annam. Sun Shiyi, the governor-general of Guangdong and Guanxi, led an expedition of fifteen thousand troops to restore the Le dynasty and put down the Tay Son rebellion. Qing documents record that he met little resistance until reaching the Annam capital in less than a month. John Wills cites Qing records revealing that once Sun and his force reached Hanoi, "they began to understand that they had not completed their conquest, that there were other major centers of power hundreds of miles further south. They lost several battles in the course of their retreat, but still seem to have come back with about 5,000 of their 8,000 men."[73] Vietnamese reports beg to differ, claiming that the Qing sent two hundred thousand troops, which were defeated badly and retreated in disarray.[74] Whatever the size of the Qing force, "the volume of [Qing] correspondence on these arrangements make it clear that this episode was a truly major embarrassment to the Qing court."[75]

The Qing reconciled and made peace with the Tay Son king, Nguyen Hue, and in 1802 the Nguyen dynasty was recognized with an imperial pardon and tributary status. When the Nguyen Anh (no relation to Nguyen Hue), fighting the Tay Son, began to rise in power, "the Qing began to ask themselves what they would do if the lord of Dong Nai (Nguyen Anh) were completely victorious."[76] Upon defeating the his rivals, Nguyen Anh changed his name to Gia Long, proclaimed himself emperor of all Vietnam, and established his capital at Hue. With his victory in 1802, the Qing recognized him as legitimate ruler of Annam. The Chinese emperor rejected Gia Long's proposed name of "Nam Viet," instead choosing "Viet Nam," to which the Vietnamese readily agreed. Brantly Womack notes: "Considering that China was always Vietnam's greatest potential threat, China's recognition of the Vietnamese court as legitimate rulers of the country was invaluable."[77] One of the conditions for recognition was that Vietnam would send tribute to China every two years and homage performed every four years, which Gia Long "faithfully observed through his reign."[78]

Truong Buu Lam writes that "the relationship was not between two equal states. There was no doubt in anyone's mind that China was the superior and the tributary state the inferior. The Vietnamese kings clearly realized that they had to acknowledge China's suzerainty and become tributaries in order to avoid active intervention by China in their internal affairs."[79] As Marr notes:

> This reality [China's overwhelming size], together with sincere cultural admiration, led Vietnam's rulers to accept the tributary system. Providing China did not meddle in Vietnam's internal affairs, . . . Vietnamese

monarchs were quite willing to declare themselves vassals of the Celestial Emperor. The subtlety of this relationship was evident from the way in which Vietnamese monarchs styled themselves "king" (*vuong*) when communicating with China's rulers, but "emperor" (*hoang de*) when addressing their own subjects or sending messages to other Southeast Asian rulers.[80]

The Manchu Pacification of Korea (*Pyôngja Horan*, 1626–1636)

By the early seventeenth century, a new state had arisen in East Asia—the Manchu state of Later Jin (K. Hu Kŭm), proclaimed in 1616. They changed the name to Qing (along with a change in their traditional ethnic identification from "Jurchen" to "Manchu") in 1636. By any reckoning, this was much more than a barbarian conglomerate of scattered tribes. It had a stable government with laws, bureaucratic structures, dependencies, and alliances (primarily with Mongol groups); considerable territory (ethnic homelands plus lands formerly held and ruled by Ming); a well-organized military; and even a respectable industrial capacity for manufacturing arms and military supplies. While it might have been content simply to conquer all of the Manchurian (now Dongbei) lands north of the Great Wall, it did not hesitate to take advantage of a sizeable internal Chinese rebellion and the suicide of the last Ming emperor to push through Ming defenses, seize Beijing and all of northern China, and successfully crush a counteroffensive by Ming loyalists (even if that last phase took them about forty years). Certainly this was a war of conquest by an East Asian state. We will return to a more detailed discussion of the Manchus and their invasion of China in chapter 7. Here we are interested in their relations with Korea.

Three and a half centuries after the Mongols invaded Japan, peoples from the northern steppes once again moved against Korea, but this time the aim was toward establishing stable relations and removing Korea as an ally of the declining Ming dynasty. The ancient predecessors of the Qing, the Jin empire (1115–1234) of Manchuria, had never invaded Korea, having signed a diplomatic agreement proclaiming the Koryŏ dynasty (959–1392) as their brother nation.[81] Much later, in 1616, the Jin leader, Nurhachi (1559–1626), formally declared war on the Ming. The Ming asked for Korean help to put down this threat, but the Korean king was not sure whom to support. Korea sent thirteen thousand men to the northwest to join with Ming forces, but they also took with them orders to wait and see which way the battle went.[82] When the Ming began to lose, the Korean forces surrendered without a fight, and the Jin released the soldiers back to Korea, requesting a resumption of their "brother" relationship of five hundred years previous. The Korean king, In-jo, denied the request.

A decade later, the Jin, having changed their name to Qing and on the verge of taking power in China, attacked Korea twice in order to secure their southern flank (known as the *chôngmyo* (1627) and *pyôngja* (1637) *horan*. After a three-month siege at Namhansan-song Castle, In-jo was forced to surrender to the Qing leader Hong Taiji and accept terms that established the Jin as equal status and "brothers" and included a nonaggression pact and guarantees of open trade between Korea and the Jin.[83] Trade was particularly important to the Jin, because they were not agricultural people and needed food to support the campaign against the Ming.

Ki-baek Lee notes that "the Qing invasion was of short duration, only a small part of Korea became a battlefield, and the damage suffered was relatively slight."[84] Indeed, the Qing could easily have conquered Korea, but its expeditions against the Korean Chosŏn dynasty were about Chosŏn's pro-Ming policies (especially active after the deposing of Prince Kwanghae in 1623 by the Sŏin faction), which were seen to be hostile to the Manchus and contrary to the policies of Kwanghae, which genuinely looked for space between Ming and the Manchus and which the Manchus had understood and appreciated.[85] But by 1627 the Sŏin and their tool, King In-jo, had allowed Ming troops into Korea; these had based themselves on islands close to Manchu territory and were provoking hostilities. The Qing leader Hong Taiji wanted to neutralize Korea before stepping up his campaign against the Ming. The 1627 campaign lasted less than two months; agreements were made for peaceful relations and allowing trade.

The 1637 invasion was much more serious.[86] The Sŏin faction had stuck to their pro-Ming stance in spite of their earlier promises to the contrary, and this time Hong Taiji did not fool around. He quickly extracted a humiliating treaty, had it carved on a huge stone in the Manchu, Mongolian, and Chinese languages, erected it on the banks of the Han, and took away three of In-jo's sons as hostages and most of the pro-Ming politicians as captives.[87] For most of them, their captivity lasted until the summer of 1644. All relations with Ming were now severed, never to be restored. However, the Chosŏn dynasty was left standing, with In-jo still on the throne and the Manchu troops gone: all that in a month or so.[88] Kenneth Lee notes that "the Qing emperor was gentle in his treatment of Korea. In 1636 the Qing received a sworn statement from the Korean king that the Qing would be the 'elder brother.'" After pacifying Korea, "the Qing never interfered with Korean internal affairs and respected the country's independence until the end of the dynasty."[89]

The Qing expeditions against the Korean Chosŏn dynasty in the early seventeenth century were aimed more at domestic consolidation, demarcation of borders, and reestablishment of the tribute system than at conquest.[90] For example, Kim notes that "it was the wild ginseng growing in the borderland that initiated the border demarcation between China and Korea."[91] He quotes Huang Taiji (the Manchu emperor from 1626 to 1643 who laid the groundwork for the Qing dynasty) criticizing the Chosŏn king In-jo in 1631 for his trade policies, writing, "the ginseng prices used to be sixteen *liang* per *jin*, but you argued that ginseng is useless and fixed the price at nine *liang*. . . . I do not understand why you would steal such useless ginseng from us."

Conclusion

Those who see the tribute system as merely symbolic instead emphasize the relative capabilities of states as an explanation of their behavior and of the overall stability of the East Asian system. This would involve putting forth two basic hypotheses: (1) that for material reasons China, despite being the most powerful actor in the system, was unable to conquer Korea or Japan; and (2) that Korea and Japan deferred to China's centrality because they saw little chance to defeat China militarily and thus preferred compromise to fighting.

However, there is a fair amount of evidence that China actually did have the material resources and logistical capabilities to conquer Korea had it wanted to; we have already seen that the only war between Korea, Japan, and China in the five centuries under study involved the Ming dispatch of one hundred thousand troops to defend Korea against a Japanese invasion. Not only could the Ming send massive numbers of troops to Korea, but at virtually the same time and on the other side of China, the Ming intervened in border disputes in Burma, suppressed a major troop mutiny in the northwestern garrison city of Ningxia, and used another two hundred thousand troops to crush an aboriginal uprising in Sichuan.[92] Rather than being constrained, it appears the Ming had more than adequate logistical and military resources to move against Korea had it so desired. For its part, Japan was able to mobilize massive numbers of troops and ships; this is further evidence that when they decided to fight, these states had the capacity to do so on a massive scale.

There is also little evidence that China was merely deterred by effective Korean (or Vietnamese) military preparations. Borders were stable, and there is a notable absence of empirical evidence that either China, Korea, or Vietnam considered war against the others a likely possibility. If realist considerations of relative capabilities were the key factor in their relationship, we should find in the historical records of Korea, Vietnam, and China extensive discussion among strategists about possible military actions and debates over how best to deal militarily with each other. However, these are absent in both the Chosŏn, Vietnamese, and the Ming veritable records. Particularly significant is that both Korea and China have extensive records of just such military calculations about how to deal with the nomads on their northern borders.

Perhaps most difficult to explain is the Japanese general Hideyoshi's invasion of Korea in 1592. Here a much smaller state invaded a close ally of the dominant power in the system. Japan and Korea ostensibly should have allied together to balance China, yet the opposite occurred. Furthermore, we have also already seen that the reasons that Hideyoshi decided to invade Korea remain unclear, although most scholars point to status or economic, not military, considerations. That is, the burden of proof is on those who believe that the distribution of capabilities was the main factor in international relations at the time, not only to supply a plausible hypothesis that explains the patterns of stability and violence at the time but, more importantly, to provide empirical evidence that would substantiate those claims.

In sum, major wars between the Sinicized states were remarkably rare by any measure. Indeed, the absence of wars, especially given the technological, organizational, and logistical capabilities of China, Korea, Vietnam, and Japan, poses a stark contrast to the expected violence and interstate war that traditional international-relations theories have taught us to expect. There was plenty of violence in early modern East Asia, to be sure, but that violence existed between the states and the different political units on their frontiers, most notably along China's long northern and western frontiers. We will return in chapter 7 to a discussion of the political and cultural ecology of the nomads. Next, we will turn to exploring the economic relations that tied the system together.

6 TRADE

International Economic Relations

I go to the Turkish shop, buy a bun,
An old Turk grasps me by the hand.
If this story is spread abroad,
You alone are to blame, little actor.
I will go, yes, go to his bower:
A narrow place, sultry and dark.
—ANONYMOUS (Korea, c. thirteenth century)

THE EAST ASIAN SYSTEM, in short, featured smaller states existing under the shadow of a preponderant hegemonic power with the material wherewithal potentially to conquer all or most of the system. Yet we have also seen that the main actors in the system were states and that they interacted with one another within an elaborate and deeply institutionalized diplomatic system that yielded considerable stability. That system was not merely a political or cultural one, however: there were also extensive economic interactions that bound these states together. All states in the system used the same Chinese-derived international rules and norms in their dealings. With China at the center of the system, some states deeply accepted Confucian ideas, while others—such as the Southeast Asian polities—merely used those rules in their relations with one another. Although this book is primarily concerned with explaining the international relations of the Sinic states within their own hegemoncentric society, because the system was so wide and interconnected, we will also discuss Southeast Asia in some detail.

China sat at the center of a vast trading network, and Chinese staple and luxury goods were desired literally around the world. The Ming era saw a rapid economic expansion of the Chinese domestic economy and market, and cotton, silk, and sugar became commodities available for sale throughout East Asia. A national Chinese internal market emerged, aided by Ming efforts to build an extensive canal system that linked the north and south and subsequent Qing investment in a series of roads that linked the east and west.

The system was geographically quite wide. China was the central trading focus of most East Asian states, but extensive trade also existed between states ranging from Japan to Java and Siam and at times even including India and the Middle East. Perhaps the most famous international trade route, of course, was the ancient Silk Road that connected China to the Middle East and beyond by way of Central Asia. In existence for well over two thousand years, that trade route was the source for the transfer of many innovations, ideas, and goods from and to China and the outside world. Yet probably more important in terms of volume was the vast maritime trade connecting Japan, Korea, and Northeast Asia to China, Southeast Asia, and India, the Middle East, and even Europe. Far from being a barrier, the ocean linked the states, peoples, and cultures of the region. In fact, the various Pacific trade routes stretched from Japan and Russia down through China, wending their ways past the Philippines and Malaysia into Indonesia. The countries in this system were part of a thriving, complex, and vibrant regional order. Janet Abu-Lughod writes:

> The literature generated both in China and abroad gives the impression that the Chinese were "not interested in" trade, that they tolerated it only as a form of tribute, and that they were relatively passive recipients. . . . This impression, however, is created almost entirely by a literal interpretation of official Chinese documents. . . . Upon closer examination, it is apparent that much more trade went on than official documents reveal, and that tribute trade was only the tip of an iceberg of unrecorded "private" trade.[1]

Trade served as a double-edged instrument of system consolidation: it facilitated both more intense state-to-state interactions and the development of domestic state institutions. The picture that emerges is one in which the various states and kingdoms of early modern East Asia were involved in an elaborate trading system, one governed by national laws, diplomacy, and protocols, with states attempting to control, limit, and benefit from trade. Thus, early modern East Asia was interconnected diplomatically, culturally, economically, and politically.

This is contrary to the conventional Western perspective that views historical East Asia as uninterested in trade and largely consisting of isolated and autarkic economies. This view came about in part because of a superficial understanding of the full nature of East Asian trade networks and partially because, as we will see in this chapter, Western states had a much more difficult time trading in East Asia than did their East Asian counterparts. The emerging new consensus holds that, far from the West's bringing trade and interaction to a somnolent East Asia in the seventeenth century, there existed a vibrant East Asian economic trading system well before the West arrived. China and its neighbors had far more interaction with one another than has been traditionally acknowledged. Recent scholarship finds that trade, both private and tributary, made up a significant portion of both government revenues and the national economies. Furthermore, trade tended to expand throughout the region following increases in Chinese power and tended to contract when China was preoccupied with internal troubles.

In general, there were four types of foreign trade: tribute, official, commercial, and illegal (smuggling and piracy). As described in chapter 4, central to the tribute system was *tribute trade*—the ceremonial exchange of gifts, presented on behalf of a ruler and returned, usually in greater amounts, by the receiving ruler. *Official trade*—as distinct from tribute trade—was conducted by embassy officials during their tribute missions. *Private trade*, or commercial trade, was the largest portion of international trade and was conducted by merchants dealing with other merchants who operated under and were regulated by the diplomatic rules of the tribute system. Both smuggling and piracy were types of *illegal trade*, and they were often indistinguishable from each other, and when state power waned, or when states imposed too restrictive rules on trade, armed merchant and trader groups unsurprisingly developed, often in collusion with local officials.

Of these, the tribute trade was the most important but also the smallest portion of total trade. The *tribute system* of diplomacy was the international institution under which states conducted other trade, and it remained the diplomatic infrastructure throughout the region and throughout the time period in question. All the states in the region used tribute relations as the basic building block of their relationships with one another. For example, Korea-Japan relations functioned under a tribute diplomatic system, and even the Manchu Qing, upon taking power in China in 1644, "always described its diplomatic functions as part of the tribute system (*chaogong tizhi*)."[2] However, tribute itself was a miniscule portion of total trade; by far the largest portion was commercial trade between merchants.

China, Korea, and Japan at various times all imposed fairly coherent maritime restrictions on trade. While each of these countries was profoundly transformed by foreign trade, they all remained both wary of unregulated foreign access to their shores and attempted to exert their own institutional and bureaucratic control over their borders. While some have seen this as mercantilism, it can just as easily be viewed as the unsurprising result of increasingly centralized state control.

Given this history, the rise of East Asia as a vital and interconnected trading region and a locus of feverish economic activity in the late twentieth century should come as no surprise. Indeed, it is not a new phenomenon but rather the reemergence of a tightly integrated and dynamic region with centuries of history as a center for economic growth and exchange. Furthermore, the deep involvement of the state in the economic and particularly foreign economic relations of their countries is also nothing new, and this pattern existed centuries before the most recent burst of economic activity.

Chinese Trade

China was the unquestioned center of international trade in early modern East Asia. Both as producer and consumer, the Chinese market was the most important factor in creating and sustaining trade. When Chinese power expanded, so did regional trade. When China was weak or focused on internal troubles, trade contracted. The "tribute system" was the official veneer behind which much larger volumes of private trade occurred, and even the tribute system itself was not a fixed set of rules and institutions but was in fact often reinterpreted and quite flexible. Although Chinese attitudes toward trade and its trading partners varied, China was heavily engaged in trade throughout the time period in question.

The Chinese experience with foreign trade began long before the Ming era. The Tang (a.d. 618–907), Song (960–1279), and Yuan (1279–1368) dynasties each oversaw expansion of their domestic and international markets, with innovations such as a change from an agrarian to a monetized economy as early as the ninth century. This era saw Chinese private traders rapidly and actively expand their ties to trade in East and Southeast Asia, the Indian Ocean, and as far as East Africa and the Persian Gulf. By 1065, over 50 percent of state revenue was in the form of money, banks and companies began to appear, and investment into commerce and industries such as textiles, metal, and ceramics increased both domestic and international consumption.[3] John Wills notes that the tenth-century Chinese city of Quanzhou was "especially known as one of the great cosmopolitan ports of these centuries; modern researchers have found tombstones in Arabic, Persian, Syriac, and Latin, and a fine *lingam* from a Siva temple. The front wall of a mosque dating from the Song is still to be seen."[4]

Song dynasty rulers built harbors, suppressed piracy, and dredged canals, opening nine ports to international trade and establishing customs houses that taxed both imports and exports. In the mid-twelfth century, customs revenue amounted to more than two million strings of copper coins, or roughly 5 percent of state revenues during the Song dynasty.[5] So extensive was trade at this time that the trading ports were referred to as the court's "southern treasury." The first southern Song emperor said: "Overseas trade is a business that can produce enormous profits. The court, if it regulates it appropriately, is able to earn at least one million guans of copper money of income . . . it should therefore follow the old and successful policy to attract private traders and develop commercial exchange."[6]

In Northeast Asia, Chinese private traders traded silk, porcelain, tea, books, and medicine in return for Japanese knives and metals and Korean cows, ginseng, furs, and wood. During this time, the size of Chinese ships ranged between 150 to 300 tons, far larger than European ships of even three centuries later. During the Mongol Yuan dynasty, trade with the Middle East surged, in part because both the Silk Road to the north was safe and also because relations with the Middle East were more stable. Gang Zhao quotes a Chinese merchant of the thirteenth century who commented that "trading and traveling to other countries were as easy as traveling within China's different provinces and counties."[7] There are even published records of the Chinese and Indian exchange rate, which implies that trade was frequent enough for such a rate to exist.

The subsequent Ming dynasty was also deeply involved in international trade, and eventually seven cities were opened as international trading ports. In 1368, Zhu Yuanzhang declared a national ban on overseas trade and outlawed nonofficial voyages abroad. This was due in part to the endemic pirate attacks along the coast, with which we will deal later, and it was also a result of an attempt to control the coastal areas, extend institutional control from the center, and defend the Ming regime from subversion by those who contested the legitimacy of Ming rule. The Ming also depended more on land taxes from peasants, and thus government revenue did not depend on trade tariffs as much as had the previous Song and Yuan dynasties. As Hui points out, "unlike the Song court, the early Ming regime did not face a strong military threat from the north and hence did not need to concentrate overwhelmingly on sea-routes for connections to the outside world."[8]

This Ming policy essentially allowed trade only to foreign-tribute missions. Even these tribute missions were allowed to participate in trade only under highly regulated conditions. A certificate (*kanhe*), or "tally," was a visa issued to countries with tribute relations with China. Presentation of the certificate distinguished the visitor from pirates. While this policy made it more difficult for Chinese to engage in trade, it also caused the consolidation of trade networks throughout the region, and in particular it magnified the importance of Chinese living *outside* of China, as they filled the void left by the retreat of Chinese from trade. As Wang Gungwu describes it:

> The number of Chinese traders who resided abroad only temporarily was drastically cut at the end of the fourteenth century. But for those who were abroad and failed to return to China immediately as well as those who defied the bans and continued to trade overseas and had to prolong their stay indefinitely, the policy ensured that they formed more stable communities and even settled down permanently.[9]

Yet the tribute and maritime restrictions did little to actually stop private trade: in 1404, 1451, 1523, 1525, 1529, and 1533, the Ming court attempted to destroy any ships made for foreign travel and publicly affirmed the ban over thirty times. Gang Zhao writes that this was "tacit acknowledgement that the law was being flagrantly violated."[10] Southern China, with its long coastline and numerous rivers, bays, and inlets that provide both harbors and hiding places, is a region ideally situated for trade. Furthermore, the southern Chinese depended on trade for their living far more than the agriculturally based northern Chinese, and the provincial governments also relied on tariffs and trade for their government revenue, giving them incentives to avoid or ignore the maritime bans.

In the sixteenth century, in response to these bans, powerful trading groups emerged and engaged in smuggling and the bribery of (or collaboration with) coastal officials. These private Chinese traders also developed extensive commercial networks throughout East Asia, however—a point to which we will return later in this chapter. The ban on maritime trade also predictably led to piracy. As an indirect indicator of the extent of Chinese trading at the time, in 1546 and 1547, Korea returned to Fujian over one thousand Chinese who had been shipwrecked on the Korean peninsula. As one Ming court official, Xie Zhaozhi, wrote: "In Suzhou and Songjiang, Shaoxing, Wenzhou, Fuzhou, Xinhua, and Zhangzhou, the local people currently ignore all sorts of risks and pursue profit by engaging in overseas trade. They view the ocean as land and so consider Japan a neighbor. They sail to Japan to trade and enjoy close relations with it."[11] This trade was "local, apolitical, and handled by private merchants."[12] Given the reality of coastal trade and smuggling, the Ming court opened the port of Yuegang in Fujian to trade in the 1540s. Trade flourished almost immediately, and by the late sixteenth century, over one hundred ships each year sailed from Yuegang to Japan, Vietnam, Siam, the Philippines, and other Southeast Asian regions. However, in general the Ming court saw private trade as a threat to their interests, even as local officials actively participated in trade.

Throughout this era, there was a constant debate among the Confucian officials as to the utility of trade. Huo Yuxia (1522–1599), an official in Guangdong, noted that "strengthening China's maritime defenses is inseparable from cherishing maritime traders." By the late sixteenth century, many coastal intellectuals were openly encouraging Chinese traders. One such example is Xu Fuyuan, appointed governor of Fujian in 1592. Xu submitted a memorial to the Ming court that emphasized that ending the maritime ban would end smuggling and that it would increase the wealth and stability of the coastal regions, in addition to allowing the Ming to gather information about Japan in particular—their politics, economy, and goals and intentions.

Lee notes that "China since the sixteenth century was even more deeply involved than Japan in trade with the larger world. Few other places produced the commodities that were universally in demand in greater quantity or variety, and few others attracted foreign traders in the same number."[13] Deng agrees: "China is often portrayed as a country isolated from the outside world, self-sufficient and insulated from capitalism . . . with marginal, if not nonexistent, foreign trade. In fact, China needed foreign trade, both by land and sea, as much as many other pre-modern societies in Eurasia."[14] Demand for Chinese goods was almost unlimited, and in particular an increasingly urbanized and commercialized Japan created a huge demand for Chinese products. In fact, Chinese goods sold for much higher prices in Japan than they did in Taiwan, which was a transshipment area (table 6.1).

Gang Deng contrasts the Chinese and European experiences, noting that mercantilism in Europe led to a "happy, flourishing marriage" between the state and the merchant class. The marriage

blossomed, with the European man-o-war often working as one partner to knock open Asia's local markets, and the European merchants func-

TABLE 6.1 Prices of goods in Taiwan and Japan in the 1660s and 1670s

Goods	Unit	Price in Taiwan	Price in Japan
Sugar	1 picul*	2 pesos	8 pesos
Cow tails		9 pesos	50 pesos
Deer fur	100 pieces	16 pesos	70 pesos
Silk	100 piculs	250 pesos	600 pesos
Silk products (*fuzhou*)		2.5 pesos	6.5 pesos
Silk products (*jinduan*)		6.25 pesos	10 pesos

*1 picul is the equivalent of about 60 kg.
Source: Gang Zhao, "Shaping the Asian Trade Network," 41.

tioning as the other partner to capture the trade. . . . On the contrary, the Chinese state cared less about maritime trade. . . . The Chinese maritime merchants had no backing most of the time from the Chinese state [which was] often distracted by the class mobility mechanisms in Chinese society. . . . There was no need for the development of the man-o-war in China since capturing an existing offshore market was never on the Chinese agenda.[15]

The tribute-trade system itself was a net loss for China, and from 1403 to 1473, the total cost to China was more than twenty-five million taels of silver, or the equivalent of seven years of national income. The Ming court purchased all the foreign goods imported on the mission, often paying prices highly inflated over the market price. Most of this official trade was actually conducted at the port of entry where the tribute missions first entered China, and while the official envoys would travel to the capital, the traders would remain in the port and conduct their trade there. For example, Gang Zhao notes that the Ming court paid twice the market price for a Japanese knife and twenty times the market price for ivory, and between 1400 and 1560, "Japan exported more than 200,000 knives to China through the tribute channel."[16] Even the tribute missions were subject to flexibility—although the Ryukyus were officially limited to one tribute mission every two years, data reveal that between 1424 and 1447 the Ryukyus sent seventy-eight missions, more than three per year. As Deng explains, these figures belie the old "trade as trib-

TABLE 6.2 Tribute missions from major Southeast Asian states, 1370–1500

	Cambodia	Champa	Java	Malacca	Palembang	Siam	Sumatra	Total
1370–1379	3	9	7	—	7	15	—	41
1380–1389	6	9	2	—	—	12	—	29
1390–1399	1	3	1	—	—	9	—	14
1400–1409	3	6	11	1	3	10	2	36
1410–1419	3	7	7	7	1	6	7	38
1420–1429	—	7	14	4	1	9	2	37
1430–1439	—	10	7	4	—	6	2	29
1440–1449	—	10	5	1	—	4	—	20
1450–1459	—	3	3	3	—	3	—	12
1460–1469	—	5	2	2	—	1	—	10
1470–1479	—	3	—	1	—	4	—	8
1480–1489	—	2	—	—	—	4	2	8
1490–1499	—	3	—	—	—	3	—	6
Total	16	77	59	23	12	86	15	288

Source: Hui, "Overseas Chinese Business Networks," 40.

ute" view: "The tributary system was a form of disguised staple trade."[17] Siam sent fifty-one tribute missions to China between 1371 and 1420, with the Ming sending fifteen missions in return. Over the next century, Siam sent another twenty-seven missions (table 6.2).[18] Six hundred and thirty junks traveled to Manila from China between 1571 and 1600.[19]

The Japanese, for example, were only permitted to send three ships and two hundred officials every ten years on tribute missions, yet the additional private goods (*fuwongwu*) they brought with them returned profit rates as much as 1,100 percent.[20] Even Japan's tribute missions were focused on economic as much as diplomatic realities. Kawazoe notes that

many have since contended that it was the income that could be gained from missions to China that motivated Japanese king Yoshimitsu (Ashikaga

TABLE 6.3 Quantities of tribute during the Ming era

Time	Country	Export to China	Quantity	Import from China	Quantity
1393	Korea	Horses	9,800	Silk cloth	19,000 rolls
1394	Cambodia	Incense	60,000 *jin* (35.8 tons)		
	Siam	Pepper	10,000 *jin* (6 tons)		
		Sappanwood	100,000 *jin* (60 tons)		
1403–1570	Mongolia	Horses	4,000*		
		Hides	100,000		
1406–1407	Japan		Copper	215×10^5 coins	
1411	Malacca			Copper coins	26×10^5
1417	Philippines			Copper coins	30×10^5

* quantities exported yearly
Source: Deng, "The Foreign Staple Trade of China in the Premodern Era," 260.

shogunate in 1403) to open relations with the Ming . . . the large gifts of copper coins, silks, brocades, and so forth that the Ming envoys brought to the shogunal court were certainly a major economic attraction. This tribute-gift exchange was in reality simply trade.[21]

The Chinese court had tried to control economic interactions and use tributary trade to take the place of private trade, but this led to extreme pressures on their budget and became a "crippling burden."[22] Furthermore, tribute missions by themselves did not meet the demand for either Chinese goods or for foreign imports. Table 6.3 shows selected estimates of the quantity of goods traded between China and its neighbors during the Ming era under the guise of tribute. During the Ming, numerous tribute missions came from Southeast Asia, although the scale of that trade was dwarfed by the illegal smuggling that went on during that period.

Wakō: *Smugglers and Pirates*

With the Ming maritime bans on Chinese trade coupled with the tremendous demand for Chinese goods, illegal trade in the form of smuggling and piracy was inevitable. The full story of this illegal trade has yet to be written, and we find as much confusion as we do fact in existing accounts. While there were certainly pirate clans that existed purely to prey upon merchants, many of those supposed "pirates" were in fact merchants who engaged in smuggling. Both pirates and smugglers have been called *wakō* (倭寇; K: *waegu*; C: *wokou*; literally, "invaders from Japan"), and these *wakō* had two major periods of activity—the mid-fourteenth century and the early seventeenth century, which coincide with the Ming and Qing maritime restrictions on trade. The *wakō* were never considered a legitimate or alternative political entity, however, and they were never a political threat to Japan, Korea, or China. Indeed, dealing with the *wakō* was one of the main factors that caused diplomatic coordination among these countries, just as the analogous problem of piracy was to do among European states in the eighteenth and nineteenth centuries.

While some were truly pirates living on the edge of society, most of the *wakō* were not actually Japanese invaders but rather armed Chinese merchants who turned to smuggling and formed sometimes vast organizations because international trade was so important to them. Stephen Turnbull calls the *wakō* "half merchant–half pirate," because "in the absence of legitimate trade, piracy and smuggling rushed to fill the vacuum."[23] One example is Wang Zhi, a smuggler along the Zhejiang coast. In the 1540s and 1550s, because of the Ming ban on private trade, he began trading activities on an island of Guangdong, where he built a large trading fleet of over one hundred ships, selling Chinese silks to Japan, the Ryukyus, Siam, and Vietnam. When Ming authorities met with Wang, he stressed that he merely wished to trade, saying that "only opening overseas trade can solve the issue of piracy."[24]

Indeed, although known as *wakō*, in fact there were numerous armed merchant groups that sprang up on the southern Chinese Fujian and Guangdong coasts. These various armed merchants, such as He Yaba, Lin Guoxin, Hong Dizhen, and Lin Daoqian, each commanded warships, trading ships, and thousands of soldiers from bases along the Chinese coast and in southern Japan and the Philippines. As one scholar concluded at the time: "Whenever the government strengthened the maritime ban, the maritime traders turned into pirates; conversely, the pirates changed into commoners whenever the restriction was loosened."[25]

True *wakō* pirates coexisted with these smugglers. The *wakō* were origi-nally petty military families from the western islands in Kyushu. Bands of as many as three thousand intruders would pillage granaries, attack towns, take slaves in Korea and China, and interrupt trade. *Wakō* roved as far south as the Yangtze Delta, Fujian, and Guangdong. The Chinese emperor Hongwu (1368–1398) warned the Japanese that he would send forces to "capture and exterminate your bandits, head straight for your country, and put your king in bonds" unless the *wakō* raids were stopped.[26] *Wakō* raids on Korea in the fourteenth century were so destructive that Koreans attacked the island of Tsushima in 1389 in an attempt to wipe out the *wakō* stronghold, destroying some three hundred ships in the process.[27] The Koreans used diplomacy as well as force and sought the cooperation of the shogunate to repress the *wakō,* sending a number of embassies in the late fourteenth century to Japan. In fact, foreign relations between Japan and Korea at this time were essentially initiated because of the piracy issue.[28]

As Kawazoe Shoji writes, "the problem of suppressing piracy and the de-velopment of the tribute system that accompanied the founding of the Ming dynasty were the common threads running through Japan's relations with Chosŏn and Ming China."[29] Official relations between Korea and Japan covered protocols about how to deal with the return of Koreans or Japanese who were captured by pirates or those (known in Korean as *pyoryumin*) who accidentally landed in the other country.[30] With the consolidation of the Ashikaga shogunate (1336–1573), the *wakō* were severely weakened, and by the early fifteenth century, they had become more a nuisance than a threat. However, two centuries later, a resurgent tide of pirates afflicted Korea and China.[31] Chinese sources note twenty-five raids from 1440 to 1550 but 467 raids from 1551 to 1560.[32] This later wave of *wakō* pirates attacked Fujian and other southern regions of China. In large part, the resurgence of pirate raids arose as the Ming dynasty was declining and unable to effectively po-lice its borders, and it caused the Ming to officially sever relations with Japan in 1621.[33]

As the central governments of East Asia became more powerful and exerted greater control over their territories and borders, the *wakō* eventually died out. Yet the importance of these merchant-pirates should not be underestimated. They caused the governments of the region to expend enormous resources in attempting to control them, prompted the governments to communicate and even collaborate at times, and also served to link the economies of the region together in ways that might not otherwise have happened.

Qing Trade Policies

Qing trade policies followed a path similar to those taken by the Ming: initially severe restrictions on trade were followed by a gradual loosening, as both the inevitability of trade became apparent and the central government established better institutional control over its borders. Although the Qing were originally Manchus and viewed as a "foreign" regime that had conquered China, they retained many Ming institutions in governing their foreign relations, and the tribute system remained in effect—with modifications—until the end of their rule in 1911. Qing rulers took power already having had a long history of trade with Korea and China. Qing predecessors such as the Jurchen had been a crucial actor in Northeast Asian trade, deeply involved in trading horses for textiles. Gang Zhao notes that the Jurchens "came to refer to trade with Ming China and Korea as the 'golden road' (*jinlu*) and 'saw it as their life blood' (*shi ruo xingming*)."[34] Indeed, the Qing had a longstanding tradition of engaging in foreign trade, and this did not change considerably when they gained control of China.

The Qing spent four decades consolidating their control of China, particularly the coastal southern areas. In 1645, having gained control of China, the Qing initially allowed trade in copper, and the court decreed that "those merchants who intend to purchase foreign copper overseas are allowed to trade with Japan and other southeastern countries."[35] Trade continued to be presented as tribute, however, and trade in silver was prohibited; that is, maritime trade still existed under heavy restrictions. The Qing court reaffirmed the centrality of tribute missions in 1672, concluding that "foreign tribute missions are allowed to trade their own goods if they carry the goods to Beijing themselves. All non-tribute trade is illegal and prohibited."[36] Despite this ban, Zhao estimates that tribute and official trade amounted to only 3 percent of total trade during the Qing dynasty.[37]

The continuing existence of Ming loyalists on Taiwan and the existence of powerful and armed merchant clans led the Qing to increase maritime restrictions. The Qing court feared that overseas Chinese might ally with Ming loyalists abroad and pose a threat to Qing rule. Thus, from 1661 to 1684 private trade was outlawed, and many civilians living along the southern coast were ordered to move inland. Yet even under these restrictions, private trade continued in the form of smuggling. One example is Shang Kexi (1604–1676), a former Ming officer who had joined the Qing and became a banner elite. He was sent to tend to affairs in Guangdong, where he quickly became involved in illegal maritime trade. His subsequent trading empire was reported to have accrued over one million silver taels.[38] Deng further notes that "Zheng Chenggong's Ming loyalist regime in Taiwan (1644–83) took part in triangular trade involving Japan, Vietnam, Cambodia, Indonesia, and the Philippines; his fleet to Japan alone comprised fifty ships a year. . . . The total profit from overseas trade each year has been estimated at 2.3–2.7 million *liang* [one *liang* was approximately 45 grams] of silver."[39]

By the 1680s, having consolidated domestic control and control of the coasts, and being convinced that private trade would benefit the Chinese economy and state budgets, the Kangxi emperor officially lifted the ban on private trade. However, Qing rulers retained the tribute system and its institutions as the diplomatic rules of the game. As Zhao notes, "although Kangxi and his court were no longer concerned with tribute as an economic issue, they continued to stress the centrality of tribute in handling *official* relationships with other countries. Kangxi effectively put an end to the tribute trade system, but he continued the tribute system."[40]

Trade quickly resumed, and a Japanese historian notes that "from 1670 onwards Chinese ships ruled the seas of East Asia."[41] Thus trade continued in both tribute and private form: between 1685 and 1722, the Ryukyus sent 110 tribute ships, and over twenty-five hundred private ships sailed between China and Japan during that same time. During the Qing dynasty, the Chinese built more than one thousand ocean-going ships each year, and Deng concludes that "pre-modern China's long-distance staple trade reveals a system of international exchange, a prototype of division of labor transcending national/ethnic territories, and great manufacturing capacity with considerable technological advancement."[42] A Chinese source estimates that although only 20 to 30 percent of total trade was actually recorded and taxed by customs officials during the seventeenth century, customs duties on trade still accounted for one-sixth of the land tax in Fujian province and almost 75 percent of the tax in Guangdong province from the 1730s to the 1790s.[43] And, by the early nineteenth century, tea exports accounted for between 13 and 14 percent of total tea production in China.[44]

Thus, although popular views of China see it as largely closed off from the outer world, the reality was much different. Both Ming and Qing China interacted on a regular basis—both formally and privately—with traders and people from around the region. The overarching institutions that governed trade were those of the tribute system—states needed to establish diplomatic relations before they were allowed to trade. While a very large amount of smuggling and illegal trade was conducted throughout this time, the smugglers knew that they were engaging in illegal activity, and while they may have disagreed with the rules and justified their own actions, this does not negate the reality that it was the tribute system that governed relations. We should remind ourselves that even today there is a considerably large market for smuggled, pirated, and illegal goods, and governments today also expend considerable effort attempting to impose rules on trade.

Korea and Japan

Korea and Japan were also heavily involved in the early modern trading system, and they also used the institutions and norms of the tributary system as the basis for diplomacy with each other and other states. Goods, ideas, and people flowed back and forth between Japan and Korea and with China and Southeast Asia, as well. There were three maritime trade routes in Northeast Asia: one came from Southeast Asia through the Ryukyus to Satsuma and then on to the Kinai region. Another route connected Japan and Korea through Tsushima, while a third, direct route connected Hakata to China. The direct route was in fact the most dangerous, because it involved open ocean travel with especially dangerous currents and was thus the least used.[45]

The Japanese demand for Chinese silk was virtually limitless, as was the corresponding Chinese demand for Japanese silver and copper. Korea traded with both Japan and China—with China through an overland route and with Japan through the island of Tsushima. Sanderson writes: "trade with China and Korea became an important part of the Japanese economy. . . . During the fifteenth and sixteenth centuries foreign trade grew rapidly in intensity and trade ventures were extended to other parts of the far east, even as far as the Straits of Malacca."[46] Both Japan and Korea, like China, imposed fairly strict maritime controls over their traders. None of these countries showed enthusiasm for free and unlimited trade, and all three attempted to exert centralized control over their borders and, with that, to control trade flows. However, state control did not aim to eliminate contact with the outside world, and indeed both Korea and Japan remained deeply involved in trade throughout the early modern era.

Tribute trade was the diplomatic structure in both Korea and Japan that created the political framework within which private and official trade could be conducted. Korea and Japan have a long history of economic and cultural exchange, and many Japanese institutions, technical and craft knowledge, and cultural ideas were originally of Korean origin or came from China by way of the Korean peninsula. Yet Korea, having direct access to China, remained more focused on Chinese trade, and its trade with the rest of Asia and Japan was never as intensive as other East Asian states. For its part, Japan had been connected to both the Southeast Asian and China trade in addition to its Korean trade for centuries before the early modern period that is the subject of this chapter.

In contrast to much of Chinese policy during the Ming and Qing eras, Korea-Japan trade was officially pluralistic: that is, it was not a state monopoly. Although tribute relations were the key diplomatic institution, both the daimyō and rich Japanese merchants were involved, as were Korean elites and merchants. Different levels of status corresponded with different rights and access. For example, following the Ming tribute system, the Korean court limited the number of ships and personnel allowed on various tribute missions. Japanese officials in the third and fourth reception grades were restricted to one or two ships per year during the 15th century, although Shogunal tribute missions were allowed three ships.[47] When a trade mission arrived in Korea from Japan, the first step was to establish diplomatic credentials, which involved a set of ceremonies. After credentials had been certified and diplomatic protocol had been followed, "high volume [official] trade began." Official trade, as separate from tribute trade, involved the purchasing of goods that had not been exchanged as tribute but rather had been brought by the Japanese. Tribute missions typically remained in Pusan for eighty-five days while trade was conducted. Korean purchasing of the excess Japanese cargo began in the fourteenth century—the Korean experience with the wakō led them to believe that if the traders did not leave happy, they might turn into pirates in order to recoup their losses somewhere else.[48] Indeed, although Japanese sent 2,369 missions to Korea between 1392 and 1608, only thirty-six of these were shogunal (the highest diplomatic rank).[49] Official amounts and type of tribute trade between Korea and Japan were fixed by treaty, and so expanding trade was only possible through private trade. As James Lewis describes it: "Tribute trade was the oldest and most important component of the trade structure, not for its volume or content but for its symbolism. . . . Koreans viewed tribute trade as a 'burden' and a favor extended to needy islanders; the significance was diplomatic not economic."[50]

As for Japan, during the Muromachi bakufu period, it is estimated that annual traffic between China and Japan was never less than forty to fifty ships annually.[51] It was during the Song dynasty in China (960–1297), for example, that the Japanese economy essentially became monetized, because trade with China brought in so much coinage that the Japanese government was forced to legalize its use. As Yamamura notes, this "had profound effects on the political, economic, and social history of Japan."[52] Despite three separate decrees by the Japanese bakufu to ban the use of coinage, the China trade was so important to the Japanese economy that by 1240 the government had allowed the use of coins in all but the northernmost province of Japan.

Copper coins were in high demand in Japan during the Ashikaga shogunate as well, and Japanese tribute missions often attempted to receive payment in copper coins rather than in the form of Chinese goods. For example, the retired shogun Yoshimasa sent a letter with a tribute mission in 1480, writing: "Nowhere in our land can a single copper coin be found. . . . We would appeal to the sympathy and mercy of our sage Emperor for a grant of . . . coins so that our urgent needs may be met."[53] The Ashikaga shogunate allowed the powerful families on the island of Tsushima to serve as their main interlocutor with Korea and used them also as Japan's main conduit for trade with Korea. The seventeenth-century Tokugawa bakufu continued this trend, and although it controlled the all-important China trade through a port directly under its control at Nagasaki, the less important Korean and Ryukyuan trade was allowed to be indirectly run by the local domains of Tshushima and Satsuma.

It was under the Tokugawa shogunate that the central government instituted its "red seal," or *shuinsen*, trade policy. The Tokugawa shogunate granted a red seal to signify the exclusive right for Japanese to trade abroad and to distinguish legitimate Japanese traders from pirates. According to the Japanese economic historian Iwao Sei'ichi, by the 1620s this volume of Japanese foreign trade with other countries exceeded China's private trade with Japan. By 1635, 350 permits had been issued—forty-three to Chinese applicants, thirty-eight to European applicants, and 259 to Japanese traders. These were large ships, carrying an average crew of 225 men.[54] By 1636, however, the Tokugawa bakufu eliminated the shuinsen trade in an attempt to control the southern daimyō, who were the main beneficiaries of foreign trade. This should not be interpreted as a closing of Japan to trade but rather an extension of central control over the periphery. While trade came under more central control, it did not disappear. Ronald Toby notes that "a 'seclusion' analysis ignores the fact that Japan is in Asia, and divorces European relations ('seclusion') from Asian relations."[55]

Trade between Japan, China, Korea, and Southeast Asia was robust, and Etsuko Kang concludes that "from the fifteenth century Japanese-Korean trade surpassed Japanese-Ming trade in quantity, and it had a greater impact on the daily life of the Japanese in western areas."[56] From the end of the sixteenth century to the eighteenth century, private trade comprised mainly Japanese silver for Chinese silks and Korean ginseng.[57] One indication of the scale of Korea-Japan trade comes from the records of So Kin, a Japanese trader well known in Korea. In 1428, private trade conducted by So Kin's envoy brought 28,000 *kun* (16,800 kg) of copper and iron to Korea, and exchanged them for 2,800 bolts of silk cloth. Kenneth Robinson reports that the trade volume for single retinues to the Korean capital in the fifteenth century was typically between seventeen and twenty metric tons to the capital, with more being left in the ports.[58]

In 1613, following the Imjin War, the Korean government placed restrictions on the size of tribute and official trade, and those limits remained in place until 1876.[59] The annual number of Japanese seal ships allowed to trade with Korea was limited to thirty by the "Kiyu agreement" of 1630. Twelve escort ships were also permitted, resulting in a total of forty-two Japanese ships being allowed to trade in Pusan. Yet trade remained robust, and Japanese imports of raw silk approached 300,000 *kin* (180 metric tons) annually during the seventeenth century, while a single Korean merchant in the nineteenth century exported between twenty-five and thirty thousand cowhides to Japan while also importing over sixty metric tons of copper, all in the space of five years.[60] Examining Korean documents, Chong estimates that between 1684 and 1710, Pusan trade averaged annual volumes of six thousand *kanme* (22,500 kilograms), as compared to nine thousand *kanme* (34,000 kilograms) of annual trade at Nagasaki. In fact, the Tsushima profits from Korean trade during the Tokugawa era were estimated to be great enough to feed the entire population of Osaka at the current rice prices.[61]

Trade with Southeast Asia was also extensive, and between 1604 and 1635, at least eighty-seven Japanese ships traded with Vietnam, fifty-four with Manila, and fifty-five with Siam.[62] The seventeenth century saw a Japanese economic boom, as its domestic economy flourished with the stability that came from political control by the Tokugawa bakufu. As John Lee concludes:

> For a little over a century since the late sixteenth century, Japan's ample reserves in precious metal, growing Japanese interest in the commodities in which the country had little or no productive capacity, and the world-

wide expansion of trade had all helped Japan trade vigorously with the outside world. Even though foreign trade ultimately declined in importance, the legacy was nevertheless lasting.[63]

During the Tokugawa era, Japanese exports in the seventeenth century are estimated to have reached between 1.5 and 10 percent of its agricultural output.[64] Von Glahn writes that "Japanese trade with China grew substantially after the Tokugawa came to power in 1600. The Tokugawa *shogun* Ieyasu aggressively pursued foreign trade opportunities to obtain strategic military supplies and gold as well as silk goods."[65] Lee stresses the "undiminished importance of a trade relationship with China and, to a lesser extent, with Korea and the Ryukyus" during the Tokugawa period.[66] The official bakufu limits on Tsushima trade were 1,080 *kanme*, showing the considerable amount of private or disguised trade that accompanied the officially sanctioned trade. In Nagasaki, the Dutch were officially limited to three thousand *kanme* and the Chinese, six thousand; trade with the Ryukyus was officially limited to one hundred and twenty *kanme*.[67] Yet here too there is suspicion that a fair amount of illegal trade went on, judging merely from the number of ships that docked each year at these ports. Chong Song-il estimates that tribute trade comprised only 10 to 20 percent of all official trade between 1614 and 1699 and of course was even smaller relative to private trade. Trade with China remained considerable during the Tokugawa era, and in 1654 alone, the Suzhou-based Zheng trading group exported four hundred thousand silver taels' worth of goods to Japan.[68] After the Qing court established full control of Taiwan in 1683, it lifted restrictions on shipping to Japan, and trade expanded even more.[69] Japanese silver dominated the East Asian regional economy, far outstripping European silver supplies.[70] In fact, after Spanish America, Japan was the second largest producer of silver in the world in the seventeenth century. Between 1684 and 1710, Tashiro Kazui reports an average annual export from Japan of 154 metric tons of copper and 22.2 metric tons of tin. Japanese silver exports from 1615 to 1625 are estimated to have amounted to between 130,000 and 160,000 kilograms, or between 30 and 45 percent of total world production of silver.[71] Table 6.4 provides estimates of the Japanese silver trade in the mid-seventeenth century. Most notable is how small the Dutch portion of the silver trade actually was. So much silver was pouring out of Japan to buy foreign goods that the government restricted silver exports beginning in 1688 and completely banned its export in 1763, attempting to promote copper instead.[72] However, this government attempt to control exports was not

TABLE 6.4 Japanese silver exports, 1648–1672 (kg)

Year	Exports to China	Exports to the Netherlands	Total silver exports	Dutch share (%)
1648	6,727.50	23,332.50	30,060.00	77.6
1649	20,452.50	20,028.75	40,481.25	49.5
1650	25,605.00	14,775.00	40,380.00	36.6
1651	17,808.75	18,360.00	36,168.75	50.8
1652	21,326.25	21,446.25	42,772.50	50.1
1653	13,188.75	23,216.25	36,405.00	63.8
1654	30,678.75	14,430.00	45,108.75	32.0
1655	17,456.25	15,007.50	32,463.75	46.2
1656	19,653.75	23,212.50	42,866.25	54.2
1657	9,187.50	28,357.50	37,545.00	75.5
1658	41,358.75	21,150.00	62,508.75	33.8
1659	72,753.75	22,350.00	95,103.75	23.5
1660	75,566.25	16,008.75	91,575.00	17.5
1661	96,633.75	20,790.00	117,423.75	17.7
1662	48,536.25	22,350.00	70,886.25	31.5
1663	20,291.25	13,770.00	34,061.25	40.4
1664	62,490.00	20,895.00	83,385.00	25.1
1665	30,157.50	25,800.00	55,957.50	46.1
1666	27,135.00	14,913.75	42,048.75	35.5
1667	17,051.25	13,402.50	30,453.75	44.0
1668	12,806.25	0.00	12,806.25	0.0
1669	1,110.00	0.00	1,110.00	0.0
1670	1,481.25	0.00	1,481.25	0.0
1671	3,562.50	0.00	3,562.50	0.0
1672	33,615.00	0.00	33,615.00	0.0

Source: von Glahn, "Myth and Reality of China's Seventeenth-Century Monetary Crisis," 443.

entirely successful, and by the mid-eighteenth century, precious-metal exports had returned to sixteenth-century levels. "During the eighteenth century," Klein writes, "Japanese exports of precious metals over the isle of Tsushima into Korea and China actually surpassed the amounts of silver that had earlier been carried away from Nagasaki by the Chinese and Dutch."[73] In fact, Iwao Sei'ichi estimates that between 1648 and 1662, Japan exported at least twelve million taels of silver to China.[74]

Japanese trade was not restricted to Northeast Asia. Leonard Andaya writes that "the Japanese were especially prominent in Ayutthaya, and by the late 1620s the trade between Siam and Japan was probably greater than Siam's total trade with other nations." In addition to a large Chinese population, between one thousand and fifteen hundred Japanese lived in a "Japanese quarter" of the city.[75] Between 1647 and 1692, 115 Siamese ships traveled to Nagasaki (table 6.5). Between 1600 and 1635, over three hundred and fifty Japanese ships traded under the vermillion seal, visiting at least nineteen ports, including Vietnam, Cambodia, Luzon, and the Malay-Indonesian archipelago. Using reports of Chinese ship captains given to Japanese officials in Nagasaki during the Tokugawa era, Yoneo Ishii estimates that during the seventeenth and eighteenth centuries, the junks that carried trade between China, Southeast Asia, and Japan had an average size of between 120 and five hundred tons, with some capable of carrying as much as twelve hundred tons of cargo. Even Tokugawa Japan was not closed to foreign trade: in 1688 alone, 173 Chinese ships and almost ten thousand Chinese merchants visited Japan.[76]

Southeast Asia exported rhino horn (Africa), turmeric (India), betony, garu-wood or lign aloes, sappan wood, spices, perfumes, medicines, and dyes to Japan. Japan exported tin, copper, sulfur, and artisans' manufactures such as fans and swords. Seventy to 90 percent of Japanese exports were metals—silver, copper, tin, and brass. Silver itself comprised about 50 percent of Japanese exports during the seventeenth century. Korea's main export was cotton, followed by silk, linen, ginseng, cowhides, and other agricultural goods. The basic outline of Japanese trade was the export of Japanese metals, first silver and then copper, in return for silk, cotton, medicines, and sugar.

One humorous example of the wide range of trade comes from 1728, when a Japanese trading ship brought two elephants from Annam as gifts for the Tokugawa emperor Yoshimune. The captain did not have an official seal allowing him to trade but was allowed in because Yoshimune had made a special request that elephants be brought to him from Southeast Asia. Marius Jansen reports that the emperor wished to see the beast (the female died soon

TABLE 6.5 Chinese and Southeast Asian ships entering Nagasaki, 1647–1692

Year	China	Taiwan	Vietnam	Siam	Cambodia	Other	Total (non-Chinese)
1647	23	1	4				6
1648	10		5	1	1		7
1649	44	1	2		1	1	5
1650	59		7		1	3	11
1651	32		9	1	3		13
1652	37		8	1	4		13
1653	37		9	2	5	3	19
1654	41		4	2	4	3	13
1655	40		2			3	5
1656	40		2			3	5
1657	32		3	3	11	2	19
1658	39		5	5	2	1	13
1659	47		2	6	4	1	13
1660	35		4	5	1	10	20
1661	32		1	3	2	1	7
1662	35	2	4	3	1	1	11
1663	33	3	4	3	3		13
1664	25	5	5		4		14
1665	10	8	11	1	3	2	25
1666	2	14	6	4	4	3	31
1667	4	11	4	3	3	2	23
1668	18	12	5	5	1	2	25
1669	15	10	5	3	1	4	23
1670	16	13	4	2	1	6	26
1671	7	20	3	2		6	31

TABLE 6.5 (*Continued*)

Year	China	Taiwan	Vietnam	Siam	Cambodia	Other	Total (non-Chinese)
1672	3	16	10	4	4	8	42
1673	6	1	3	1	2	7	14
1674	7	6	3	2		3	14
1675	7	11	3		2	6	22
1676	7	8	3	3		3	17
1677	7	13	6	2		1	22
1678	9	8	3	3		3	17
1679	13	8	7	2	1	1	19
1680	5	7	7	6	1	4	25
1681	0	5	2		1	1	9
1682	5	9	3	6	1	2	21
1683	2	13	3	6		3	25
1684	7		6	5		4	15
1685	77		1	3		4	8
1686	96		6	3	1	5	15
1687	130	2		1	1	3	7
1688	173	4	4	2	2	6	18
1689	66	1	6	2	2	2	13
1690	77	2	6	3	1	5	17
1691	76	2	5	3	2	2	14
1692	63	1	2	3	3	1	10
Total	1549	217	207	115	84	131	755
Annual average	34.4	4.8	4.6	2.6	1.9	2.9	16.8

Source: Gang Zhao, "Shaping the Asian Trade Network," 59–60.

after arrival in Japan), but there was a problem: only court-rank officials were allowed to meet the emperor. The elephant was granted Fourth Imperial Rank (*Juyon'i Konan Hakuzo*, higher than most daimyō), and thus the emperor could see the wonderful import.[77]

Thus, evidence from both Japan and Korea reveals that both countries were heavily involved in international trade. This involvement necessitated both domestic laws, such as licenses for officially approved traders, and international diplomacy, such as agreements on how much trade and how many ships would be allowed each year.

Southeast Asia

Southeast Asia illustrates that processes of trade encouraged both interstate relations and domestic institution building. By the time of the Song dynasty, trade with Southeast Asia had expanded to become a major source of wealth and revenue for the Song state coffers. Sea trade generated considerable income for the government through customs duties, and the Yuan dynasty sometimes subsidized traders' voyages, in return for which they received up to 70 percent of the trip's profits.[78] In the ninth century, the Tang governor Gao Pian dredged the Gulf of Tonkin in order to make it passable for shipping.[79]

From roughly 1400 to the eighteenth century, the expansion of international trade within Southeast Asia and between Southeast Asia and China, Japan, and Northeast Asia resulted in a regionwide process of territorial consolidation and centralization of royal authority.[80] Frank notes that "at least a half dozen trade dependent cities—Thang-long in Vietnam, Ayutthaya in Siam, Aceh on Sumatra, Bantam and Mataram on Java, Makassar on Celebes—each counted around 100,000 inhabitants plus a large number of seasonal and annual visitors."[81] Chinese records indicate three main trading routes—one from China to Vietnam, the Malay peninsula, and western Indonesia; a second from China to Luzon, the Sulu zone, and onward to Borneo and the Moluccas; and finally a third route linking the two other routes.

Extensive trade relations also facilitated population flows, particularly as Chinese emigrated to Southeast Asia in search of economic opportunities. In fact, there was more international migration in early modern East Asia than is generally recognized. For example, the Chinese population in Jakarta approached 20 percent of the total population. Upward of ten thousand Chinese lived in Manila by the seventeenth century, and by 1750, the number of Chinese living in Manila had quadrupled to over forty thousand.[82]

The center of international trade was, of course, China. Even after the Ming ban on private overseas trade, Southeast Asian "illicit and third-party operations plus official tribute mission continued to send a vast array—in terms of volume, probably considerably larger than western trade—to the expanding networks of south China."[83] By the sixteenth century, Chen Bisheng estimates that there were over one hundred thousand Chinese living outside China, and significant Chinese communities developed in Vietnam, Cambodia, Siam, the Philippines, Surabaya, Java, Brunei, and Sulu. Mostly traders or small businessmen, they became the backbone of the China–Southeast Asia trade.[84] By the start of the nineteenth century, that number had swelled to almost one million ethnic Chinese living in Southeast Asia. With the increase in their numbers came more solidified trade networks, merchant groups, and institutional presence. In fact, as table 6.6 shows, Chinese ships far outnumbered Indian ships to Luzon, even during the maritime ban enacted by the Qing. These Chinese traders took advantage of the desire for Chinese goods, as well as their own trade networks, to dominate trade throughout the region.

As in Northeast Asia, trade in Southeast Asia was regulated by royal monopolies. Siam provides a case in point. By the seventeenth century, the Siamese capital of Ayutthaya had become a center of regional economic activity, sending deer hides, tin, lac, and rare woods to China, Japan, and South Asia, in return for firearms, precious metals, Indian and Persian textiles, and Chinese silk.[85] China-Siam trade provided perhaps half of the royal income by the late eighteenth century.[86] The Siamese central civil administration had four working departments—Treasury, Palace, Land, and City. Treasury was in charge of overseeing foreign trade, and consisted of royal warehouses, factories, tax and duties collectors, and the "port master."[87] The Siamese royal port department was divided into two sections. One dealt with the Chinese trade and often employed a Chinese merchant as *phra klang*, or minister in charge of foreign trade; the other section was headed by a Muslim.

> The Chinese were outside the system by which all freedmen (*phrai*) were registered in a specific district under a lord. . . . The Chinese were therefore able to move freely throughout the country . . . they came to manage successful commercial enterprises or to run government enterprises, such as tin-mining and state overseas trade . . . the Siamese court used Chinese as port officials, captains and navigators of royal junks, and purchases and sellers of overseas consignments.[88]

TABLE 6.6 Chinese and Indian trading ships to Luzon Island, 1581–1760

	Chinese ships	Indian ships
1581–1590	102	—
1591–1600	119	1
1601–1610	290	—
1611–1620	49	9
1621–1630	73	—
1631–1640	325	1
1641–1650	162	3
1651–1660	68	—
1661–1670	57	2
1671–1680	49	13
1681–1690	89	38
1691–1700	171	35
1701–1710	204	34
1711–1720	94	24
1721–1730	123	38
1731–1740	152	31
1741–1750	116	12
1751–1760	134	14

Source: Hui, "Overseas Chinese Business Networks," 42.

By the early eighteenth century, the number of Chinese ships calling at Siam had steadily increased to between ten and twenty per year, and Siam exported tin to meet an "almost insatiable" Chinese demand.[89] One European trader at the time wrote:

The Chinese . . . bring them the most valuable commodities; and, at the same time, allow their own people to disperse themselves unto a great number of foreign parts, whither they carry their silks, porcelain, and other curious manufactures and knickknacks, as well as their tea, medicinal roots, drugs, sugar, and other produce. They trade into most parts of East India; they go to Malacca, Achen, Siam, etc. No wonder then that it is so opulent and powerful.[90]

As Cushman emphasizes, "Siam's exports should not be seen as marginal luxuries, but as staple products intended either for popular consumption or for the manufacture of consumer goods by the Chinese."[91] Due to growing population in eighteenth-century China, rice imports from Southeast Asia grew rapidly, and by 1750 the Chinese were importing over ten thousand tons of rice from Southeast Asia.[92] By 1767, the Chinese community in Siam numbered perhaps thirty thousand.

During the late sixteenth century, trade between Manila and China reached an estimated annual value of eight hundred thousand *liang* of silver (one *liang* was approximately forty grams).[93] China imported horses from India, cloves and other spices from Java, and numerous other goods such as ebony, coral, and timber. "Chinese voyaging in the Indian Ocean was well-established before the much-publicized voyages of Zheng He."[94] Between 1604 and 1635, the Japanese recorded 335 ships sailing officially to Southeast Asia, and even in the late seventeenth century, two hundred ships arrived in Nagasaki every year.[95] At its peak, over 250,000 deerskins were imported from Luzon each year, decimating the local deer population in Luzon, and by the eighteenth century, Japanese traders turned their attention to Siam instead.

Although there is evidence of Vietnam-Japan trade as early as 1330, Vietnam had become Japan's "most important trading partner" by the seventeenth century, with the value of trade probably exceeding six hundred thousand taels of silver annually, with at least 124 Japanese ships licensed to trade visiting Vietnam between 1604 and 1635. The number of unlicensed ships was probably greater.[96] The Gulf of Tonkin region was an active trading zone that ranged from the Guanxi coast and the island of Hainan down to northern Champa, with horses, salt, and oxen being major items traded.[97] Vietnamese goods have been found in the Philippines, Sulawesi, and other Javanese regions. One source notes that up to half of Vietnam's twelfth-century population came from China, although that number is probably exaggerated.[98]

The fifteenth century saw the largest Southeast Asian ships, some two hundred to five hundred tons, carrying trade between Japan, China, and Southeast Asia. Although the Ming had banned private trade from 1433 to 1567, enforcement was lax, and there is extensive evidence that private and illegal trade continued almost unabated during the Ming dynasty. Indeed, between 1580 and 1680, private Chinese traders made at least five thousand trips to the Philippines alone, and the total commercial value of this trade exceeded one hundred million Spanish pesos.

As Victor Lieberman concludes, "instead of a late seventeenth-century retreat from foreign trade, we find a change in emphasis from Indian Ocean to Chinese networks, and a general intensification after 1710 . . . [and] movement from high value, low bulk trade to the opposite mix."[99] The Ryukyus were a central part of this trade, situated as they are between Japan and China. Especially with the official Ming ban on trade, the Ryukyus took on an expanded role as entrepot, sending at least seventeen trade missions to Ayutthaya, eight to Palembang, and six to Java between 1430 and 1442.[100] With the lifting of the Ming ban on trade in 1567, fifty large junks (two hundred tons or more) each year plied their trade between Fujian and Southeast Asia, and by 1597 the number of junks had grown to 117. Half of these junks were licensed for the Philippines and beyond, and half for continental Southeast Asia (among them Siam, Vietnam, and Cambodia) as well as Java and Sumatra.[101]

Rather than viewing early modern East Asian states as isolated and autarkic, we find a vibrant regional, as well as global, trading system. This system was extensive—China was clearly the central and most important economy, but trade throughout the region was much greater than has traditionally been recognized. This trade necessitated and facilitated both domestic and international consolidation.

The West

Evidence on the relative importance of trade with the West suggests, moreover, that relations among Asian states continued to outweigh more sporadic interactions with outside powers. In contrast to Japan's continued incorporation into active trade in the region, Western trade—mainly Dutch and Portuguese traders—was simply never as important as has been believed. The annual Portuguese share of silver exports was usually less than 10 percent of total exports.[102] The Dutch were actually pushed out once the East Asian system stabilized by the end of the eighteenth century. Indeed, in 1639, the Tsushima daimyō told the Korean government that "because commerce with the Portuguese has been banned from this year, we must seek more broadly trade with other foreign nations besides them, and [the *shogun*] has ordered us to trade with your country even more than in the past."[103] Thus, Klein concludes that "during the eighteenth century . . . the East China Sea saw the reestablishment of its traditional self as it more or less retired from the world [European] market."[104] Numerous estimates compiled by researchers on different regions, periods, and markets show the overwhelming bulk of trade occurring within Asia as opposed to between Asian states and Europe. Klein's assessment is typical: "European penetration into the maritime space of the China sea was marginal . . . weak and limited."[105]

Europeans and Americans began to arrive in significant numbers in the sixteenth and seventeenth centuries as Renaissance missionaries and traders. In 1557, the Portuguese gained a permanent colony on Macau, which they held until 1999. Ferdinand Magellan came to Cebu in the Philippines in 1521; two weeks later, tribal warriors killed him, in what is known locally as "the first anti-colonial war in East Asia."[106] Slowly European states began to conquer and colonize various political spaces in East Asia. Dutch East India Company colonies or outposts were later established in Atjeh (Aceh) in 1667, Macassar in 1669, and Bantam in 1682. The company established its headquarters at Batavia (today Jakarta) on the island of Java, and the Dutch East India Company maintained a trade post in Japan, on Deshima, from 1641 to 1857. With the Treaty of Saigon in 1862, the Vietnamese emperor ceded to France three provinces of southern Vietnam to form the French colony of Cochinchina.

As the Europeans began to compete with the Chinese trade networks in Southeast Asia, they had a very difficult time. Gang Zhao notes that "wherever Dutch traders landed, Chinese businessmen soon appeared to compete with them. Because the Chinese traders had a longer history of trade with the local people, were more aware of their needs, and had a wider commercial network, they generally won."[107] For example, even in Jakarta (Batavia), a Dutch colony, the annual average number of Chinese ships arriving for trade far exceeded the number of Portuguese ships (table 6.7).

The Dutch provided only 20 percent of Siam's imports during the seventeenth century, and "in total volume, European trade [with Siam] probably remained inferior to that of Indian Muslim and more especially Persian merchants."[108] Indeed, George Smith estimates that Siamese trade, in both volume and value, was probably greater than Dutch trade.[109] Heather Sutherland observes that in Indonesia, "despite their military strength and wide-ranging commercial apparatus, the Dutch East India Company could not compete effectively with the Asian trade networks . . . they were marginal, whereas the

TABLE 6.7 Chinese and Portuguese ships to Jakarta
(Batavia), annual averages, 1681–1793

	Chinese	Portuguese	Total
1681–1690	9.7	1.8	11.5
1691–1700	11.5	1.6	13.1
1701–1710	11.0	2.9	13.9
1711–1720	13.6	5.9	19.5
1721–1730	16.4	9.0	25.4
1731–1740	17.7	4.8	22.5
1741–1750	10.9	4.1	15.0
1751–1760	9.1	1.8	10.9
1761–1770	7.4	2.4	9.8
1771–1780	5.1	3.0	8.1
1781–1790	9.3	3.9	13.2
1791–1793	9.5	3.0	12.5

Source: Blusse, Strange Company, 123.

TABLE 6.8 Relative amounts of salt trade with Melacca
by origin of traders (%)

	1699/1700	1735/1736
Chinese	38.7	45.3
Malayans	26.2	19.3
Javanese	16.3	13.0
Portuguese	9.4	10.4
Burghers	5.8	6.0
Moors	—	4.1
English	2.7	1.6
Other	0.8	0.3

Source: Hui, "Overseas Chinese Business Networks," 59.

Chinese were absolutely central."[110] Table 6.8 shows that the salt trade was also dominated by the Chinese and other Southeast Asians. Although European trade was important, it was never the dominant form of trade in East Asia. This does not mean, however, that interactions with Europe were unimportant or that they had no consequences. Much recent scholarship is emphasizing the interconnectedness of the global system, demonstrating that as early as 1300, economic trends and events in Europe, Arabia, Southeast Asia, and China affected one another.

Conclusion

Even into the twentieth century, scholars such as Takeshi Hamashita have explored the nature of the economic and diplomatic linkages made in East Asia and have argued that Japan challenged China within the Confucian international order, not outside of it. According to Hamashita, prosperity from the post–Imjin War economic boom, smuggling, and commercialism that prospered outside the tribute-trade system was not a collapse of the system but a sign of its success, which resulted from the strong demand for Chinese goods. Refuting the commonly held view that the arrival of Western great-power politics in Asia marked a sharp disjuncture from the traditional Sinocentric order, he argues that the tribute-trade system was far stickier and more persistent than normally assumed. Based on the examination of a series of treaties signed during this period,[111] he makes a further claim that not only were the tribute-trade system and the Western-style treaty order compatible but also that the tribute concept tended to subsume the Western treaty concept even into the twentieth century.[112]

Thus the economic and diplomatic system of East Asia was far more integrated, extensive, and organized than the conventional wisdom allows. From at least the Song era of the tenth century to the end of the Qing dynasty in the nineteenth century, there existed a vibrant and integrated trading and foreign-relations system in East Asia that ran from Japan through Korea to China and extended from Siam through Vietnam and the Philippines. So extensive was this regional economic and diplomatic order that it had domestic repercussions, such as the monetization of the Japanese economy. The Dutch and the Portuguese had less of an influence than is normally thought. It was only when China began to crumble in the nineteenth century that this system finally broke apart.

Research on trade patterns and diplomacy indicates a high level of system interaction in East Asia that was relatively independent of the simultaneously developing European system. As Hamashita contends, it is necessary to see "Asian history as the history of a unified system characterized by internal tribute/tribute-trade relations, with China at the center," stressing that a

> fundamental feature of the system that must be kept sight of is its basis in commercial transactions. The tribute system in fact paralleled, or was in symbiosis with, the network of commercial trade relations, [and] the entire tribute system and interregional trade zone had its own structural rules which exercised systematic control through silver circulation and with the Chinese tribute system in the center.[113]

7 FRONTIERS

Nomads and Islands

If you're an atheist in Minnesota, the god you don't believe in is Lutheran.
—GARRISON KEILLOR

THE DIFFERENCE between a border and a frontier is the difference between a line and a space. Borders are fixed—a clear line that separates
two different political spaces, with clear rights and responsibilities on both
sides of the line. In contrast, a frontier is a zone—an ambiguous area where
political control, organization, and institutions gradually diminish and inter-
mingle with other ideas, institutions, rules, and peoples. While some political
relationships in early modern East Asia were demarcated by lines, and these
proved to be remarkably stable, other historical relationships were mediated
by space, and these proved to be more conflictual.

This book is focused on borders, the states that demarcated and controlled
them, and the rules and norms that they devised to govern their interactions
during a particular time and place in East Asia. As we have seen, a political
entity coherent enough to define itself over geography and to negotiate a fixed
line and border with another entity requires considerable organization, institutionalization, and a set of ideas shared with the other political entity, so that
the two parties can actually agree on a border, view each other as legitimate,
and agree on the rights and responsibilities of both sides. In early modern
East Asia, Sinic states had political organization and shared cultural values,
China had clear borders with both Vietnam and Korea, and these combined
for long periods of stability.

Yet these Sinic states, sharing a worldview that I have called "Confucian,"
were not the only political actors in the system. Coexisting with these ma-

jor Sinicized states were many different types of political units that resisted China's civilizational allure, most notably the various pastoral, highly mobile tribes and seminomadic peoples in the northern and western steppes (variously known as Mongols, Khitans, Jurchens, Uighurs, Tibetan nomads, and others). These various peoples and polities engaged in long-running endemic skirmishing with the Sinicized states.[1]

As David Wright asks, "Why all the fighting?"[2] Although popular imagination sees the nomads prowling like hungry wolves outside the Great Wall, attacking randomly and whenever possible, there was in fact a logic to Chinese (and Korean) interactions with the nomads.[3] China and the nomads existed along a vast frontier zone, and the disparate cultural and political ecology of the various nomads and China itself led to a relationship that, although mostly symbiotic, never resulted in a legitimate cultural or authority relationship between the two. Creating civilization also entailed creating the idea of an other, the "barbarian," in contrast to "civilization." These nomads had vastly different worldviews and political structures than the Sinicized states. They rejected Chinese ideas of civilization, such as written texts or settled agriculture, and they were playing a different international game by different rules. Thus crafting enduring or stable relations was difficult. The frontier was only turned into a border when other states, such as Russia, began to expand eastward in the eighteenth century, leaving the nomads with nowhere to move.

Although there was considerable stability between the Sinicized states, these same East Asian states did expand into areas that were not controlled by other states. Just as the United States expanded into largely empty areas, so did China (and Korea, Vietnam, and Japan). In fact, China's centuries-long westward expansion, so ably described by Peter Perdue, is strikingly similar to America's nineteenth-century westward expansion.[4] In both cases, large and powerful states with populous and urbanized east coasts expanded into sparsely populated, ethnically different western "frontier areas" and obliterated the native inhabitants. In both cases, this was seen as a natural and inevitable process of taming their western frontiers and bringing order and civilization to largely "wild" areas. Furthermore, in both the U.S. and Chinese cases, once borders with recognizable states were settled (Mexico and Canada; Korea and Vietnam), they did not attempt to conquer them.

There was another type of frontier in early modern East Asia. Although popular imagination has focused more on the nomads to the north and west of China, frontiers existed in many other places. Particularly important for this book were the maritime borders between states. For understandable reasons, these were not ever demarcated formally before the advent of the modern Westphalian system, and they have proved to be the most enduringly difficult areas to demarcate even today.

While nomads to the north and west of China and Korea were a constant nuisance, maritime frontiers were demarcated only in the most obvious of ways. Thus, land "obviously" Japanese was considered to be Japanese; land obviously Chinese or Korean was considered to be Chinese or Korean. Between these countries were a number of islands, bodies of water, and uninhabited rocks that historically had little value or meaning to the people at the time, and thus they remained undefined and unclaimed. In the modern contemporary world, it is these frontiers—not nomads—that cause the most trouble.

Nomads

Why did threats come from frontiers and not borders? Why did states lack the intention to conquer China, unlike small bands of farmer-warriors? It is taken basically for granted that Vietnam and Korea posed no military threat to China, while the mobile "nomads" posed a continual threat. Thus much of our scholarship and memory about warfare in this time period naturally enough focuses on those nomadic threats. But we should ask why this is the case. Why did these small marauders pose such a threat to China while, perhaps just as importantly, the states did not?

If the explanation is merely that Korea and Vietnam were too small to consider balancing, attacking, or conquering China, then we must ask why an even smaller, poorer, less organized, and less populous group could have entertained such ambitions. As Frederick Mote writes about China:

> An enemy from without had to have a base in the nearer steppe (for that time, no other enemies need be considered) from which to utilize the comparative advantages of mobile warfare over positional warfare of fixed battle lines. The external enemy also would need to have in place a system for governing sedentary subjects, as it acquired them, in order to take full advantage of its superior striking force. If it could not do that, it would remain a raiding, plundering force but would not become a conquering power.[5]

In fact, for most of the time period covered in this book, the various nomadic tribes did *not* have any ambition to conquer China. For the most part, nomads engaged in border skirmishes, trading, and raiding, as we saw in chapter 5. Peter Perdue notes that "it was almost never the ambition of a steppe leader to conquer China itself. Steppe leaders staged raids on the Chinese frontier to plunder it for their own purposes."[6]

Social Organization

It is unwise to generalize about the pastoral nomads of various ethnicities, languages, and social structures that populated the vast northern steppe and who ranged from the Pacific Ocean to India and Turkey. In fact, there were many types of peoples who lived north of China. Not all were nomads, and not all political organization was tribally based. Manchuria was home to many disparate peoples, languages, and cultures, and Crossley notes that "the result was not the refinement of a homogenous people and culture from heterogeneous sources, but the settlement of the uneven terrain of the region by culturally diverse groups who on occasion wove their lineages and federations together."[7] Crossley notes that "in the 1500s . . . the result was a complex, multi-layered cultural milieu in which Mongolian political and cultural influences mixed with traditional Jurchen economic life and the radiating attractions of the Chinese trading towns."[8] Indeed, Tibetans, Uighurs and Zhungar Mongols to the west, Khitans and Mongols to the north, and Manchus to the Northeast were all types of "nomads."

The basic political unit was the family or clan, which herded sheep and rode horses. This basic herding unit was highly mobile and formed the core of the economic and political life of the northern steppe. Large nomadic groups were difficult to sustain, because grazing their animals required adequate water, and so peoples tended to disperse, leading to inherently decentralized social structures—central authority made sense "only when there was an opportunity for regular military exploitation of other communities."[9]

Occasionally, a group of these clans would coalesce into a more enduring and centralized political unit, although these tended to be based on the charisma and personality of the ruler and thus were thus short lived; "tribal rivalries and fragmentation were common."[10] Even the Zhungar empire, which emerged in the late seventeenth century, had only "an increasingly 'statelike' apparatus of rule" and never developed the same centralization or institutionalization as did the Sinicized states.[11] Crossley notes that the division between sedentary and nomadic economies and peoples was never clear, with hunting, fishing, and gathering coexisting with occasional sedentary agricultural practices. Those living closer to the Chinese tended to be governed by Chinese practices and institutions: "[the Jurchens, like the Khitans before them] were governed in Chinese and according to Chinese political traditions."[12]

However, there did occasionally arise more enduring political structures, often in response to events in China. Thomas Barfield argues that nomads "were forced to develop their own peculiar form of state organization in order to deal effectively with their larger and more highly organized sedentary neighbors."[13] Although loosely organized internally, with the tribal structure remaining intact, the leader dealt with China, looking for the material benefits that the nomads could not provide for themselves.

Such structures were inherently less enduring than the states of China, Korea, and Vietnam, due simply to the fact that the basic units remained mobile and nomadic. The most famous nomad was, of course, the Mongol leader Chinggis (Genghis) Khan, who united the tribes of Mongolia by force in 1206 and embarked upon a classic "conquest dynasty." It survived by eating up more and more land and conquered and actually governed Chinese territory. Having conquered China, the Mongols took the dynasty name Yuan (1234–1368) and adopted Chinese-style institutions and administration with which to rule China. Yet Chinggis Khan did not begin with the aim of seizing and holding territory, and it was not until Kubilai Khan (the grandson of Chinggis Khan) took power that the Mongols established enduring administrative institutions.[14] Yet change was not as lasting as it might have been. Kubilai Khan ruled through the existing Chinese bureaucracy instead of supplanting the existing Sinic civilization. The Yuan dynasty then continued on to attack Persia, Baghdad, European Crusaders in the Holy Land, Japan, Vietnam, and Burma. Yet the Mongols had never prepared for enduring rule over a sedentary culture like China's, and, as David Wright notes, "by the 1350s Yuan rule over China was so disorganized and decentralized that a native Chinese insurgent named Zhu Yuanzhang was able to overthrow the dynasty in 1368."[15]

There is also a distinction between the mobile and more nomadic peoples of the open steppe to the northwest and the peoples of the northeastern frontier zone, who lived in close proximity to China and had a mixed culture that incorporated aspects of sedentary, Chinese-influenced life along with their more nomadic culture and society. Thus, a proto-Manchurian people known as the Khitan came into power and became known as the Khitan-Liao (916–1125). The Khitans ruled over Manchuria and southern Mongolia. Khitans "retained, at least in official policy, a strong attachment to the principles of nomadic life and a toleration for traditional segmented political structures."[16]

The majority of nomads were illiterate, even though at various times "the peoples of Central and Northern Asia were acquainted with both the phonetic systems of Western Asia and the ideographic system of Eastern Asia," and the "Jurchen who founded the Jin empire devised writing systems in which ideographic writing derived from Chinese was combined with phonetic elements."[17] Unfortunately, the use of the Jurchen script died out, so that by 1444, the eastern Jurchens wrote to the Ming court, saying: "Nobody out here in the forty garrisons understands Jurchen script, so please write to us in Mongolian from now on."[18] The Khitans did have their own script for writing their own language, but it was heavily influenced by Chinese concepts.

The Mongols and Khitans never used the Chinese system of examinations, nor did they link "status or achievement to time-consuming attainments in civil or literary pursuits."[19] The Jurchens destroyed the Khitans and survived for a century as the Jin dynasty (1126–1234), located to the north of China, but that too fell apart almost as quickly as it had formed.[20] The Jurchens themselves were a loose group of people who divided themselves into various more local groupings, and after the Jin empire dissolved, its descendants became the Qing, and it was not until Nurhaci unified the various peoples of northern Manchuria that they came to see themselves as one identity.

In sum, the nomads for the most part were scattered, mobile tribes composed of small numbers of families. They would occasionally cooperate for some purpose or when a local strongman was able to unify a few groups, but on the whole they remained far less institutionalized and organized than the states to their south. They had a wide variety of cultural influences but always existed in the shadow of China, and to a lesser extent Korea, and their more settled societies.

Trade and Raids Along the Frontier

That major wars of conquest along China's northern frontier were rare did not mean that violence was completely absent.[21] In particular, controlling borders, stabilizing frontier areas, and dealing with those peoples outside borders has been a major part of being a state in every region in the world. Japan, surrounded by water, had a comparatively easier time establishing and controlling borders, once its own internal frontiers had incorporated the major islands of Japan, although Japan did have to contend with pirates. It was the Chinese and Koreans that dealt with frontier problems most often, and they attempted to stabilize their frontiers and turn them into borders through a combination of four practices: offense, defense, diplomacy, and trade.

At its core, the Chinese-nomad relationship was about trade. Nomads needed three things from agricultural China: grains, metals, and textiles, and they would trade, raid, or engage in tribute to gain them. Chinese strength was a key factor in the rise of nomadic empires: "nomadic imperial confederacies came into existence only in periods when it was possible to link themselves to the Chinese economy . . . when China fell into severe disorder and economic decline it was no longer possible to maintain this relationship and the steppe devolved into its component tribes."[22] Chinese strength stabilized nomadic life, and the two existed in an interacting and related manner. Perdue notes that "the collapse of a Chinese dynasty threatened the stability of the steppe empire. This relationship explains why, for example, the Uighurs intervened to keep the Tang dynasty alive."[23] Because a strong and stable China provided the possibility of enduring relations with the nomads through trade or raids, when China fell into internal division, the nomadic empires tended to fall as well.

For its part, China used offense (as Johnston emphasizes), defense (the Great Wall), trade, and diplomacy in attempting to deal with the nomads.[24] The Chinese weighed the costs of warring with the nomads against the problems of trading with them. Sechin Jagchid argues that when trade was more advantageous, the nomads traded. When trade was difficult, they raided China's frontier towns to get the goods they needed. Thomas Barfield agrees that the nomads were dependent upon the Chinese, but he sees the key factor as domestic politics within the Mongols—a strengthening of the chieftain–regional ruler link.[25] In contrast, Anatoli Khazanov points out that "conquest, when and where it was possible, was the most profitable way for pastoral nomads to secure the items they needed from civilized societies."[26] As Sechin Jagchid and Van Jay Symons write, "when the nomads felt they were getting too little or the Chinese felt they were giving too much compared to the relative power of each participant, war broke out."[27]

Some dynasties fought the nomads; others used trade and created markets. A successful stabilization strategy required creation of frontier trade, markets, intermarriage, tribute exchange, and payments and titles to the nomads— often determined by the relative power of the Chinese and the nomads. Many of the arguments about whether to trade or war with the nomads mirror debates held today about how to deal with an implacable enemy. On one side were those who felt that trading with the nomads merely enriched them but did not prevent them from invading in the future. Barfield argues, for example, that refusing to engage the nomads only exacerbated tensions along the frontier. He writes:

> with the memory of the Mongol invasion still fresh, the Ming . . . adopted a policy of non-intercourse, fearing the nomads wished to replace the Ming in China. The nomads responded by continually raiding the frontier, subjecting the Ming to more attacks than any other Chinese dynasty. When the Ming finally changed its policy to accommodate [and trade with] the nomads, the attacks largely ceased and the frontier remained at peace.[28]

In this way, the Ming made the largest contributions to a defensive strategy, by expanding and repairing the Great Wall.

Why did the Ming Chinese not initially trade with the nomads? Yang Chi-sheng, a counselor for the Ming Ministry of Military Affairs, summed up the problems faced by the Chinese in deciding whether to trade with the nomads:

> When we send an important minister to carry gold and silk to the border, they may not abide by the agreement and refuse to come. Or, because of the markets they may attack the customs area and invade. Or, they may send their masses to invade and say that it was done by other tribes . . . [horses are the only good they sell, but] horses are purchased only for expeditions against the barbarians. If the markets lead to peace, then where are the horses to be used? Moreover, why should the barbarians give us good horses?[29]

Furthermore, the nomads had little to exchange with China in terms of trade. Although the Chinese conceit that they "possessed everything they need" (*ti ta wu po*) was clearly an overstatement, it was also true that the nomads could usually offer only horses or sheep in return for Chinese goods. Trade along the border was also difficult to monitor and tax, and the central Chinese government actually relied little on taxing trade, so it served no purpose. They also felt that trading with the nomads would strengthen them, making them more dangerous, or that allowing trade could lead to nomads making even more excessive demands.[30]

In addition, there were those who felt that trading with the nomads after they had attacked so often was an insult to the Ming court. As one mandarin wrote in 1550, "the dignified Celestial Court's [is] disgracing itself by trading with dogs and sheep . . . [trade is] nothing but a large bribe to maintain an improper peace for a short time."[31]

On the other side were those who argued for allowing frontier trade, emphasizing that opening markets would make the nomads more dependent upon Chinese goods, thus reducing their incentives to fight; that trade could "win the hearts and minds of the nomads"; and that military action was extremely costly. David Wright points out that "raiding was in fact probably the easiest way for the nomads to get what they needed from China, but they were astute enough to know that they very often could not get away with this for very long."[32] Yet it was not always that nomads preferred trading over raiding, but trade may not have satisfied all of the "average" nomad's desires: "is the profit from the horse trade sufficient to meet the needs of the multitude? If not, why should they observe words spoken in vain and harness themselves?"[33] Often the benefits of trade were monopolized by the leader and his close associates and not distributed evenly, as it would be during a raid.[34]

During the Ming dynasty, Toghtobukha, a nomad leader in the northwest, argued against attacking the Ming: "All of our food and clothing depend on the great Ming. How can we do this and survive?"[35] Indeed, the Uighurs had become so dependent on the Tang dynasty that they came to the aid of a weak ruler when he was threatened. Barfield notes that "Uighurs, for example, were so dependent on this revenue that that they even sent troops to put down internal rebellions in China . . . with the exception of the Mongols, 'nomad conquest' occurred only after the collapse of central authority in China left no government to extort."[36]

During the Ming dynasty, although the nomads were a continual raiding problem, Perdue concludes that "no Mongol really aspired to rule the entire steppe. China was a target for raiding and plunder, but not a genuine goal of conquest."[37] Perhaps the best example of this dynamic was the Mongol chieftain Esen's capture of Emperor Zhengtong (r. 1436–1449) in 1449. A Chinese refusal to grant greater trade and tribute missions requests to Esen caused him to attack the border at Datong, in Shanxi. Zhengtong personally led a massive army on a "ridiculous" expedition into the steppes, where Esen captured him after a series of Ming blunders. Instead of continuing his attack on Beijing, Esen took twenty thousand taels from the Datong commander and then returned to the steppe. Two months later, Esen attacked Beijing, but by this time Zhengtong's brother had been made emperor, and "the new emperor was not particularly eager to have his brother back." Esen himself was "quite anxious to unload his illustrious captive, now useless to him." In negotiations over the emperor, Esen said, "Why did you lower the price of horses and why did you often deliver worthless and spoiled silk? In addition, many of my envoys disappeared without a trace and never returned home." Eventually, in return for the resumption of trade, Esen sent Zhengtong back, and, after staging a coup against his brother, Zhengtong ruled as the Tianshun emperor until 1464.[38]

Diplomacy in the form of tribute relations was also an option for China. Yet nomadic acceptance of the tribute system was minimal and at most an arms-length means toward an economic end rather than a full-blown embrace of the full meaning, legitimacy, and authority of the tribute system. The Chinese gave titles and gifts to the nomads to entice them to trade and to deter aggression.[39] Some rulers of northern tribes were willing to submit to tributary status and engage in trade, such as Altan Khan (?–1583). Although originally he had conducted numerous raids along China's northern frontier, by 1571 Altan Khan had established peaceful relations with the Ming, and in return for the opening of two stable frontier markets, his ruling clan accepted ranks and titles from the Ming court. In this way, the nomads involved themselves in and understood the larger Chinese tribute system and the rules and hierarchy it represented.[40]

Endemic frontier skirmishes stemmed not only from differences in political, military, and economic power but also from identity and deeply held cultural beliefs. Alexander Woodside notes a Chinese "fear of frontiers, as much as the desire to colonize them." David Wright concludes:

> China's failure to solve its barbarian problem definitively before the advent of the Manchu Qing dynasty was a function neither of Chinese administrative incompetence nor of barbarian pugnacity, but of the incompatibility and fixed proximity between very different societies, ecologies, and worldviews. Many statements in historical records strongly suggest that the Chinese and the Nomads had clear ideas of their differences and were committed to preserving them against whatever threats the other side posed.[41]

Nomads were willing to trade with the Chinese, but they had no intention of truly taking on Chinese norms and cultures, as opposed to the Koreans,

Vietnamese, and Japanese. Peter Perdue points out that "the frontier zone was a liminal space where cultural identities merged and shifted, as peoples of different ethnic and linguistic roots interacted for common economic purposes. Most Han Chinese officials found this environment hostile, abhorrent, and alien."[42]

Chinese-nomad relations once again remind us how crucial ideas are to the outbreak of war. Material power is important, but just as important are the beliefs and identities that serve to define a group, state, or people. China was able to develop stable relations with other units that adopted similar identities: states that conducted diplomacy in the Chinese style and that "looked like states" to the Chinese. But those political units that rejected China's vision of the world were much harder to deal with. In the modern world, this still holds true: we think that if everyone could be like us, even if they don't look like us, we would get along.

In sum, much of the Chinese use of force was not for conquest but to control borders and reestablish stable neighboring states and kingdoms. When China felt powerful and deemed the use of force to be effective, it would fight. At other times, China would attempt trade or diplomacy. Thus, there was no inherent "culture of peacefulness" in China, as Iain Johnston rightly points out. But it is noteworthy that wars of conquest were rare.

Although China's problems with its northern border are most well known, the Chinese also fought occasional wars to stabilize their other borders with Burma, Siam, and other shifting states. For example, in the early 1760s, a Burmese king began to encroach on China's border regions, and from 1764 to 1770, the Qing fought the Burmese. When in 1770 the Burmese king offered to return to his former tributary status, Emperor Qianlong agreed.[43]

The Manchu Conquest of China

The major exception were the Manchus. Descended from the Jurchens, the Manchus were never Mongols, and for long stretches of time their economic agenda was comparable to Chosŏn, Ming, and other more settled societies. Indeed, the Manchu conquest of the Ming was more opportunism than design, and while ruling China and absorbing some of the traditional Han institutions, they retained unique Manchu elements, as well. Although Manchu worldviews and identities never completely Sinicized, they used many of the institutional forms and discursive style of traditional Chinese dynasties in dealing with the neighboring states.[44]

The story of the Qing conquest of China has been examined in much greater detail elsewhere, and here I am concerned mainly with describing the rise of the Qing state in the early seventeenth century and, in particular, in focusing on the unlikely nature of their success against the Ming. "Manchu" as a distinct political and cultural identity did not appear until the creation of the Qing empire in the early seventeenth century. And before that time, few would have predicted that a major threat to China would come from the various scattered tribes in the northeast.

Although often conflated, Manchus and Mongols were fairly distinct peoples, and both are only the most recognizable and well known of the many varied tribes and clans that populated the vast northern steppes over the past thousand years. Originally composed of various Jurchen tribes, by the late sixteenth century the Manchus had become organized along clan-based lines. As Pamela Crossley notes: "This does not mean that the Manchu identity was inauthentic or illusory. . . . Manchus' sense of themselves as a distinct nationality, with a history, language, and culture, could not be separated from the growth of the state which institutionalized the components of that identity."[45] In fact, the people who became known as "Manchus" included Mongols, Jurchens, Khorchins, Kharachins, Turkic and Tungusic peoples of Manchuria, and even Chinese and Koreans, who were "woven into the conquest elite" as the Qing consolidated power.[46]

The basic form of social and political organization of the Manchus was the *mukun*, or clan, although it was not necessarily family based. Crossley notes that "it appears that the Jurchens had no native institution that went higher than the *mukun*, or social cooperative/clan." In Jin times, the *mukun* were united for command purposes into superunits.[47] Villages usually comprised twenty households or less, with great distances between villages. These villages tended to rely on hunting and pelting and would relocate after several years "to exploit fresh gathering areas and animal populations."[48] Some of the largest villages were more sedentary and comprised fifty or so families. Political organization was loose. Families were the basic unit, although political organization was not necessarily based on kinship: clans were formed by association.

Raids were frequent, and "no man left his own village without bow and arrows, and if possible a sword, to defend himself against murder or kidnapping."[49] Villages were often raided by other villages and incorporated into the victorious village. "The local head of the village, or *beile*, was dependent upon his ability to continue to gain and distribute booty, grain, and protection."[50] Strongmen could temporarily organize some scattered tribes into a powerful force, but this was inherently unstable. Thus, there was only sporadic political control or interaction beyond the village level, and very little literacy among the people. "Individuals who could write any Chinese characters of the Mongolian syllabary were extremely rare."[51]

The late sixteenth century saw the emergence of Nurhaci (1559–1626), a leader capable of transforming these scattered villages into a cohesive and enduring national unit that eventually became the Manchus. Nurhaci began his military career as a clan chieftain with a few hundred men, attacking other local Jurchen tribes and slowly gaining local power in eastern Manchuria. Most scholarship agrees that at the beginning he had neither a grand vision of conquering China nor a messianic goal to unite the Jurchens and create a nation. However, by his early thirties Nurhaci had established a local political base, gained a larger appetite, and began to court the Mongols as allies. In 1607, a confederation of Khalkha Mongols in central Mongolia named him "khan" and accepted him as a leader. His sons and grandsons married Mongol wives, and the two ethnic groups began to collaborate. Originally, Nurhaci also cooperated with the Ming, even offering to help their efforts against the Japanese during the Imjin War. He also encouraged trade with China and quickly took control of the tribute relations with China, thus enriching himself and his followers.[52]

During the 1590s, Nurhaci introduced the "banner system," whereby different fighting units were organized under different-colored military flags. By 1615, Nurhaci had acquired three hundred *niru*—basic fighting units composed of three hundred men—or approximately ninety thousand men. It was at this time that Nurhaci declared himself the founding emperor of a new dynasty, named Jin, or "gold." This was his most obvious challenge to Ming rule. Upon his death in 1626, his eighth son, Hong Taiji (1592–1643), won a power struggle and became the leader of the Jin. Hong created governing institutions and continued promoting the idea of the Manchus as a single people. More opportunistic than strategic, the Jin, soon renamed the Qing, attacked bases in northern China and slowly began to expand their influence southward. With the help of numerous Ming collaborators, in 1644 the Qing had conquered Beijing and declared a new dynasty.

As Frederick Mote describes it:

> A careful reading of history makes it clear that the circumstances of the Ming collapse . . . were not brought about by any general disintegration

of government and society. Far from it. The fall of the Ming was, in short, caused by an accumulation of political errors, not by the underlying element of the system's inadequacies. It obviously could survive the latter; the subsequent centuries of Qing continuation of the basic Ming structure shows that the inherited structure, for all its faults, could still sustain vigorous governing.[53]

Upon conquering the Ming, "the Qing ... quickly learned to express themselves in what was considered 'Confucian' idiom, exerted themselves to restore and enhance the literary resources of the society, and from the middle seventeenth to the middle eighteenth century worked ceaselessly to flatter and co-opt the bureaucratic elite."[54] The Jurchens had dabbled with bilingual examinations based on the Chinese model in the early seventeenth century, and between the conquest of Liaodong in 1621 and the end of the seventeenth century, an enormous bureaucracy developed to keep track of banner genealogies, stipends, promotions, trials, and other aspects of ruling the vastness of China. John Wills notes that in the "final triumphs of Chinese continentality under the Qing ... ambitious men from Yunnan or Guangdong found irresistible the possibility of passing the great imperial examinations and rising in the bureaucracy."[55]

This mixture of Manchu and Ming ideas, institutions, and people would continue throughout the Qing dynasty. While the Ming institutions—the Six Boards and the censorate, for example—remained, their influence now declined as other Manchu institutions also became important. Most importantly, "after the conquest [of the Ming], the Eight Banners was retained as part of the administrative structure of Qing government, its ranks restricted to the original Qing populations and their descendants, exclusive of Han Chinese civilians."[56] However, as we have seen, in international relations the Qing kept the same basic rules, institutions, and norms as had previous Chinese dynasties. They viewed the world hierarchically, status and cultural achievement were key ranking features, and Qing hegemony was as unquestioned as had been Ming hegemony before it.

Although the Qing had its roots in the frontier areas to the northeast, they still faced the same problems of controlling their borders and frontiers as had the previous Ming rulers. China under the Qing expanded into unincorporated areas to the west, adding the province of Xinjiang and other sparsely populated areas. But the Qing, like the Ming before them, did not attempt to conquer Korea, Japan, or Vietnam. Pamela Crossley notes that "no neighboring state of sufficient magnitude stopped the expansion cold, yet there was enough resistance to keep the conquest authorities vigilant and resourceful."[57] Peter Perdue notes that "the story of the eighteenth-century Qing empire is of an effort to seal off this ambiguous, threatening frontier experience once and for all by incorporating it within the fixed boundaries of a distinctly defined space, and by drawing lines that clearly demarcated separate cultures."[58]

Most notably, the Qing conquered Tibet and present-day Xinjiang province, the location of the Mongol Zhungar empire. This westward expansion involved decades of fighting, expansion, and discussion. For example, in 1717 Zhungar Mongols under the leadership of Galdan Tseren attacked Tibet and captured Lhasa after a Tibetan opened the gates from the inside. Galdan killed the Tibetan leader and captured the Dalai Lama. The Tibetans appealed to the Qing for help, and the Qing drove Galdan from Tibet, installing their own Dalai Lama from Qinghai. After three decades of sporadic fighting, the Qing had consolidated their control over Tibet. The Qing also fought border wars with the Jinchuan, on the western frontier. The Qing did not attempt to rule this "mountainous and mostly sparsely populated land directly" and only intervened when fighting between local chieftains threatened to destabilize the region. In 1747 and later in 1776, the Qing fought arduous campaigns to pacify the region, ultimately capturing the chief leader of the Jinchuan forces and executing him in Beijing.

In sum, the difficulty of crafting longstanding and enduring relations between the nomads and China was a function not only of different political organizations and economic motives but also of deeply held and enduring cultural differences. Stability was only ensured when China, Russia, and other states expanded their political control outward and essentially obliterated the nomads, who were left with nowhere else to move.

Maritime Frontiers

Just as it is important to explain why some regions were not considered threats while others were, it is also important to explain why some geographic areas were not contested or demarcated while others were. Thus, while the history of land borders and frontiers was clearly an issue in premodern East Asia, maritime borders were generally not contested. Maritime borders differed quite substantially from land borders—water is "literally a gulf, a gap, where people can pass on ships *but not live permanently*. There is no continuum of intermixing of peoples and cultures like that across a land frontier."[59]

In this way, early modern East Asian maritime borders—Taiwan, Dokdo, the Senkakus, the Spratlys—were not an issue between states. They did not exist back then, and states did not feel the need to demarcate ownership and territory over a space where no one lived and where there was no way to fix a border. The differences on either side of a body of water could be striking: one went from being an insider to an outsider, and the changes were immediate upon landing on a different shore. Indeed, it likely would have seemed "obvious" to anyone at the time where Japan ended and Korea began—it would be as obvious as the water between them. Who was Chinese, who was Korean, and who was Japanese would have seemed self-evident at the time, even while we may know that these categories are politically and culturally determined.

Today, of course, the biggest problems in East Asia concern the formal demarcation of these maritime borders. Japan has disputes with every one of its neighbors: with Russia over the Kurile islands, with Korea over the Dokdo/Takeshima islands, and with China over the Senkakus/Diaoyus. Taiwan's status as a political entity is unclear. And a dozen countries, six of them major countries, contest the ownership of various islands in the South China Sea. The modern press, commentary, social beliefs, and political governments all characterize these disputes as "historical"; that is, they are characterized as disputes over who "owned the islands first." Thus, governments and people spend enormous resources on trying to prove their historical claims through maps, archeology, and other historical means.

However, to call these "historical" disputes is a mischaracterization and obfuscates more than it illuminates. While some dispute is actually about historical facts, such as whether the Nanjin massacre actually occurred, much is not about historical fact but rather about the meaning of those facts. That is, historical disputes have arisen from the changing and unresolved identities and political relationships in the region and the manner in which national narratives have dealt with history. The debate is over how history is remembered and characterized in the present, and it is merely the most obvious indicator for how Japan and its neighbors view one another, themselves, and their roles in the region. Indeed, the issues would be much easier to solve if they really were about history: just find better historians and archeologists. But while history is the proximate cause, it is the underlying mistrust between the neighboring countries about not only the intentions of other states but also their underlying identities that is the real cause of friction. Because of the unresolved current political relations, it is not surprising that history is resurfacing as an issue.

For example, territorial disputes are not about who owned the islands first. Were one side be somehow able to definitely prove initial ownership, it would not have the slightest effect on the beliefs of the other side. Second and more importantly, the issue arises because historically, sovereignty over uninhabited rocks was not an issue, and thus border demarcation among the ancient kingdoms was categorically different than it is today. Applying modern, Westphalian concepts of territorial sovereignty back into the past of the tribute system has little utility, because these concepts did not exist back then.

Thus, a key question when we consider maritime frontiers is: did anybody really think about Dokdo, Taiwan, and the Senkakus as important islands back then? Formally demarcating a maritime border out into the sea might have seemed ludicrous to the people at the time. The case of the island of Tsushima provides a good case study in this sense, because it was a nebulous and ambiguous space that lay between Korea and Japan. But because people lived there, over the centuries Korea and Japan began to develop some sense of whose island it really was and how to deal politically and economically with the people there. Thus Korean and Japanese officials spent considerable time demarcating what Tsushima was: whether it was Korean or Japanese, how the inhabitants on the island were to be treated, and what laws and political spaces would govern the people. And, while there have been occasional Korean attempts to claim Tsushima as Korean, as we have seen previously, in general it has been clear that it operated, more or less, within Japanese political space. There is no mention of Tsushima as Korean territory in the *Samguk Yusa*—a history of the Korean kingdoms from the seventh to tenth centuries, nor is there any mention of Tsushima in the *Sejong sillok chiriji* (History of Sejong's Era).[60] In fact, the residents of Tsushima were under political control by the Japanese court and its residents required diplomatic credentials in order to enter the Korean mainland. In contrast, "Tsushima's identity in the eyes of the Edo *bakufu* were clear: it was intermediary and trading partner with the sole foreign regime [Korea] that maintained official intercourse with Japan from the earliest years of the Tokugawa Ieyasu's rule to the arrival of Perry."[61] Although there had been a difference of opinion between Korea and Japan as to Tsushima's identity, two things are notable: first, it was actually discussed extensively at the time, and second, it was resolved satisfactorily.

Contrast this attention paid to Tsushima during the early modern era with the almost complete lack of attention paid to the islets of Dokdo, or Takeshima, as they are known in Japanese. These small rocks were uninhabited at the time, and the best evidence that nobody at the time cared about

Dokdo is the relative lack of official communication between Korea and Japan about these tiny islands. Scholars and politicians today are left with the most slim evidence: a Jesuit map that happens to call the island Dokdo instead of Takeshima, for example. We have nothing like the voluminous records about Tsushima, and that in itself is the best clue that working backward in time to figure out who "originally" owned Dokdo is unlikely to provide any definitive answers.

Similarly, questions about Taiwan, the Senkakus/Daiuyo, and other uninhabited spaces are really a modern creation. Maritime frontiers in the early modern era were not contested, because it was probably unthinkable at the time both that one could control the space—or that one needed to. The governments at the time attempted to control their land borders, and this included entry into their ports and their land from the sea. But in general, it appears that the conception of space ended at the beach and did not extend outward into the Pacific Ocean.

Taiwan historically was not a formal province of China but was considered either a part of Fukien province or was administered by Chinese officials assigned from Beijing. Official Chinese records in the eighteenth century refer to Taiwan as a "frontier area."[62] Although clearly a "part" of China, Taiwan was not considered a part of Han China, yet it was also not a separate political entity, as were Korea and Vietnam. Thus, although nominally independent, Taiwan was a part of China. Furthermore, Taiwan has traditionally served as a refuge for the losers of mainland strife. In 1644, the Ming loyalists retreated to Taiwan to harass the triumphant Qing.[63] Led by Admiral Koxingga, the Ming loyalists used Taiwan as a base from which they hoped to oust the Qing. Although the Qing eventually subdued the Ming loyalists on Taiwan, Taiwan was not made a formal province of China until 1886.

These maritime frontiers were not clearly delineated until the twentieth century, and even now they remain in dispute. This is a modern, *political* problem, not an ancient, historical issue. The historical disputes are as much about whose side of the story gets told and is a process of working backward and reading into history ideas and concepts that did not exist at the time.

Conclusion

Turning frontiers into borders is one element of state expansion and state control into previously weakly institutionalized areas. Yet it is more than that: as we have seen, creating a "nation-state" requires more than a state; it also requires a sense of nation. As Peter Perdue puts it: "Fixing people in place territorially requires material and organizational resources: border guards, passports, visas. Fixing people psychologically requires intellectual and cultural resources: nationalist symbols, rewritten history."[64]

To fix a border is to decide, culturally and politically, what goes on one side of the border and what goes on the other side. This requires knowledge about *both sides* of the border. We rarely see borders with frontiers, simply because the *other* does not yet exist in a stable or enduring enough form. Borders can only be created when there are two sides, and if there are two sides, the other side in some ways must be seen as legitimate, enduring, and worthy of respect. If not, instability will always be right around the corner.

China and Korea established enduring and stable relations with each other but had a much more difficult time dealing with the nomads. This led to endemic skirmishes and instability along their frontiers. The struggle of the Chinese during the Qing era was a struggle to turn the frontier into a fixed border and expand institutional control outward from the center. This process of fixing borders has been largely completed, at least on land. But the maritime borders, where nobody lives, have now become an issue.

A good comparison for China's historical relations with the nomads and its interventions is the historical relationship that the United States had with its western frontier and the current difficulty that it has in demarcating its southwestern border. Even today, the United States is building its own "great wall" in an attempt to divide itself clearly and decisively from Mexico. There are, of course, political differences between the United States and Mexico, but the cultural and economic geography of the southwest merges the two, and building a massive three-thousand-mile wall and spending billions of dollars has done little to stem the flow of people across this space. The United States is devoting considerable resources to controlling its southern border: over seventeen thousand personnel are devoted to patrolling it. In Southern California, the construction of 140 miles of pedestrian and vehicle fencing cost over $500 million in 2008.[65] While clearly not a frontier, it does remind us that even in the modern world, borders are not as stable or fixed as we might think.

8 LESSONS

History Forward and Backward

Life can only be understood backward; but it must be lived forward.
—SØREN KIERKEGAARD

IN THE FUTURE, there is absolutely no possibility of a return to the tribute system of international relations that existed centuries ago. Yet we might still ask: How does the past affect the present? How does the present affect the past? Ultimately, we care about what happened centuries ago in East Asia because of what it might tell us about our own situation today. Normally, we view history as moving forward from past to present, and we see the events of the past affecting the way the think about or act in the present. In this way, we might ask whether there are any historical roots to the way East Asians behave or what they believe today and how those roots might affect their contemporary foreign relations. Yet history also works backward: after all, we learn about and remember events in the past by looking over our shoulders and shaping interpretations after the fact. And in this way, whose side of the story gets told in the present affects our knowledge of the past. Different stories emphasize, glorify, or condemn different people, events, and actions.

History both forward and history backward is central to the contemporary international relations of East Asia. The question of whether history affects the present comes with asking whether there is anything unique or distinctive about East Asia. That is, we might assume that all people and states are essentially the same, and because of modernization, globalization, and industrialization, all East Asian states and peoples want, perceive, and act essentially the same as do Western states and peoples. But we also might ask whether history, culture, language, religion, and context have any bearing on how East

Asian leaders and peoples view and interact with one another and the rest of the world. It might be that distinctive memories, patterns, or beliefs have an effect on contemporary East Asian international relations, and acknowledging this may help our explanations and understandings.

On the other hand, the question of how the present affects our memories of history presents itself in the myriad of ways in which the contemporary states of East Asia dispute how history is remembered, characterized, and claimed. Thus, many of the current problems these states are wrestling with are often posed as historical issues: claims over territory, glorified ancient kingdoms, and control over how various historical events are remembered. Yet these are not historical issues; they are disputes over whose side of the story gets told, how it gets told, and who privileges what parts of history and who ignores other parts.

It is certainly worth asking to what extent history is important in explaining contemporary East Asian international relations, and it is also worth asking whether we can truly explain contemporary East Asian relations without having knowledge of this history. This is especially pertinent because the traditional East Asian order was replaced by the Western, Westphalian order in less than a century. Despite wrenching and disruptive change, the ancient Asian states adjusted quickly—and perhaps better—to the new order than did peoples or governments anywhere else around the globe. Within decades, Japan had succeeded in this new international order, and within a century Korea, China, Taiwan, and other East Asian states had also become "successful" by most modern measures. Rapid industrialization, relatively stable political systems, and dynamic societies are all hallmarks of the contemporary East Asian states. Given the profound changes that took place, we might wonder whether anything of the old order remains. Of particular interest is how China, the source of much of the East Asian order, has adjusted and changed in this modern Westphalian system. Given China's historical political, economic, and cultural centrality, and given how quickly the Chinese economy has come to once again dominate the East Asian region, how China manages its contemporary international relations is of immense practical importance for regional stability and prosperity.

The tribute system and the Confucian order, which have roots that are over two thousand years old and lasted in their most fully developed form for well over six centuries, collapsed within the space of a few decades upon the full arrival of European colonial powers in the late nineteenth century. Economic relations between Europe and Asia had been in existence for well over one thousand years, and the Silk Road to the north and the numerous maritime trading routes to the south had encouraged interaction. But Western powers had arrived in force by the nineteenth century and proceeded to colonize most of Asia, from the Middle East through India to Australia and as far north as the outskirts of China.[1] The British colonized Hong Kong, the Malay peninsula, Australia and New Zealand, Burma, India, and deeply influenced Siam. France colonized much of Indochina, including Vietnam and Cambodia. The Dutch took Indonesia, the Spanish (and then the United States) conquered the Philippines, and the Portuguese possessed Macao.

In the late nineteenth century, the Chinese tribute connections of Burma, Siam, Vietnam, Ryukyu, and Korea "all vanished as European, American, and Japanese power forced the Chinese and their former tributaries to accept the Westphalian multi-state system."[2] China itself was forced to give special access (the "unequal treaties") to certain European countries. In Northeast Asia, only Korea and Japan avoided being colonized by European powers. But this was due less to any inherent strength of these countries and more to the fact that they had little desired by the West.[3] Indeed, by the late nineteenth century, the Americans, Russians, Chinese, and Japanese were keenly interested in dominating Korea as a geopolitical and economic access point to Northeast Asia.[4]

Between 1841 and 1979, East Asia experienced interstate wars, colonization, anticolonial independence wars, struggles with state building, domestic insurgencies, ethnic violence, the cold war, and a massive U.S. military, economic, and social presence. Revolutions in China overthrew first the Qing and then the Kuomintang; anticolonial wars erupted in Vietnam, Indonesia, Malaysia, and the Philippines. Now there were new national states, born modern, in the post–World War II era. Maps were redrawn, and different ethnic groups thrown together as new nation-states appeared under one government. Why one group became independent with its own nation and another was subsumed was as much a matter of chance as it was design.

The end of the twentieth century saw a return to stability throughout much of the region. After 150 years of tumult, the East Asian region was becoming more stable, prosperous, and peaceful. First Japan and then the "newly industrializing countries" such as South Korea, Taiwan, Malaysia, and Indonesia made rapid strides toward economic modernization. After the numerous wars of the late nineteenth and early twentieth centuries, only two states feared for their survival—North Korea and Taiwan. Many countries in the region had stabilized their modern borders and crafted nascent national political institutions and national identities.

How the Past Affects the Present: Are We All Westphalians Now?

Perhaps of most interest is how studying early modern East Asia might influence what we think about the region today and, in particular, what we think about China's rapid rise and how the other states in the region are reacting. It is popular to call the twenty-first century the "Pacific century" and to argue that the locus of power is shifting from the Atlantic to the Pacific, with first Japan and now China as "number one."[5] The most common way of studying history is to see what roots, pathways, or tendencies existed in the past and seeing whether the past affects the present. Studying East Asian history provides some important clues and suggestive ideas.

Those who grew up in the West learn a specific type of history. Whether knowing about the European roots of the United States, or that classical music means Bach and Beethoven, or seeing museums and galleries devoted to Italian artists and French painters, this is the world that Westerners inhabit. For Americans, this might mean studying in Europe during one's junior year of college, knowing vaguely about historical figures such as Napoleon or about legends such as King Arthur, or believing that America is built on "Judeo-Christian" values.

It is not hard to realize that East Asians inhabit a different world. There is a thin layer of skilled East Asian English-language speakers who are truly globalized, but even today, the overwhelming majority of Japanese, Chinese, and Koreans do not have serviceable English-language skills, not to mention the Vietnamese, Malaysians, and others. Even those from Hong Kong or Singapore, who believe that studying in the United States or taking the British O-level exams is the height of intellectual achievement, still grow up in a world where the center is East Asia and not Europe. Their maps do not center on the West; they center on East Asia. Their classical music is as likely to be Beijing opera or *samulnori* as it is to be Western, and peoples from this region know about *feng shui* (whether or not they believe in it) and know vaguely that their societies are built on "Confucian" values. The historical dramas they watch on television, their museums, and the stories they hear from grandparents are Asian, not Western. Indeed, Martin Jacques writes that "it is striking how relatively little East Asia has, in fact, been Westernized. . . . China has enjoyed a quite different history to that of the West . . . it is banal to believe that China's influence on the world will be mainly economic: on the contrary, its political and cultural effects are likely to be at least as far-reaching."[6]

This leads to an important question: have East Asian countries, peoples, and leaders completely internalized and been socialized into Western, Westphalian ideas? East Asian views, identities, and expectations—as influenced as they are by the West—emerged from their own historical experiences and intellectual worldviews. It might thus be surprising to expect that their beliefs and norms about state behavior would completely derive from a Western model.

Yet new ideas have flooded into East Asia over the past 150 years: Sun Yat-sen, a Chinese revolutionary, studied in Hawaii and San Francisco and famously incorporated ideas from Abraham Lincoln and Alexander Hamilton into his republican vision for a modern China. The Vietnamese independence activist Ho Chi Minh studied in France, and the Korean independence activist Dosan Ahn Chang Ho lived in Los Angeles; both learned Western ideas about politics, equality, and independence before returning home. Universities based on the European model began to coexist with and then replace the Confucian academies that had traditionally been the centers of education and learning in East Asia. Tokyo University was founded in 1877, combining traditional and Western education; Beijing University was founded in 1898 during the "hundred days reform," a movement that attempted to introduce Western-style learning into China. In Korea, U.S. missionaries founded Ewha University in 1886 and Yonsei University in 1885. The Philippines and Korea were also particularly receptive to Christianity, and throughout East Asia Christianity rapidly became a viable religious and social force.

Indeed, the West has had a profound influence on East Asia. On the one hand, we tend to take for granted that all states are now Westphalian and to guide their expectations and theories based on that assumption. On issues such as economic development and territorial integrity, scholars view East Asian states as Westphalian. As Muthiah Alagappa argues, "it is the Asian states that most clearly approximate the Westphalian state."[7] East Asian diplomats, scholars, and businessmen certainly know how to speak the right language and stress that they know the right concepts and were educated at Western universities. By the beginning of the twentieth century, what was taken for granted—institutions, dress, clothes, and so on—had changed fundamentally. In Japan, Korea, and China, there was intense discussion and debate about how best to translate the Western concept of "sovereignty." Seo-hyun Park notes that in the 1870s, "the translation of the term sovereignty was chosen carefully to symbolize the power and authority of the state so that they could compete with the Western powers, and to a lesser extent, China."[8] So extensive was the role of the Berkeley economics department during the 1970s on the governing of East Asian states that Indonesian economic bureaucrats were called the "Berkeley mafia." China and South Korea send more students to study in the United States than any other country, and Seoul National University graduates earned more U.S. doctorates between 1997 and 2007 than students from any other foreign university.[9]

On the other hand, it might be worth asking whether these Western values have penetrated to the core of East Asian beliefs. There is a genuine question about East Asian worldviews and values and the degree of East Asian acceptance of "global" norms and ideas, whether it be issues of human rights, Internet control, democracy, biodiversity, economic issues such as capital and current accounts, energy and climate-change policy, or intellectual-property rights. Scholars and military planners ask whether Chinese "strategic culture" affects its foreign relations.[10] This is reflected in U.S. calls on China to become a "responsible stakeholder." This U.S. attempt to change China's identity has been underway for many years. Alastair Iain Johnston has noted: "The Clinton administration's strategy of constructive engagement was, for some, aimed at pulling China into the 'international community,' and exposing it to new norms of the market and domestic governance."[11] Former Clinton Defense Secretary William Perry had made similar claims a decade earlier, arguing that "engagement is the best strategy to ensure that as China increases its power, it does so as a responsible member of the international community."[12] Others have harshly criticized China precisely because of its values, citing human-rights abuses and its authoritarian government as reasons why China is both dangerous and unpredictable.

While these debates are often focused on politics at the domestic level, it is also worth considering how they are affecting the larger international system. An enduring strand of literature sees East Asian cultures as both different and consequential, perhaps most famously characterized by Samuel Huntington as "the West against the rest."[13] But even major East Asian leaders such as Singapore's Lee Kwan-yew and Kim Dae-jung have debated whether there is anything distinctive about "Asian values," and certainly many policymakers and scholars see cultural distinctiveness as a key aspect to working with East Asian states and peoples.[14] Indeed, an entire industry of "how to do business in China/East Asia/Korea/Japan" books[15] would be worthless if there were not distinctive and enduring differences about East Asian business organization, mindsets, and institutions (and numerous consultants and fixers would be out of a job—not necessarily a bad thing!).

In terms of economics, an enormous literature has attempted to explain why, in the late twentieth century, Japan, Korea, Taiwan, and other East Asian states managed to "catch up" to the West. Mainly focused on actions taken in the 1960s—and occasionally exploring the role of Japanese colonialism in the early twentieth century—this debate has been fruitful and spurred advances in economics, institutional analysis, political science, and sociology.[16] As we have seen, the early modern East Asian international order involved extensive trade and diplomatic relations, in well-developed form, many centuries before the arrival of the West. And the evidence presented in this book suggests that explaining current East Asian economic dynamism at least requires asking whether it is really anything new or whether there were much deeper historical roots that laid the foundation for subsequent growth.

Much of the contemporary organization, international economic integration, and institutional capacity of East Asian states existed centuries earlier. These institutions were not created from whole cloth in the twentieth century but were built upon deeply ingrained ideas about the proper role of institutions, government, and society and the proper way to manage relations with each other. In this way, explanations for the modern economic development of these countries and their rapid reintegration with China appears to have historical roots.

Viewed in the historical context of this book, such economic dynamism and success is actually nothing new. If anything, the most different and anomalous era of East Asia was the last century, when these states were not powerful, coherent, and wealthy. From this perspective, we might not be so surprised that they managed this remarkable economic growth when given the opportunity: after all, long before the West, Korea, Japan, China, and Vietnam were already functioning, organized, and coherent societies with complex bureaucratic states. The West may have arrived at an economic and political system that gave it a temporary lead in production and power, but it is also not surprising that the Asian states managed to incorporate, modify, and update those ideas.

How the past affects the present is surely an open question, and we are unlikely to answer it definitely here. But it is worth asking whether East Asia's past has any effect on its modern preoccupations, perceptions, goals, or intentions. Perhaps the most prudent conclusion to draw is one that avoids either extreme. That is, East Asian peoples want what most people in modern societies want—security, safety, status, and wealth—and they have also learned what and how contemporary international relations works. There are still some things that make us all the same. But at the same time, how their cultures and values have evolved and the specifics of how they view themselves, their relations with their neighbors, and their place in the world are also partly a function of their own particular history, and we would be wise to acknowledge that fact.

How the Present Affects the Past

Just as important as how the past affects the present is the question of how the present affects the past. We tend to think of history as an objective and unchanging set of facts and figures that moves chronologically and linearly. While this is true in many respects, there is another way in which history matters. That is, whose side of the story gets told is often far more important than any objective facts or events. As anyone who has disagreed with a spouse over what happened at the Johnsons' dinner party knows, history is subject to multiple interpretations and perspectives.

Another way to say this is that we decide in the present how to remember the past, what lessons to draw, what parts of the past to emphasize and celebrate, and what parts of the past to ignore or overlook. We also concoct stories and myths about our past that shape our view of ourselves and our place in the world and, in many ways, this creation of history is more important than whatever the historical reality might have been. Viewed in this context, we can see that East Asians are all in the midst of attempting to write their own histories. The states studied here—in particular China, Korea, Vietnam, and Japan—all have long, glorious histories. But they are also in the process of defining and crafting those national histories and beliefs and visions about their place in the world.

But history has been subject to multiple rewritings and reinterpretations. For example, do Koreans and Vietnamese remember and glorify the centuries in which they were loyal tributaries of the various Chinese dynasties? Or does that imply slavish obsequiousness and weakness?[17] Should Koreans glorify their military exploits against Japan in 1592 and against the nomads to the north? Should the Vietnamese downplay their relations with China and emphasize their military exploits against their Southeast Asian neighbors? Do the Japanese recognize and value the Chinese influence over their entire history, or do they emphasize the separateness of Japan from China?[18] As for

China itself, does it glorify a history of stable relations with its neighbors or rather emphasize a century of exploitation at the hands of the West?

Indeed, the arrival of the West and its different norms and institutions of international relations presented these East Asian countries with enormous challenges. Much of the old, tributary system of international relations was almost instantly reinterpreted to be considered "backward" or "despotic," and East Asian countries quickly learned the new norms of international relations. In particular, those Western norms of equality and sovereignty meant that much of East Asian history needed to be reinterpreted and presented to the West in ways that dignified and elevated East Asian countries to a similar status as Western ones. The modern view of nation-states as inherently equal is clearly at odds with the historical tribute system that differentiated states in a hierarchy. To admit historical subordination to China in the modern world was thus an invitation for colonization, imperialism, or worse. Thus, much of the twentieth century has involved a process of East Asian governments and peoples engaging in nationalistic writing of their history in ways aimed at convincing themselves and others that they were worthy of the equality that Western nations enjoyed, and along with it, the rights and respect that they enjoyed, as well.

In this new set of global norms, a subordinate position to China was "obviously" a sign of weakness, even though it had previously been a sign of cultural and civilizational strength. Thus the twentieth century saw Vietnamese writers ignore and downplay the nine preceding centuries of close emulation of and relations with China in favor of a historiography that emphasized the few battles that Vietnam had fought against China. In Korea, the humiliation of colonization by Japan led historians to emphasize how masculine and strong Korea had been in the past. In this modern context, the centuries in which Korea had been a close subordinate of China was reinterpreted as weakness and toadying. To counteract this, historians reached back fifteen centuries into their past to claim a relationship with the Koguryo kingdom (37 b.c.–a.d. 668), which straddled present-day China and Korea. This new nationalist historiography downplayed the centuries of stability and close relations with China in favor of a tenuous relationship to the Koguryo kingdom, which was actually crushed by combined Chinese (Tang) and Korean (Silla) forces.

For their part, Japanese writers emphasized their difference from China and their similarity to the West. Being the first non-Western country to industrialize (the Meiji restoration) and the first to defeat a Western great power in a war (the Russo-Japanese War), the Japanese were more easily able to

tions on the part of its East Asian neighbors, that could change. Furthermore, although China has embarked on a very clear policy of reassuring its neighbors and attempting to make very clear that its economic and political development need not be a threat to the region or the world, these assurances are met with some skepticism around the region. Will China show restraint, wisdom, and a willingness to provide leadership and stability for the region? Or will it merely use its power to pressure and bully other states? That has not yet become clear and is the source of other regional states' uneasiness with China's rise. While many are willing to give China a chance and wait and see, few take the Chinese government's statements at face value.

Thus, more important for future stability than the regional balance of power and whether China continues its economic and political growth is the question of whether the East Asian states can develop a clear and *shared* set of beliefs and perceptions about one another's intentions and their relative positions in the regional and global order. That is, although it is natural for contemporary scholars to focus on yardsticks such as economic size and military spending, the research presented in this book leads to the conclusion that more important factors are the intentions and beliefs that states have about one another. As we have seen, key factors in international relations are what the hierarchy is in terms of a rank order of states and whether or not states view one another's relative status in that hierarchy as legitimate.

By these criteria, then, China has a long way to go before becoming a leader. Although China may already be—or may soon become—the largest economic and military power in East Asia, it has virtually no cultural or political legitimacy as a leading state. The difference between China at the height of its hegemony five centuries ago and China today is most clearly reflected in the fact that nobody today thinks that China is still the civilizational center of the world. Although China may have been the source of a long-lasting civilization in East Asia in the distant past, today it has no more civilizational influence than does modern Greece. Ancient Greek ideas and innovations had a central influence on Western civilization, and Greek concepts such as democracy and philosophy continue to be influential today. Yet contemporary Greece has no discernible "soft power," and few people look to Greece for leadership in international relations. In the same way, few contemporary East Asian states or peoples look to China for cultural innovation or for practical solutions to present problems, and although China self-consciously promotes its own soft power, the real question is whether other states and peoples will accept it.

Can China ever return to its position as a center of cultural and political innovation, where other states admiringly look to it as model, guide, and inspiration? There is grudging respect for Chinese economic accomplishments over the past three decades, to be sure. But there is just as much wariness about Chinese cultural and political beliefs. Will Chinese nationalism become brittle, confrontational, insecure, and defensive, or will it eventually return to the self-confidence of centuries ago? The Chinese people—as evidenced by the hysterical response to protests about Tibet in the spring and summer of 2008—show that they are far from comfortable with their own position in the world and how they are perceived by others. Will the Chinese Communist Party cling to its power indefinitely, or will it eventually find a way to craft some type of peaceful transition from authoritarianism?

It is impossible to predict how Chinese beliefs about themselves and their place and role in the world will evolve, and it will depend on an enormous number of factors: how the Chinese Communist Party responds to changing domestic and international circumstances; whether domestic economic growth continues in any manner whatsoever for the next few decades or whether China experiences an economic crisis of some kind; domestic Chinese actions toward its own people; how society changes given the one-child policy, increasing levels of education and rates of foreign travel, and the current domestic inequalities; and how specific incidents with other regional and global actors are resolved. That is, Chinese society and its views about itself, its economy, its government, and its relations with its neighbors are all still in flux and as yet have not achieved the stability that would allow us to predict its future with confidence.

On the part of other East Asian states, how and whether they accept China will depend on their own beliefs about themselves and their relations with China. For example, although few Japanese fear another great-power war in East Asia, the Japanese are used to seeing themselves as the leader in East Asia and as the most important Asian country. Whether Japanese can adjust to an increasingly important China, and how the two countries come to view each other, will have enduring repercussions for regional stability. Will Japan and China be "co-leaders" in East Asia? Will Japan accede to being second to China, as it did centuries ago? And regarding Korea and Vietnam, recent history has radically altered their relations with China, despite their long histories as close followers. New nationalist histories in both Korea and Vietnam no longer emphasize their cultural debt to China but rather emphasize their differences from and in some ways superiority to China. Whether these two countries can live comfortably in the shadow of China or prefer to seek a status equivalent to China and how they manage their relations with the United States and Europe are both questions that we cannot yet answer with confidence.

Given the changes in the international system and the central place of the United States, there is almost no chance that China will become the unquestioned hegemon in East Asia. Too much has changed for that to happen, and the United States—even as it adjusts to changing circumstances—is not going to disappear from the region. The United States remains too central and too powerful, and American (and Western) ideals have become too deeply accepted around the globe for the United States not to be important. Perhaps the most important question is whether the United States, with its very Western way of viewing the world, and China, with a potentially more Eastern way of viewing the world, can come to some type of accommodation and agreement on each others' roles and their relations with each other. While to date both the United States and China are working to accommodate each other and stabilize their relations, that process is far from complete. How these two countries manage East Asian leadership, the status they accord each other, and how other regional countries come to view them will be central aspects of whether or not the future of East Asian international relations is one of increasing stability.

NOTES

1. The Puzzle: War and Peace in East Asian History

1. Swope, "Crouching Tigers, Secret Weapons," 41.

2. Ibid., 13. The Spanish armada consisted of thirty thousand troops on 130 ships and was defeated by twenty thousand English troops. This comparison is made explicitly by Hawley, *The Imjin War*, xii. See also Turnbull, *Samurai Invasion*.

3. I should note that I am using the modern social-science term "hegemon," not the Chinese term *bawang* (霸王), which refers to a powerful person at a time when there is not a legitimate dynasty in place, such as Xiang Yu before the Han Dynasty was established. Thanks to Liam Kelley for this point.

4. Even the nomads valued Chinese stability, and Mears, "Analyzing the Phenomenon of Borderlands from Comparative and Cross-Cultural Perspectives," 8, notes: "Nomadic confederacies . . . seemed best served by the preservation of a stable Chinese regime." See also Perdue, *China Marches West*, 521.

5. Krasner, "Organized Hypocrisy in Nineteenth-Century East Asia," 173.

6. Reus-Smit, "The Constitutional Structure of International Society and the Nature of Fundamental Institutions," 557; Ruggie, "Continuity and Transformation in the World Polity," 261–285.

7. Lloyd, *The Passport*.

8. Waltz, "The Emerging Structure of International Politics," 77. See also Kaufman, Little, and Wohlforth, eds., *The Balance of Power in World History*; Osiander, "Sovereignty, International Relations, and the Westphalian Myth"; and Mearsheimer, *The Tragedy of Great Power Politics*. On balancing in East Asia, see Friedberg, "Ripe for Rivalry"; Betts, "Wealth, Power, and Instability"; and Brzezinski and Mearsheimer, "Clash of the Titans."

9. Friedberg, "Ripe for Rivalry," 7.

10. Rudolph, *State Formation in Asia*, 2; Buzan and Amitav, "Why Is There No Non-Western International-Relations Theory?"

11. Exceptions are Johnston, *Cultural Realism*; and Hui, *War and State Formation*.

12. Wolferen, *The Enigma of Japanese Power*; Prestowitz, *Trading Places*.

13. Frank, *ReOrient*; Anderson, *The Spectre of Comparisons*.

14. For an excellent summary, see Miller, "Some Things We Used to Know About China's Past and Present."

15. Dudden, *Troubled Apologies Among Japan, Korea, and the United States*.

16. Schmid, "Rediscovering Manchuria."

17. Wills, for example, identifies institutions in addition to beliefs and values, and in particular he identifies many exceptions, modifications, and changes in the tribute system, warning against "overgeneralizing" the tribute system model. Wills, *Embassies and Illusions*, 21–22, 173. See also Wills, "Tribute, Defensiveness, and Dependency," 225–229.

18. An extraordinary diversity of peoples, cultures, and polities existed on the northern steppes, and for expositional ease I refer to these in the text as "nomads," although the term is far from satisfactory.

19. The phrase is from Elisseef, "The Middle Empire, A Distant Empire, and Empire Without Neighbors," 60–64. For example, Jakov Smith and Richard von Glahn only discuss warfare and diplomacy in passing in Smith and von Glahn, eds., *The Song-Yuan-Ming Transition in Chinese History*. New research on the Qing focuses more on ethnic diversity than on foreign relations per se, an exception being Peter Perdue. Crossley, *Empire at the Margins*; Giersch, *Asian Borderlands*; Peter Perdue, *China Marches West*.

20. Johnston, *Cultural Realism*, x. Similar China-centered work is Hui, "China's Rise in Comparative-Historical Perspective."

21. Edward Keene argues that nineteenth-century Europe was operating in the context of two very different international societies: there was one set of rules that applied to the European states, and there was a very different set of rules that regulated Europe's relations with the outside "uncivilized" world. Keene, *Beyond the Anarchical Society*.

22. Waltz, *Theory of International Politics*, 81–88.

23. Wohlforth, "The Stability of a Unipolar World." See also Layne, "The Unipolar Illusion"; Pape, "Soft Balancing Against the United States"; and Lieber and Alexander, "Waiting for Balancing."

24. Fairbank and Teng, "On the Ch'ing Tributary System," 139, 141.

25. Fairbank, "Tributary Trade and China's Relations with the West," 135; Fairbank, *Trade and Diplomacy on the China Coast*, 32. Quoted in Hevia, *Cherishing Men from Afar*, 10.

26. Hevia, *Cherishing Men from Afar*, 14.

27. Taylor, "China and Vietnam," 271; Wills, *Embassies and Illusions*, 188.

28. Kelley, *Beyond the Bronze Pillars*, 18.

29. Hevia, "Tribute, Asymmetry, and Imperial Formations," 11.

30. Kelley, *Beyond the Bronze Pillars*, 26.

31. Hevia, *Cherishing Men from Afar*, 15, quoting Wills, *Embassies and Illusions*, 189.

32. Rossabi, ed., *China Among Equals*.

33. Crossley, *China as a Strategic Idea*, 7.

34. Barfield, *The Perilous Frontier*; Jagchid and Symons, *Peace, War, and Trade Along the Great Wall*; Curtin, *The Mongols*.

2. Ideas: Hierarchy, Status, and Hegemony

1. Lebow, *A Cultural Theory of International Relations*, 4.

2. Waltz, *Theory of International Politics*; Weber, *Hierarchy Amidst Anarchy*; Paul, "Sovereignty, Survival, and the Westphalian Blind Alley in International Relations."

3. Lake, "Escape from the State of Nature," 54.

4. Weber, *Economy and Society*.

5. Wendt and Friedheim, "Hierarchy Under Anarchy," 697.

6. The question of leadership is prevalent in the international-relations literature. See, for example, Calder, "China and Japan's Simmering Rivalry"; Terada, "Forming an East Asian Community"; Obama, "Renewing American Leadership"; Nye, "Transformational Leadership and U.S. Grand Strategy"; Sutter, "China's Rise."

7. Hurrell, "Rising Powers and the Question of Status in International Society," 2.

8. Samuels, *Machiavelli's Children*; Lebow, *A Cultural Theory of International Relations*; Wohlforth, "Unipolarity, Status Competition, and Great-Power War."

9. Onuf, *World of Our Making*, 278.

10. Johnston, *Social States*, 82. Gould, "The Origins of Status Hierarchies," defines status as "the honor or prestige attached to one's position in society."

11. Lebow, *A Cultural Theory of International Relations*, 64.

12. Fearon, "Domestic Politics, Foreign Policy, and Theories of International Relations," 294.

13. Weber, "The Profession and Vocation of Politics," 356, quoted in Lebow, *A Cultural Theory of International Relations*, 20; Harsanyi, *Essays on Ethics, Social Behavior, and Scientific Explanation*, 204, quoted in Wohlforth, "Unipolarity, Status Competition, and Great-Power War," 3.

14. Lebow, *A Cultural Theory of International Relations*, 64, 67.

15. Hurrell, "Rising Powers and the Question of Status in International Society," 5.

16. Coggins, "States of Uncertainty."

17. Wendt, "Anarchy Is What States Make of It; Buzan, "From International System to International Society"; Little, "The English School's Contribution to the Study of International Relations."

18. Hurd, "Legitimacy and Authority in International Politics," 389, 392.

19. Holland, "McCain Would Exclude Russia from G8 Nations."

20. Donnelly, "Sovereign Inequalities and Hierarchy in Anarchy," 154, fig. 2.

21. Mastanduno, "Hegemonic Order, September 11, and the Consequences of the Bush Revolution," 179.

22. Clark, "How Hierarchical Can International Society Be?" 6. For realist versions of hegemony, see Layne, "The Unipolar Illusion," 11–12; Mearsheimer, *The Tragedy of Great Power Politics*, 40; Haugaard, "Power and Hegemony in Social Theory," 62.

23. Ikenberry and Kupchan, "Socialization and Hegemonic Power," 283. David Lake notes that hegemony "rests on a bargain between the ruler and the ruled premised on the former's provision of a social order of value sufficient to offset the latter's loss of freedom." Lake, "Escape from the State of Nature," 54.

24. Joseph, *Hegemony*, 1.

25. Lake, "American Hegemony and the Future of East-West Relations," 28. See also Hurd, *After Anarchy*, 78–79.

26. Mastanduno, "Incomplete Hegemony," 145.

27. Clark, "Towards an English-School Theory of Hegemony"; Cronin, "The Paradox of Hegemony."

28. Lake, "The New Sovereignty in International Relations," 304. See also Clark, "How Hierarchical Can International Society Be?" 14.

29. Fearon, "Rationalist Explanations for War," 379–414.

30. Baud and Van Schendel, "Toward a Comparative History of Borderlands," 214; Adelman and Stephan, "From Borderlands to Borders"; Batten, *To the Ends of Japan*.

31. Samuels, *Machiavelli's Children*; Lebow, *A Cultural Theory of International Relations*; Wohlforth, "Unipolarity, Status Competition, and Great-Power War."

32. Hurd, "Breaking and Making Norms," 194.

33. Lake, "Escape from the State of Nature," 53.

3. States: The Confucian Society

1. Weber, *Economy and Society*, 1:54.

2. Woodside, *Lost Modernities*, 1.

3. Wills, "South and Southeast Asia, Near East, Japan, and Korea," 1.

4. Wigan, "Culture, Power, and Place," 1187.

5. Naval History and Heritage Command, Department of the Navy, "USS *Constitution*: Chronology," http://www.history.navy.mil/faqs/faq68-2.htm.

6. Osiander, "Sovereignty, International Relations, and the Westphalian Myth"; Krasner, *Sovereignty*.

7. Woodside, "Territorial Order and Collective-Identity Tensions in Confucian Asia," 193.

8. Di Cosmo, *Ancient China and Its Enemies*, 94.

9. Lewis, *The Early Chinese Empires*, 1.

10. Standen, *Unbounded Loyalty*, 30.

11. Keyes, "The Peoples of Asia," 1171.

12. Brindley, "Barbarians or Not?"; Giersch, "A Motley Throng"; Abramson, *Ethnic Identity in Tang China*.

13. Strange, "An Eleventh-Century View of Chinese Ethnic Policy," 237.

14. Kelley, "Vietnam as a 'Domain of Manifest Civility' (Van Hien Chi Bang)," 68.

15. Wills, "The South China Sea Is Not a Mediterranean," 5.

16. Woodside, *Lost Modernities*, 1.

17. Ibid., 6.

18. Mote, ed., *The Cambridge History of China*.

19. Woodside, *Lost Modernities*, 62.

20. McNeill, *The Pursuit of Power*, 106.

21. Wong, *China Transformed*, 98–99.

22. Standen, *Unbounded Loyalty*, 1.

23. Ibid, 30.

24. Kelley, *Beyond the Bronze Pillars*, 34–35.

25. Woodside, *Lost Modernities*, 6.

26. Woodside, "Territorial Order and Collective-Identity Tensions in Confucian Asia," 199.

27. Cho, "Diglossia in Korean Language and Literature."

28. Kim, *The Last Phase of the East Asian World Order*, 40; Cumings, "The Historical Origins of North Korean Foreign Policy," 3.

29. Deuchler, *The Confucian Transformation of Korea*, 29.

30. Ibid., 83.

31. Duncan, *The Origins of the Choson Dynasty*, 208.

32. Deuchler, *The Confucian Transformation of Korea*, 292.

33. Park, *Between Dreams and Reality*, 1.

34. Kang, *Crony Capitalism*, 78–81.

35. Woodside, *Lost Modernities*, 2.

36. Ibid., 23.

37. Gari Ledyard, posting on Korea Web, March 22, 2006 (koreanstudies@koreaweb.ws).

38. Deuchler, *The Confucian Transformation of Korea*; Lieberman, *Strange Parallels*.

39. Lee, *A New History of Korea*, 175.

40. Lee, *A New History of Korea*, 176.

41. Lieberman, "Local Integration and Eurasian Analogies," 539.

42. Ibid.

43. Karnow, *Vietnam*, 111.

44. Ibid., 113.

45. Nationalist Vietnamese historians often point to these earlier struggles as extending the concept of "Vietnam" back long before there was any centralized political rule. Although the idea of Vietnamese resistance to foreign aggression has become the accepted nationalist history, it is fairly difficult to conceive of the peoples in a.d. 40 as "Vietnamese" in any way that we use the term today.

46. Womack, *China and Vietnam*, 122.

47. See, for example, Hansen, *Changing Gods in Medieval China*.

48. Lieberman, *Strange Parallels*, 360.

49. Whitmore, "The Rise of the Coast," 117.

50. Quoted in Womack, *China and Vietnam*, 124.

51. Vuving, "The References of Vietnamese States and the Mechanisms of World Formation."

52. Taylor, "The Literati Revival in Seventeenth-Century Vietnam," 14.

53. Whitmore, "Literati Culture and Integration in Dai Viet," 675.

54. Whitmore, "Vietnamese Embassies and Literati Contacts," 5.

55. Ibid., 6.

56. Whitmore, "China Policy in the New Age," 4.

57. Vuving, "The References of Vietnamese States and the Mechanism of World Formation"; Taylor, *The Birth of Vietnam*.

58. Pollack, *The Fracture of Meaning*, 3.

59. Keene, "Literature," 383; quoted in Pollack, *The Fracture of Meaning*, 3.

60. Pollack, *The Fracture of Meaning*, 3.

61. Farris, "Trade, Money, and Merchants in Nara Japan."

62. Wills, "South and Southeast Asia, Near East, Japan, and Korea," 10.

63. Howell, "Review of Bruce Batten," 760.

64. Cited in Batten, *To the Ends of Japan*, 30.

65. Ibid., 34–35.

66. Wills, "South and Southeast Asia, Near East, Japan, and Korea," 10; Shiveley et al., *The Cambridge History of Japan*.

67. Cited in Yamamura, "Introduction," 11.

68. Grossberg, *Japan's Renaissance*, 2.

69. Osamu, *Sino-Japanese Relations in the Edo Period*.

70. Jansen, *China in the Tokugawa World*, 65, 228.

71. Toby, "Rescuing the Nation from History," 228.

72. Jansen, *China in the Tokugawa World*, 56.

73. Whitmore, "Literati Culture and Integration in Dai Viet."

74. Taylor, "The Literati Revival in Seventeenth-century Vietnam," 2.

75. Whitmore, "Literati Culture and Integration in Dai Viet," 671.

76. Liam Kelley, personal communication, July 30, 2009.

77. Whitmore, *Vietnam, Ho Quy Ly, and the Ming*; Wolters, *Two Essays on Dai-Viet in the Fourteenth Century*.

78. Lieberman, *Strange Parallels*, 381.

79. Whitmore, "Literati Culture and Integration in Dai Viet," 675.

80. Lieberman, "Local Integration and Eurasian Analogies," 484.

81. Karnow, *Vietnam*, 117.

82. Lieberman, *Strange Parallels*, 382.

83. Whitmore, *Vietnam, Ho Quy Ly, and the Ming*, 17.

84. Nguyen, *Viet Nam*, 66.

85. Grossberg, "From Feudal Chieftains to Secular Monarch."

86. Steenstrup, "The Middle Ages Survey'd," 239.

87. Robinson, "Policies of Practicality," 3.

88. Batten, *To the Ends of Japan*, 44.

89. Reid, "An 'Age of Commerce' in Southeast Asian History," 10.

90. Toby, "Rescuing the Nation from History," 208.

91. Batten, *To the Ends of Japan*.

92. Park, *Between Dreams and Reality*.

93. Thanks to Gari Ledyard for these insights.

94. Deuchler, *The Confucian Transformation of Korea*, 292.

95. Quoted in ibid., 123.

96. Chega, "A Reexamination of the Civil-Service Examination System," 26–28.

97. Wolters, "Le Van Huu's Treatment of Ly Than Ton's Reign (1127–1137)."

98. Lieberman, *Strange Parallels*, 341.

99. Lieberman, "Local Integration and Eurasian Analogies," 513.

100. Collcutt, "Kings of Japan?"

101. Mass, "The Early Bakufu and Feudalism," 262.

102. Batten, *To the Ends of Japan*, 42.

103. Toby, "Rescuing the Nation from History," 202.

104. Pollack, *The Fracture of Meaning*, 7.

105. Wills, "South and Southeast Asia, Near East, Japan, and Korea," 25.

106. Pollack, *The Fracture of Meaning*, 7.

107. Lieberman, "Local Integration and Eurasian Analogies," 477.

108. Smits, *Visions of Ryukyu*.

109. Abu-Lughod, *Before European Hegemony*, 303.

110. Wolters, *History, Culture, and Region in Southeast Asian Perspectives*; Hall, "An Introductory Essay on Southeast Asian Statecraft in the Classical Period."

111. Stuart-Fox, *A Short History of China and Southeast Asia*, 29.

112. Lieberman, *Strange Parallels*, 393.

113. Day, "Ties That (Un)Bind," 390.

114. Christie, "Negeara, Mandala, and Despotic State."

115. Rafael, *Contracting Colonialism*, 146.

116. Lieberman, *Strange Parallels*, 33.

117. Day, "Ties That (Un)Bind," 384–409.

118. Reid, "An 'Age of Commerce' in Southeast Asian History," 3.

119. Ryan, *The Making of Modern Malaysia and Singapore*, 1. See also Bakar, "Malaysian Perceptions of China."

120. Ryan, *The Making of Modern Malaysia and Singapore*, 13.

4. Diplomacy: The Tribute System

1. Keyes, "The Peoples of Asia"; Fiskesjo, "On the 'Raw' and 'Cooked' Barbarians of Imperial China."

2. Kelley, *Beyond the Bronze Pillars*, 28.

3. Mastanduno, "Incomplete Hegemony," 145.

4. Hevia, *Cherishing Men from Afar*, 124, 132–133.

5. Yoo, *Chosŏnjo taeoe sasangui hurum*.

6. Quoted in Hevia, *Cherishing Men from Afar*, 118.

7. Zhenping, *Ambassadors from the Islands of Immortals*.

8. Hevia, *Cherishing Men from Afar*, 124.

9. Smits, *Visions of Ryukyu*, 36.

10. Son, *Chosŏn sidae hanil gwangywe yonku*; Kang, *Diplomacy and Ideology in Japanese-Korean Relations*, 6–9.

11. Kelley, *Beyond the Bronze Pillars*, 2.

12. Hevia, *Cherishing Men from Afar*, 24.

13. Choi, *Chŏngkwa Chosŏn*; Choi, *Myŏngchong sidae chunghan kwanggyesa yŏngu*.

14. Swope, *A Dragon's Head and a Serpent's Tail*, 43; Haboush and Deuchler, eds., *Culture and the State in Late Chosŏn Korea*, 68.

15. Wills, "South and Southeast Asia, Near East, Japan, and Korea," 18.

16. Lee, *A New History of Korea*, 189.

17. Hevia, *Cherishing Men from Afar*, 50.

18. Kelley, *Beyond the Bronze Pillars*, 182.

19. Anderson, *The Rebel Den of Nùng Trí Cao*, 8.

20. Wills, "South and Southeast Asia, Near East, Japan, and Korea," 20.

21. Quoted in Kelley, *Beyond the Bronze Pillars*, 60–61.

22. Wills, "Great Qing and Its Southern Neighbors."

23. Robinson, "Policies of Practicality," 31.

24. Ibid., 30.

25. Whitmore, "Vietnamese Embassies and Literati Contacts," 6.

26. Robinson, "Policies of Practicality," 31.

27. Wills, "The South China Sea Is Not a Mediterranean," 16.

28. Whitmore, "Vietnamese Embassies and Literati Contacts," 1–2.

29. Quoted in Kelley, *Beyond the Bronze Pillars*, 66.

30. Kazui, "Foreign Relations During the Edo Period," 286.

31. Shoji, "Japan and East Asia," 425; Kang, *Diplomacy and Ideology in Japanese-Korean Relations*, 18.

32. Kim, *The Last Phase of the East Asian World Order*, 15.

33. Fogel, *Articulating the Sinosphere*, 102–107.

34. Wills, "South and Southeast Asia, Near East, Japan, and Korea," 19.

35. Kelley, *Beyond the Bronze Pillars*, 66.

36. Ibid., 72.

37. Quoted in Tana, "A View from the Sea," 88.

38. Kelley, *Beyond the Bronze Pillars*, 36.

39. Simmons, "Rules Over Real Estate," 827. See also Fravel, "Regime Insecurity and International Cooperation."

40. Wendt and Friedheim, "Hierarchy Under Anarchy," 704.

41. Kim, "Ginseng and Border Trespassing Between Qing China and Chosŏn Korea"; Roh, *Yŏmong oegyosa*; Lee, *Koryŏ sidaeui chŏngch'i pyŏndonggwa daeoejŏngch'aek*; Ha, "Chosŏn jeongi-ui daeil gwangye."

42. Kenneth Robinson notes that pirates attacked the southern Korean coast over five hundred times between 1350 and 1392. Robinson, "Policies of Practicality," 1.

43. Deuchler, *The Confucian Transformation of Korea*, 292; Yoo, *Chosŏnjo taeoe sasangui hurum*.

44. Deuchler, *The Confucian Transformation of Korea*, 107.

45. Lee, *A New History of Korea*, 189.

46. Duncan, "The Social Background of the Founding of the Chosun Dynasty," 57–58.

47. T'aejo Sillok, "Admonition to the New King," 1:40a–42b, quoted in Lee, ed., *Sourcebook of Korean Civilization*, 1:483–485.

48. Lee, *A New History of Korea*, 189.

49. Ledyard, "Cartography in Korea," 290.

50. Quoted in Lee, ed., *Sourcebook of Korean Civilization*, 234.

51. Personal communication from Gari Ledyard, October 30, 2007.

52. Gari Ledyard, posting on Korea Web, March 22, 2006 (koreanstudies @koreaweb.ws).

53. Taylor, "The Early Kingdoms," 147.

54. Anderson, *The Rebel Den of Nùng Trí Cao*, 145.

55. Whitmore, "Cartography in Vietnam," 492.

56. Kelley, *Beyond the Bronze Pillars*, 81.

57. Quoted in ibid., 83.

58. Wills, "Great Qing and Its Southern Neighbors."

59. Ibid.

60. Ledyard, "Confucianism and War"; Adriana Boscaro, *One Hundred and One Letters of Hideyoshi*.

61. All three authors are referenced in von Verschuer, "Looking from Within and Without," 540.

62. Ibid., 555.

63. Wills, "Great Qing and Its Southern Neighbors."

64. Quoted in ibid.

65. Ryan, *The Making of Modern Malaysia and Singapore*, 18.

66. Arrighi et al., "Historical Capitalism, East and West."

67. Thanks to Greg Noble for this point.

68. Crossley, personal communication, February 15, 2008.

69. Pak Chega, "On Revering China," in Lee, ed., *Sourcebook of Korean Civilization*, 2:87.

70. Schottenhammer, "Japan: The Tiny Dwarf?" 10.

71. Mizuno, "Japan and Its East Asian Neighbors."

72. Kelley, *Beyond the Bronze Pillars*, 93.

73. Deng, "The Foreign Staple Trade of China in the Pre-Modern Era"; Hamashita, *China, East Asia, and the Global Economy*.

74. Smits, *Visions of Ryukyu*, 36.

75. Wyatt, *Thailand*, 104.

76. Wills, "Great Qing and Its Southern Neighbors."

77. Ibid.

78. Ibid.

79. Robinson, "Centering the King of Chosŏn"; Kang, *Diplomacy and Ideology in Japanese-Korean Relations*, 50–51.

80. Quoted in Luc, "An Early Trade Coin."

81. Robinson, "Policies of Practicality," 6, 27.

82. Ha, "Chosun chongi ui tae-il kwangye."

83. Swope, "Deceit, Disguise, and Dependence," 763.

84. Robinson, "Centering the King of Chosŏn," 109–125.

85. Lewis, *Frontier Contact Between Chosun Korea and Tokugawa Japan*, 21.

86. Robinson, "Policies of Practicality," 80–81.

87. von Verschuer, "Looking from Within and Without," 538.

88. Ibid., 548.

89. Mizuno, "Japan and Its East Asian Neighbors," 51.

90. Ibid., 40.

91. Ibid., 47.

92. Ibid., 58.

93. Quoted in ibid., 71.

94. Ibid., 84.

95. Ibid., 36.

96. Lewis, *Frontier Contact*, 26.

97. Kelley, *Beyond the Bronze Pillars*, 49.

98. Ibid., 189–190.

99. Wills, "South and Southeast Asia, Near East, Japan, and Korea," 24.

100. Toby, "Reopening the Question of Sakoku," 351.

101. Mizuno, "Japan and Its East Asian Neighbors," 115.

102. Ibid., 120.

103. Ibid., 147.

104. Ibid., 148–149.

105. Toby, *State and Diplomacy in Early Modern Japan*.

106. Kim, *The Last Phase of the East Asian World Order*, 15.

107. Wray, "The Seventeenth-Century Japanese Diaspora," 2.

108. Howe, *The Origins of Japanese Trade Supremacy*, 40.

109. Klein, "The China Seas and the World Economy Between the Sixteenth and Nineteenth Centuries," 69.

110. Wray, "The Seventeenth-Century Japanese Diaspora," 12.

111. Toby, *State and Diplomacy in Early Modern Japan*, xvi.

112. Kim, *The Last Phase of the East Asian World Order*, 15.

113. Ishii, *The Junk Trade from Southeast Asia*, 2.

114. John Wills, "South and Southeast Asia, Near East, Japan, and Korea," 25.

115. Smits, *Visions of Ryukyu*, 21.

116. Ibid., 22.

117. Sakai, "The Satsuma-Ryukyu Trade and the Tokugawa Seclusion Policy," 392.

118. Mizuno, "Japan and Its East Asian Neighbors," 170.

5. War: The Longer Peace

1. Herbst, "War and the State in Africa," 124.

2. Gaddis, *The Long Peace*.

3. Childs Kohn, *Dictionary of Wars*.

4. Woodside, "Territorial Order and Collective-Identity Tensions in Confucian Asia," 191–221, 194.

5. Perdue, *China Marches West*, 521.

6. Kaufman, "The Fragmentation and Consolidation of International Systems," 176.

7. Waley-Cohen, "Commemorating War in Eighteenth-Century China," 869–899.

8. Johnston, *Cultural Realism*, 234; Van de Ven, "War and the Making of Modern China," 737; Shu, *The Rise of Modern China*.

9. An important question, requiring further research, would explore when and why states used force in combination with other strategies against the northern tribes.

10. Kwanten, *Imperial Nomads*.

11. Johnston, *Cultural Realism*.

12. Grimmet, "Instances of Use of United States Armed Forces Abroad, 1798–2001."

13. Johnston, *Cultural Realism*, claims there were on average 1.12 foreign wars per year during the Ming. See also Zundorfer, "Ming China, the Imjin Waeran, and the Dynamics of Peace and War in East Asia."

14. Duncan, "The Uses of Confucianism in Modern Korea," 432.

15. Swope, *A Dragon's Head and a Serpent's Tail*, 9.

16. Sarkees, Wayman, and Singer, "Inter-State, Intra-State, and Extra-State Wars," 58; Gleditsch et al., "Armed Conflict 1946–2001."

17. Childs Kohn, *Dictionary of Wars*, 565; Dupuy and Dupuy, *The Harper Encyclopedia of Military History*; Davis, *Encyclopedia of Invasions and Conquests*.

18. People's Liberation Army, *Zhongguo lidai zhanzheng nianbiao*. To supplement and extend the database, I used a number of other sources, chief among these Childs Kohn, *Dictionary of Wars*.

19. The entire dataset in English, created from the author's translation of the *Zhongguo lidai zhanzheng nianbiao*, along with a detailed discussion of different sources, how to measure wars in East Asia, and caveats about using PLA sources, is available by e-mailing the author.

20. The only previous Japanese use of force on the continent came nine centuries earlier, in a.d. 663, when Tang and Silla crushed Yamato Japanese forces sent to support Paekche.

21. Van de Ven, "War and the Making of Modern China," 737; Waley-Cohen, "Commemorating War in Eighteenth-Century China"; Shu, *The Rise of Modern China*.

22. Mote, *Imperial China*, 611.

23. Perdue, *China Marches West*, 520.

24. Giersch, *Asian Borderlands*.

25. The Spanish armada consisted of thirty thousand troops on 130 ships and was defeated by twenty thousand English troops, as noted by Hawley, *The Imjin War*, xii. See also Turnbull, *Samurai Invasion*; Lee, *Imjin waeransa yŏngu*.

26. Park, "War and Peace in Premodern Korea," 6.

27. Lee, *Korea and East Asia*, 99.

28. Lee, *A New History of Korea*, 210.

29. Ibid.

30. Hawley, *The Imjin War*, 409; Swope, "Crouching Tigers, Secret Weapons."

31. Ledyard, "Confucianism and War," 84; Myungki, *Imjin waerangwa hanjung kwangye.*

32. Swope, *A Dragon's Head and a Serpent's Tail*, 63.

33. Ibid, 64–65.

34. Berry, *Hideyoshi*, 216.

35. Ibid., 212.

36. Quoted in Swope, *A Dragon's Head and a Serpent's Tail*, 58.

37. Quoted in ibid.

38. Ibid., 38.

39. Deng, "The Foreign Staple Trade of China in the Premodern Era," 254.

40. Kang, *Diplomacy and Ideology in Japanese-Korean Relations*; quoted in Swope, *A Dragon's Head and a Serpent's Tail*, 63.

41. Berry, *Hideyoshi*, 278.

42. Naohiro, "The Sixteenth-Century Unification," 71.

43. Lee, *A New History of Korea*, 210.

44. Naohiro, "The Sixteenth-Century Unification," 77.

45. Hawley, *The Imjin War*, 22–24, 76.

46. Swope, "Deceit, Disguise, and Dependence," 769.

47. Ibid., 780.

48. Swope, "Deceit, Disguise, and Dependence," 780; Berry, *Hideyoshi*, 217.

49. Roland, "Review of Kenneth Chase, *Firearms.*"

50. Swope, "Deceit, Disguise, and Dependence," 781.

51. Elisonas, "The Inseparable Trinity," 293.

52. Park, "War and Peace in Premodern Korea," 6.

53. Roy, *Taiwan*, 17–19.

54. Osamu, *Sino-Japanese Relations in the Edo Period*, 254.

55. Deng, "The Foreign Staple Trade of China in the Pre-Modern Era"; Hamashita, *China, East Asia, and the Global Economy.*

56. Chan, "The Chien-wen, Yung-lo, Hung-hsi, and Husan-te reigns, 1399–1435," 230.

57. Womack, *China and Vietnam*, 128.

58. Nguyen, *Viet Nam*, 63.

59. Quoted in Stuart-Fox, *China and Southeast Asia*, 90.

60. Karnow, *Vietnam*, 116.

61. Lieberman, *Strange Parallels*, 375.

62. Womack, *China and Vietnam*, 129.

63. Quoted in Kelley, *Beyond the Bronze Pillars*, 84.

64. Whitmore, "Vietnamese Embassies and Literati Contacts," 6.

65. Womack, *China and Vietnam*, 132–133.

66. Quoted in Tana, "A View from the Sea," 94–95.

67. Nguyen, *Viet Nam*, 63.

68. The Mongol Kublai Khan invaded Vietnam and was defeated in the thirteenth century, and in the fourteenth and fifteenth centuries, Vietnam fought an arduous and ultimately successful war against Champa, in what is now southern Vietnam.

69. Womack, *China and Vietnam*, 118.

70. Ibid.

71. Ibid., 134.

72. Wills, "Great Qing and Its Southern Neighbors, 1760–1820."

73. Ibid.

74. Womack, *China and Vietnam*, 136.

75. Wills, "Great Qing and Its Southern Neighbors, 1760–1820."

76. Ibid.

77. Womack, *China and Vietnam*, 135.

78. Kenny, *Shadow of the Dragon*, 37.

79. Lam, "Intervention Versus Tribute in Sino-Vietnamese Relations, 1788–1790," 178.

80. Marr, *Vietnamese Tradition on Trial*, 49.

81. Lee, *Korea and East Asia*, 110.

82. Lee, *A New History of Korea*, 215.

83. Lee, *Korea and East Asia*, 112.

84. Lee, *A New History of Korea*, 216.

85. Lee, *Korea and East Asia*, 112; Choi, *Myŏngchong sidae chunghan kwanggyesa yŏngu*.

86. The invasion is often wrongly dated 1636 because of a forced equivalence of the Western solar and Eastern lunar years. The Manchus crossed the Amnok river on Twelfthmoon 11 or 12 lunar, which corresponds to January 6 or 7, 1637, solar. Manchu envoys reached Namhansŏng, where the king had fled, on 12.15, or January 10; the Manchu military siege began on 12.19 (January 14); and the king surrendered on 12.27 (January 22). Thanks to Gari Ledyard for this point.

87. Choi, *Chŏngkwa Chosŏn*.

88. Han, *Imjin oerangwa Hanjung kwangye*.

89. Lee, *Korea and East Asia*, 113.

90. Han, *Imjin Yeoran-gwa Han-jung gwangye*.

91. Kim, "Ginseng and Border Trespassing Between Qing China and Chosŏn Korea."

92. Swope, *A Dragon's Head and a Serpent's Tail*, 15.

6. Trade: International Economic Relations

1. Abu-Lughod, *Before European Hegemony*, 317.

2. Zhao, "Shaping the Asian Trade Network," 189.

3. Lo, "Maritime Commerce and Its Relations to the Sung Navy," 61.

4. Wills, "South and Southeast Asia, Near East, Japan, and Korea," 15.

5. Lo, "Maritime Commerce and Its Relations to the Sung Navy," 64.

6. Quoted in Zhao, "Shaping the Asian Trade Network," 33.

7. Ibid., 29.

8. Hui, "Overseas Chinese Business Networks," 34.

9. Gungwu, *China and the Overseas Chinese*, 85.

10. Zhao, "Shaping the Asian Trade Network," 39.

11. Quoted in ibid.

12. Lee, "East Asia in the Age of Global Integration," 17.

13. Lee, "Trade and Economy in Preindustrial East Asia, c. 1500–1800," 14.

14. Deng, "The Foreign Staple Trade of China in the Premodern Era," 254.

15. Deng, *Maritime Sector, Institutions, and Sea Power of Premodern China*, 212.

16. Zhao, "Shaping the Asian Trade Network," 199.

17. Deng, "The Foreign Staple Trade of China in the Pre-Modern Era," 254; Beckwith, "The Impact of the Horse and Silk Trade on the Economies of T'ang China and the Uighur Empire."

18. Reid, "An 'Age of Commerce' in Southeast Asian History," 5.

19. Hui, "Overseas Chinese Business Networks," 39.

20. Smits, *Visions of Ryukyu*, 435–436.

21. Zhao, "Shaping the Asian Trade Network," 40.

22. Ibid., 45.

23. Turnbull, *Pirates of the Far East*, 17.

24. Quoted in Zhao, "Shaping the Asian Trade Network," 46.

25. Quoted in ibid.

26. Elisonas, "The Inseparable Trinity," 241.

27. Lee, *Korea and East Asia*, 97.

28. Ha, "Chosŏn jeongi-ui daeil gwangye"; Kang, *Diplomacy and Ideology in Japanese-Korean Relations*, 25.

29. Shoji, "Japan and East Asia," 430.

30. Min et al., "Hanil-gan Pyoryuminae gwanhan yongu."

31. Elisonas, "The Inseparable Trinity," 250, emphasizes that although called *wakō*, many of the pirates were actually Chinese and located along the coasts of China itself.

32. Jansen, *China in the Tokugawa World*, 6.

33. Kang, *Diplomacy and Ideology in Japanese-Korean Relations*, 2.

34. Zhao, "Shaping the Asian Trade Network," 113.

35. Quoted in ibid., 127.

36. Quoted in ibid., 212.

37. Ibid., 219.

38. Ibid., 131.

39. Deng, "The Foreign Staple Trade of China in the Premodern Era," 254.

40. Zhao, "Shaping the Asian Trade Network," 221.

41. Quoted in ibid., 25.

42. Deng, "The Foreign Staple Trade of China in the Premodern Era," 283.

43. Andaya, "Interactions with the Outside World and Adaptation in Southeast Asian Society," 349.

44. Lee, "East Asia in the Age of Global Integration," 16.

45. Lewis, *Frontier Contact Between Chosŏn Korea and Tokugawa Japan*, 88.

46. Sanderson, *Social Transformations*, 153.

47. Robinson, "Policies of Practicality," 47.

48. Lewis, *Frontier Contact Between Chosŏn Korea and Tokugawa Japan*.

49. Robinson, "Policies of Practicality," 2.

50. Lewis, *Frontier Contact Between Chosŏn Korea and Tokugawa Japan*, 91.

51. Toby, "Reopening the Question of Sakoku," 325.

52. Yamamura, "The Growth of Commerce in Medieval Japan," 358.

53. Quoted in Atwell, "A Seventeenth-Century 'General Crisis' in East Asia?" 663.

54. Jansen, *China in the Tokugawa World*, 19.

55. Toby, "Reopening the Question of Sakoku," 325.

56. Kang, *Diplomacy and Ideology in Japanese-Korean Relations*, 28.

57. Lewis, *Frontier Contact Between Chosŏn Korea and Tokugawa Japan*.

58. Robinson, "Policies of Practicality," 75.

59. Lewis, *Frontier Contact Between Chosŏn Korea and Tokugawa Japan*.

60. Lee, "East Asia in the Age of Global Integration," 8; Lewis, *Frontier Contact Between Chosŏn Korea and Tokugawa Japan*.

61. Toby, *State and Diplomacy in Early Modern Japan*, xxviii.

62. Reid, "An 'Age of Commerce' in Southeast Asian History," 10.

63. Lee, "East Asia in the Age of Global Integration," 10.

64. Lee, "East Asia in the Age of Global Integration," 8; Howe, *The Origins of Japanese Trade Supremacy*, 40.

65. von Glahn, "Myth and Reality of China's Seventeenth-century Monetary Crisis."

66. Lee, "Trade and Economy in Preindustrial East Asia, c. 1500–1800," 7.

67. Lewis, *Frontier Contact Between Chosŏn Korea and Tokugawa Japan*, 97.

68. Zhao, "Shaping the Asian Trade Network," 61.

69. Ishii, *The Junk Trade from Southeast Asia*, 6–11; Ikeda, "The History of the Capitalist World-System vs. the History of East-Southeast Asia."

70. Reid, *Southeast Asia in the Age of Commerce, 1450–1680*, 27.

71. Seiichi, "Japanese Foreign Trade in the Sixteenth and Seventeenth Centuries," 10.

72. Hall, "Notes on the Early Qing Copper Trade with Japan."

73. Klein, "The China Seas and the World Economy Between the Sixteenth and Nineteenth Centuries," 67.

74. Zhao, "Shaping the Asian Trade Network," 57.

75. Andaya, "Interactions with the Outside World and Adaptation in Southeast Asian Society, 1500–1800," 351.

76. Deng, *Maritime Sector, Institutions, and Sea Power of Premodern China*, 183.

77. Jansen, *China in the Tokugawa World*, 37–38.

78. Hui, "Overseas Chinese Business Networks," 34.

79. Tana, "A View from the Sea," 84.

80. Lieberman, "Local Integration and Eurasian Analogies."

81. Frank, *ReOrient*, 97; Reid, *Southeast Asia in the Age of Commerce, 1450–1680*.

82. Andaya, "Interactions with the Outside World and Adaptation in Southeast Asian Society," 349.

83. Lieberman, "Local Integration and Eurasian Analogies," 490.

84. Hui, "Overseas Chinese Business Networks," 16.

85. Pombejra, "Ayutthaya at the End of the Seventeenth Century," 254.

86. Lieberman, "Local Integration and Eurasian Analogies," 494.

87. Viraphol, *Tribute and Profit*, 20.

88. Andaya, "Interactions with the Outside World and Adaptation in Southeast Asian Society," 349–350.

89. Pombejra, "Ayutthaya at the End of the Seventeenth Century," 263; Pombejra, "Princes, Pretenders, and the Chinese Phrakhlang," 119.

90. Quoted in Viraphol, *Tribute and Profit*, 54.

91. Cushman, *Fields from the Sea*, 78.

92. Viraphol, *Tribute and Profit*, 100–101.

93. Atwell, "International Bullion Flows and the Chinese Economy c. 1530–1650," 68–90.

94. Prak, *China's Seaborne Trade with South and South-East Asia*.

95. Frank, *ReOrient*, 106; Klein, "The China Seas and the World Economy Between the Sixteenth and Nineteenth Centuries," 76; Howe, *The Origins of Japanese Trade Supremacy*, 37.

96. Luc, "An Early Trade Coin"; Li, *Nguyen Cochinchina*, 88–89; Wheeler, "Rethinking the Sea in Vietnamese History."

97. Tana, "A View from the Sea," 89.

98. Ibid., 100.

99. Lieberman, *Strange Parallels*, 291.

100. Reid, "An 'Age of Commerce' in Southeast Asian History," 6.

101. Ibid., 9.

102. Klein, "The China Seas and the World Economy Between the Sixteenth and Nineteenth Centuries," 76.

103. Quoted in Toby, *State and Diplomacy in Early Modern Japan*, 9.

104. Klein, "The China Seas and the World Economy Between the Sixteenth and Nineteenth Centuries," 70.

105. For example, see Frank, *ReOrient*, 101; van Leur, *Indonesian Trade and Society*, 125; Klein, "The China Seas and the World Economy Between the Sixteenth and Nineteenth Centuries," 86.

106. Numerous books have been written about this era. Perhaps the most interesting is Thomson, *Sentimental Imperialists*.

107. Zhao, "Shaping the Asian Trade Network," 53.

108. Lieberman, *Strange Parallels*, 287.

109. Smith, *The Dutch in Seventeenth-Century Thailand*, 111.

110. Sutherland, "Believing Is Seeing," 138.

111. These treaties include the 1876 Treaty of Kangwha between Korea and Japan, the 1882 Regulations for Maritime and Overland Trade Between Chinese and Korean Subjects, and the 1885 Tianjin Treaty between China and Japan.

112. Hamashita, *China, East Asia, and the Global Economy*.

113. Hamashita, "The Tribute Trade System and Modern Asia," 92.

7. Frontiers: Nomads and Islands

1. China-nomad relations have been the focus of extensive research. See Perdue, *China Marches West*; Mears, "Analyzing the Phenomenon of Borderlands from Comparative and Cross-Cultural Perspectives"; Crossley, *Empire at the Margins*; Crossley, *The Manchus*; Barfield, *The Perilous Frontier*; Sechin and Symons, *Peace, War, and Trade Along the Great Wall*; Khazanov, *Nomads and the Outside World*.

2. Quoted from Wright, "The Northern Frontier," 58.

3. Robinson, "From Raiders to Traders."

4. Perdue, *China Marches West*.

5. Mote, *Imperial China, 900–1800*, 783.

6. Perdue, *China Marches West*, 520.

7. Crossley, *The Manchus*, 17.

8. Ibid., 24.

9. Khazanov, "Characteristic Features of Nomadic Communities in Eurasian Steppes," 123.

10. Perdue, *China Marches West*, 520; Crossley, *The Manchus*.

11. Perdue, *China Marches West*, 518.

12. Crossley, *The Manchus*, 21.

13. Barfield, *The Perilous Frontier*, 7.

14. Shu, *The Rise of Modern China*.

15. Wright, "The Northern Frontier," 74.

16. Crossley, *The Manchus*, 22.

17. Ibid., 36.

18. Ibid., 38.

19. Ibid., 22.

20. Jagchid and Symons, *Peace, War, and Trade Along the Great Wall*, 18.

21. Kenneth Robinson, "From Raiders to Traders."

22. Barfield, *The Perilous Frontier*, 9.

23. Perdue, *China Marches West*, 521.

24. Barfield, *The Perilous Frontier*; Khazanov, *Nomads and the Outside World*.

25. Barfield, *The Perilous Frontier*; Jagchid and Symons, *Peace, War, and Trade Along the Great Wall*.

26. Khazanov, *Nomads and the Outside World*.

27. Jagchid and Symons, *Peace, War, and Trade Along the Great Wall*, 1.

28. Barfield, *The Perilous Frontier*, 16.

29. Quoted in Jagchid and Symons, *Peace, War, and Trade Along the Great Wall*, 90.

30. Ibid., 4.

31. Quoted in ibid., 89.

32. Wright, "The Northern Frontier," 63.

33. Quoted in Jagchid and Symons, *Peace, War, and Trade Along the Great Wall*, 95.

34. Johnston, *Cultural Realism*, 234; Van de Ven, "War and the Making of Modern China," 737.

35. Quoted in Jagchid and Symons, *Peace, War, and Trade Along the Great Wall*, 49.

36. Barfield, *The Perilous Frontier*, 9.

37. Perdue, *China Marches West*, 57.

38. This story is paraphrased from ibid., 58–60.

39. Rossabi, *China Among Equals*.

40. Kwanten, *Imperial Nomads*.

41. Wright, "The Northern Frontier," 76.

42. Perdue, *China Marches West*, 41.

43. Lococo, "The Qing Empire," 130.

44. Crossley, *The Manchus*; Elliot, *The Manchu Way*.

45. Crossley, *The Manchus*, 6.

46. Ibid., 9.

47. Ibid., 27.

48. Ibid., 41.

49. Ibid., 42.

50. Ibid.

51. Ibid., 44.

52. Zhao, "Shaping the Asian Trade Network."

53. Mote, *Imperial China*, 802.

54. Crossley, *The Manchus*, 106.

55. Wills, "The South China Sea Is Not a Mediterranean," 6.

56. Elliot, *The Manchu Way*, 39.

57. Crossley, *The Manchus*, 108.

58. Perdue, *China Marches West*, 41–42.

59. Wills, "The South China Sea Is Not a Mediterranean," 10.

60. Lewis, *Frontier Contact*, 25.

61. Ibid., 24.

62. Copper, *Taiwan*, 21.

63. Spence, *The Search for Modern China*, 50; Copper, *Taiwan*.

64. Perdue, *China Marches West*, 43–44.

65. McCombs, "U.S.-Mexico Border Fence Comes at High Cost."

8. Lessons: History Forward and Backward

1. Thomson, *Sentimental Imperialists*; Iriye, *Japan and the Wider World*.

2. Wills, "South and Southeast Asia, Near East, Japan, and Korea," 33.

3. Suganami, "Japan's Entry Into International Society."

4. Larsen, *Tradition, Treaties, and Trade*; Dudden, *Japan's Colonization of Korea*.

5. Gibney, *The Pacific Century*; Vogel, *Japan as Number One*; Fishman, *China, Inc.*

6. Jacques, *When China Rules the World*, 13–15.

7. Alagappa, *Asian Security Order*, 87. See also Pyle, *Japan Rising*, 18.

8. Park, "The Language of Sovereign-Nationalism in Japanese and Korean Security," 5.

9. Institute for International Education, *Open Doors: Report* 2008.

10. Johnson, "China's Strategic Culture."

11. Johnston, *Social States*, 13.

12. Perry, "U.S. Strategy: Engage China, Not Contain It."

13. Huntington, "The Clash of Civilizations"; Katzenstein, ed., *Civilizations in World Politics*.

14. Zakaria, "A Conversation with Lee Kwan-yew"; Kim, "Is Culture Destiny?"

15. Some of the best books in this vein include Hall and Hall, *Hidden Differences*; Hodgson, Sano, and Graham, *Doing Business with the New Japan*; McGregor, *One Billion Customers*; Clissold, *Mr. China*.

16. Haggard, "Institutions and Economic Growth in East Asia"; Wade, "States, Markets, and Industrial Policy." On the colonial era, see Kohli, "Where Do High-Growth Political Economies Come From?"; Haggard, Kang, and Moon, "Japanese Colonialism and Korean Development."

17. Schmid, "Rediscovering Manchuria."

18. Suzuki, *Civilization and Empire*.

BIBLIOGRAPHY

Abramson, Marc S. *Ethnic Identity in Tang China*. Philadelphia: University of Pennsylvania Press, 2008.

Abu-Lughod, Janet. *Before European Hegemony: The World System a.d. 1250–1350*. Oxford: Oxford University Press, 1991.

Adelman, Jeremy, and Aron Stephan. "From Borderlands to Borders: Empires, Nation-States, and the Peoples in Between in North American History." *American Historical Review* 104, no. 3 (1999): 814–841.

Alagappa, Muthiah. *Asian Security Order: Normative and Instrumental Features*. Stanford, Calif.: Stanford University Press, 2003.

Andaya, Leonard. "Interactions with the Outside World and Adaptation in Southeast Asian Society, 1500–1800." In *The Cambridge History of Southeast Asia, Volume One: From Early Times to c. 1800*, ed. Nicholas Tarling, 1–57. Cambridge: Cambridge University Press, 1992.

Anderson, Benedict. *The Spectre of Comparisons: Nationalism, Southeast Asia, and the World*. London: Verso, 2002.

Anderson, James. *The Rebel Den of Nùng Trí Cao*. Seattle: University of Washington Press, 2007.

Arrighi, Giovanni, et al. "Historical Capitalism, East and West." In *The Resurgence of East Asia, 500, 150, and 50 Year Perspectives*, ed. Giovanni Arrighi, Takeshi Hamashita, and Mark Selden, 259–333. London: Routledge, 2003.

Atwell, William. "International Bullion Flows and the Chinese Economy c. 1530–1650." *Past and Present* 95 (1982): 68–90.

———. "A Seventeenth-Century 'General Crisis' in East Asia?" *Modern Asian Studies* 24, no. 4 (October 1990): 661–682.

Bakar, Ibrahim Abu. "Malaysian Perceptions of China." *Historia Actual Online* 7 (Spring 2005): 93–105.

Barfield, Thomas. *The Perilous Frontier: Nomadic Empires and China, 221 b.c. to a.d. 1757*. Oxford: Basil Blackwell, 1989.

Batten, Bruce. *To the Ends of Japan: Premodern Frontiers, Boundaries, and Interactions*. Honolulu: University of Hawai'i Press, 2003.

Baud, Michiel, and Willem Van Schendel. "Toward a Comparative History of Borderlands." *Journal of World History* 8, no. 2 (1997): 211–242.

Beckwith, C. I. "The Impact of the Horse and Silk Trade on the Economies of T'ang China and the Uighur Empire." *Journal of the Economic and Social History of the Orient* 34 (1992): 183–198.

Berry, Mary Elizabeth. *Hideyoshi*. Cambridge, Mass.: Harvard University Press, 1982.

Betts, Richard K. "Wealth, Power, and Instability: East Asia and the United States after the Cold War." *International Security* 18, no. 3 (Winter 1993): 34–77.

Blusse, Leonard. *Strange Company: Chinese Settlers, Mestizo Women, and the Dutch in VOC Batavia*. Leiden: KITV, 1986.

Boscaro, Adriana. *One Hundred and One Letters of Hideyoshi*. Tokyo: Sophia University, 1975.

Brindley, Erica Fox. "Barbarians or Not? Ethnicity and Changing Conceptions of the Ancient Yue (Viet) Peoples (~400–50 b.c.)." *Asia Major* 16, no. 1 (2003): 1–32.

Brzezinski, Zbigniew, and John Mearsheimer. "Clash of the Titans." *Foreign Policy* 146 (January/February 2005): 46–50.

Buzan, Barry. From International System to International Society: Structural Realism and Regime Theory Meet the English School. *International Organization* 47, no. 3 (1993): 327–352.

Buzan, Barry, and Acharya Amitav. "Why Is There No Non-Western International-Relations Theory? An Introduction." *International Relations of the Asia-Pacific* 7, no. 3 (2007): 287–312.

Calder, Kent. "China and Japan's Simmering Rivalry." *Foreign Affairs* (March/April 2006): 129–140.

Chan, Hok-lam. "The Chien-wen, Yung-lo, Hung-hsi, and Husan-te Reigns, 1399–1435." In *The Cambridge History of China*, vol. 7: *The Ming Dynasty, 1368–1644, Part I*, ed. Frederick Mote and Denis Twitchett. Cambridge: Cambridge University Press, 1988.

Chega, Pak. "On Revering China." In *Sourcebook of Korean Civilization*, vol. 2: *From the Seventeenth Century to the Modern Period*, ed. Peter Lee, 86–88. New York: Columbia University Press, 2006.

———. "A Reexamination of the Civil-Service Examination System." In *Sourcebook of Korean Civilization*, ed. Peter Lee, 2:26–28. New York: Columbia University Press, 1996.

Childs Kohn, George. *Dictionary of Wars*. Rev. ed. New York: Facts on File, 1999.

Cho, Young-mee Yu. "Diglossia in Korean Language and Literature: A Historical Perspective." *East Asia: An International Quarterly* 20, no. 1 (Spring 2002): 3–23.

Choi, So-Ja. *Chŏngkwa Chosŏn: Kunsae dongasia-ui sangho insik* [Qing and Chosŏn: Mutual Perceptions in Premodern Asia]. Seoul: Hyeanh, 2005.

———. *Myŏngchong sidae chunghan kwanggyesa yŏngu* [Study on Sino-Korean Relations During Ming-Qing Periods]. Seoul: Ewha Women's University Press, 1997.

Christie, Jan Wisseman. "Negeara, Mandala, and Despotic State: Images of Early Java." In *Southeast Asia in the Ninth to Fourteenth Centuries*, ed. David G. Marr and A. C. Milner. Singapore: Institute of Southeast Asian Studies, 1986.

Clark, Ian. "How Hierarchical Can International Society Be?" Manuscript, Aberystwyth University, 2009.

———. "Towards an English-School Theory of Hegemony." Manuscript, Aberystwyth University, 2009.

Clissold, Tim. *Mr. China: A Memoir*. New York: HarperCollins, 2005.

Coggins, Bridget. "States of Uncertainty: Secession, Recognition, and Constitutive Sovereignty." Manuscript, Dartmouth College, 2009.

Collcutt, Martin. "Kings of Japan? The Political Authority of the Ashikaga Shoguns." *Monumenta Nipponica* 37, no. 4 (Winter 1982): 523–529.

Copper, John. *Taiwan: Nation-State or Province?* Boulder, Colo.: Westview Press, 1990.

Cowan, C. D., and O. W. Wolters, eds. *Southeast Asian History and Historiography: Essays Presented to D. G. E. Hall*. Ithaca, N.Y.: Cornell University Press, 1976.

Cronin, B. "The Paradox of Hegemony: America's Ambiguous Relationship with the United Nations." *European Journal of International Relations* 7, no. 1 (2001): 103–130.

Crossley, Pamela. *China as a Strategic Idea: An Overview*. Unpublished manuscript, Dartmouth College, Hanover, N.H., 2008.

———. *Empire at the Margins: Culture, Ethnicity, and Frontier in Early Modern China*. Berkeley: University of California Press, 2006.

———. *The Manchus*. Cambridge, Mass.: Blackwell, 1997.

Cumings, Bruce. "The Historical Origins of North Korean Foreign Policy." Paper prepared for the Conference on North Korean Foreign Policy in the Post–Cold War Era. 1996.

Curtin, Jeremiah. *The Mongols: A History*. Westport, Conn.: Greenwood Press, 1972.

Cushman, Jennifer. *Fields from the Sea: Chinese Junk Trade with Siam During the Late Eighteenth and Early Nineteenth Centuries*. Ithaca, N.Y.: Cornell University Press, 1993.

Davis, Paul K. *Encyclopedia of Invasions and Conquests: From Ancient Times to the Present*. Santa Barbara, Calif.: ABC-CLIO, 1996.

Day, Tony. "Ties That (Un)Bind: Families and States in Premodern Southeast Asia." *Journal of Asian Studies* 55, no. 2 (May 1996): 384–409.

Deng, Gang. "The Foreign Staple Trade of China in the Premodern Era." *International History Review* 19, no. 2 (1997): 253–283.

———. *Maritime Sector, Institutions, and Sea Power of Premodern China*. Santa Barbara, Calif.: Greenwood Press, 1999.

Deuchler, Martina. *The Confucian Transformation of Korea: A Study of Society and Ideology*. Cambridge, Mass.: Harvard University Press, 1992.

Di Cosmo, Nicola. *Ancient China and Its Enemies: The Rise of Nomadic Power in East Asian History*. Cambridge: Cambridge University Press, 2002.

Donnelly, Jack. "Sovereign Inequalities and Hierarchy in Anarchy: American Power and International Society." *European Journal of International Relations* 12, no. 2 (2006).

Dudden, Alexis. *Japan's Colonization of Korea: Discourse and Power*. Honolulu: University of Hawaii Press, 2005.

———. *Troubled Apologies Among Japan, Korea, and the United States*. New York: Columbia University Press, 2008.

Duncan, John. *The Origins of the Choson Dynasty*. Seattle: University of Washington Press, 2000.

———. "The Social Background of the Founding of the Chosun Dynasty: Change or Continuity?" *Journal of Korean Studies* 6 (1988–1989).

———. "The Uses of Confucianism in Modern Korea." In *Rethinking Confucianism: Past and Present in China, Japan, Korea, and Vietnam*, ed. Benjamin A. Elman, John B. Duncan, and Herman Ooms, 432–462. Los Angeles: Asia Institute, University of California, 2002.

Dupuy, R. Ernest, and Trevor Dupuy. *The Harper Encyclopedia of Military History: From 3500 b.c. to the Present*. 4th ed. New York: HarperCollins, 1993.

Elisonas, Jurgis. "The Inseparable Trinity: Japan's Relations with China and Korea." In *The Cambridge History of Japan: Early Modern Japan*, ed. John Hall. Cambridge: Cambridge University Press, 1988.

Elisseef, Vadime. "The Middle Empire, a Distant Empire, and Empire Without Neighbors." *Diogenes* 42 (1963): 60–64.

Elliot, Mark. *The Manchu Way: The Eight Banners and Ethnic Identity in Late Imperial China*. Stanford, Calif.: Stanford University Press, 2001.

Fairbank, John K. "Tributary Trade and China's Relations with the West." *Far Eastern Quarterly* 1 (1942): 129–149.

Fairbank, John K. *Trade and Diplomacy on the China Coast*. Stanford, Calif.: Stanford University Press, 1953.

Fairbank, John K., and S. Y. Teng. "On the Ch'ing Tributary System." *Harvard Journal of Asiatic Studies* 6 (1941): 135–246.

Farris, William Wayne. "Trade, Money, and Merchants in Nara Japan." *Monumenta Nipponica* 53, no. 3 (1998): 303–334.

Fearon, James D. "Domestic Politics, Foreign Policy, and Theories of International Relations." *American Review of Political Science* 1 (1998): 289–313.

———. "Rationalist Explanations for War." *International Organization* 49, no. 3 (1995): 379–414.

Fishman, Ted C. *China, Inc.: How the Rise of the Next Superpower Challenges America and the World*. New York: Simon and Schuster, 2005.

Fiskesjo, Magnus. "On the 'Raw' and 'Cooked' Barbarians of Imperial China." *Inner Asia* 1 (1999): 139–168.

Fogel, Joshua A. *Articulating the Sinosphere: Sino-Japanese Relations in Space and Time*. Cambridge, Mass.: Harvard University Pres, 2009.

Frank, Andre Gunder. *ReOrient: Global Economy in the Asian Age*. Berkeley: University of California Press, 1998.

Fravel, Taylor. "Regime Insecurity and International Cooperation: Explaining China's Compromises on Territorial Disputes." *International Security* 30, no. 2 (2005) :46–83.

Friedberg, Aaron. "Ripe for Rivalry: Prospects for Peace in a Multipolar Asia." *International Security* 18, no. 3 (1993): 5–33.

Friedman, Thomas L. *The World Is Flat: A Brief History of the Twenty-First Century*. New York: Farrar, Straus & Giroux, 2005.

Gaddis, John Lewis. *The Long Peace: Inquiries Into the History of the Cold War*. Oxford: Oxford University Press, 1989.

Gibney, Frank. *The Pacific Century: America and Asia in a Changing World*. New York: Scribner's, 1992.

Giersch, Charles. *Asian Borderlands: The Transformation of Qing China's Yunnan Frontier*. Cambridge, Mass.: Harvard University Press, 2006.

———. "A Motley Throng: Social Change on Southwest China's Early Modern Frontier, 1700–1880." Journal of Asian Studies 60, no. 1 (February 2001): 67–94.

Gleditsch, Nils Petter, et al. "Armed Conflict 1946–2001: A New Dataset." *Journal of Peace Research* 39, no. 5 (2002): 615–637.

Gould, Roger. "The Origins of Status Hierarchies: A Formal Theory and Empirical Test." *American Journal of Sociology* 107, no. 5 (2002): 1143–1178.

Grimmet, Richard F. "Instances of Use of United States Armed Forces Abroad, 1798–2001." CRS Report for Congress, Congressional Research Service, February 5, 2002.

Grossberg, Kenneth. "From Feudal Chieftains to Secular Monarch: The Development of Shogunal Power in Early Muromachi Japan." *Monumenta Nipponica* 31, no. 1 (1976): 29–49.

———. *Japan's Renaissance: The Politics of the Muromachi Bakufu*. Cambridge, Mass.: Harvard East Asian Monographs, 1981.

Ha, U-bong. "Chosŏn jeongi-ui daeil gwangye" [Early Chosŏn's Foreign Policy Toward Japan]. In *Kangjwa hanilgwangye-sa* [Lectures on Korea-Japan Relations], ed. Cho Hang-rae, Ha U-bong, and Son Seung-chol. Seoul: Hyonumsa, 1994.

Haboush, Jahyun Kim, and Martina Deuchler, eds. *Culture and the State in Late Chosŏn Korea*. Cambridge, Mass.: Harvard University Press, 1999.

Haggard, Stephan. "Institutions and Growth in East Asia." *Studies in Comparative Development* 38, no. 4 (December 2004): 53–81.

Haggard, Stephan, David Kang, and Chung-in Moon. "Japanese Colonialism and Korean Development: A Critique." *World Development* 27, no. 6 (June 1997): 867–881.

Hall, Edward, and Mildred Hall. *Hidden Differences: Doing Business with the Japanese*. New York: Anchor Books, 1987.

Hall, John. "Notes on the Early Qing Copper Trade with Japan." *Harvard Journal of Asiatic Studies* 12 (December 1949): 444–461.

Hall, Kenneth. "An Introductory Essay on Southeast Asian Statecraft in the Classical Period." In *Explorations in Early Southeast Asian History: The Origins of Southeast Asian Statecraft*, ed. Kenneth Hall and John K. Whitmore, 1–25. Ann Arbor: University of Michigan, 1976.

Hamashita, Takeshi. *China, East Asia, and the Global Economy: Regional and Historical Perspectives*. London: Routledge, 2008.

———. 1994. "The Tribute Trade System and Modern Asia." In *Japanese Industrialization and the Asian Economy*, ed. A. J. H. Latham and Heita Kawakatsu, 91–107. London: Routledge, 1994.

Han, Myungki. *Imjin waerangwa hanjung kwangye* [The Imjin War and Sino-Korea Relations]. Seoul, Yoksa Bipyongsa, 1999.

Hansen, Valerie. *Changing Gods in Medieval China, 1126–1276*. Princeton, N.J.: Princeton University Press, 1990.

Harsanyi, John. *Essays on Ethics, Social Behavior, and Scientific Explanation*. Dordrecht, Holland: D. Reidel, 1976.

Haugaard, M. "Power and Hegemony in Social Theory." In *Hegemony and Power: Consensus and Coercion in Contemporary Politics*, ed. M. Haugaard and H. H. Lentner, 45–66. Lanham, Md.: Lexington Books, 2006.

Hawley, Samuel. *The Imjin War*. Berkeley: University of California Press, 2005.

Herbst, Jeffrey. "War and the State in Africa." *International Security* 14, no. 4 (Spring 1990): 117–139.

Hevia, James L. *Cherishing Men from Afar: Qing Guest Ritual and the Macartney Embassy of 1793*. Durham, N.C.: Duke University Press, 2005.

———. "Tribute, Asymmetry, and Imperial Formations: Rethinking Relations of Power in East Asia." Paper prepared for the USC U.S.-China Institute Conference on History and China's Foreign Relations, February 17, 2008.

Hodgson, James, Yoshihiro Sano, and John Graham. *Doing Business with the New Japan: Succeeding in America's Richest International Market.* 2nd ed. Lanham, Md.: Rowman and Littlefield, 2007.

Holland, Steve. "McCain Would Exclude Russia from G8 Nations." *Reuters* (October 15, 2007). http://www.reuters.com/article/politicsNews/idUSN153696202 0071015.

Howe, Christopher. *The Origins of Japanese Trade Supremacy: Development and Technology in Asia from 1540 to the Pacific War.* London: Hurts, 1996.

Howell, David L. "Review of Bruce Batten." *Pacific Affairs* 77, no. 4 (Winter 2004): 759–760.

Hui, Po-keung. "Overseas Chinese Business Networks: East Asian Economic Development in Historical Perspective." Ph.D. dissertation, State University of New York at Binghamton, 1995.

Hui, Victoria. "China's Rise in Comparative-Historical Perspective: Tianxia Datong or Tianxia Daluan?" Manuscript, University of Notre Dame, 2008.

———. *War and State Formation*, Cambridge: Cambridge University Press, 2004.

Huntington, Samuel P. "The Clash of Civilizations." *Foreign Affairs* (Summer 1993).

Hurd, Ian. *After Anarchy: Legitimacy and Power in the United Nations Security Council.* Princeton, N.J.: Princeton University Press, 2007.

———. "Breaking and Making Norms: American Revisionism and Crises of Legitimacy." *International Politics* 44 (2007):194–213.

———. "Legitimacy and Authority in International Politics." *International Organization* 53, no. 2 (1999): 379–408.

Hurrell, Andrew. "Rising Powers and the Question of Status in International Society." Paper presented at the annual meeting of the International Studies Association, New York, February 15–18, 2009.

Ikeda, Satoshi. "The History of the Capitalist World-System vs. the History of East-Southeast Asia." *Review* 19, no. 1 (1996): 49–78.

Ikenberry, John G., and Charles A. Kupchan. "Socialization and Hegemonic Power." *International Organization* 44, no. 3 (Summer 1990): 283–315.

Institute for International Education. *Open Doors: Report 2008.* http://opendoors .iienetwork.org/page/131583.

Iriye, Akira. *Japan and the Wider World: From Mid-Nineteenth Century to the Present.* London: Longman, 1997.

Ishii, Yoneo. *The Junk Trade from Southeast Asia: Translations from the Tosen Fusetsu-gaki, 1674–1723.* Singapore: Institute of Southeast Asian Studies, 1998.

Iwao, Seiichi. "Japanese Foreign Trade in the Sixteenth and Seventeenth Centuries." *Acta Asiatica* 30 (1976): 1–19.

Jacques, Martin. *When China Rules the World: The End of the Western World and the Birth of a New Global Order.* New York: Penguin, 2009.

Jagchid, Sechin, and Van Jay Symons. *Peace, War, and Trade Along the Great Wall: Nomadic-Chinese Interaction Through Two Millennia.* Bloomington: Indiana University Press, 1989.

Jansen, Marius. *China in the Tokugawa World.* Cambridge, Mass.: Harvard University Press, 1992.

Johnson, Kenneth D. "China's Strategic Culture: A Perspective for the United States." Strategic Studies Institute, United States Army War College, June 2009. http://www.strategicstudiesinstitute.army.mil/pubs/display.cfm?PubID=924.

Johnston, Alastair Iain. *Cultural Realism: Strategic Culture and Grand Strategy in Chinese History.* Princeton, N.J.: Princeton University Press, 1995.

———. *Social States: China in International Relations, 1980–2000.* Princeton, N.J.: Princeton University Press, 2007.

Joseph, Jonathan. *Hegemony: A Realist Analysis.* London: Routledge, 2002.

Kang, David C. *Crony Capitalism: Corruption and Development in South Korea and the Philippines.* Cambridge, Mass.: Cambridge University Press, 2002.

Kang, Etsuko. *Diplomacy and Ideology in Japanese-Korean Relations from the Fifteenth to the Eighteenth Century.* New York: St. Martin's Press, 1997.

Karnow, Stanley. *Vietnam: A History.* New York: Viking, 1991.

Katzenstein, Peter, ed. *Civilizations in World Politics: Plural and Pluralist Perspectives.* New York: Routledge, 2009.

Kaufman, Stuart. "The Fragmentation and Consolidation of International Systems." *International Organization* 51, no. 2 (Spring 1997): 173–208.

Kaufman, Stuart, Richard Little, and William Wohlforth, eds. *The Balance of Power in World History.* London: Palgrave, 2007.

Kazui, Tashiro. "Foreign Relations During the Edo Period: Sakoku Reexamined." *Journal of Japanese Studies* 8, no. 2 (1982): 283–306.

Keene, Donald. "Literature," in *An Introduction to Japanese Civilization,* ed. Arthur E. Tiedermann. New York: Columbia University Press, 1974.

Keene, Edward. *Beyond the Anarchical Society: Grotius, Colonialism, and Order in World Politics.* Cambridge: Cambridge University Press, 2002.

Kelley, Liam C. *Beyond the Bronze Pillars: Envoy Poetry and the Sino-Vietnamese Relationship.* Honolulu: University of Hawai'i Press, 2005.

———. "Vietnam as a 'Domain of Manifest Civility' (*Van Hien Chi Bang*)." *Journal of Southeast Asian Studies* 34, no. 1 (February 2003): 63–76.

Kenny, Henry. *Shadow of the Dragon: Vietnam's Continuing Struggle with China and Its Implications for U.S. Foreign Policy.* Washington, D.C.: Brassey's, 2002.

Keyes, Charles. "The Peoples of Asia: Science and Politics in the Classification of Ethnic Groups in Thailand, China, and Vietnam." *Journal of Asian Studies* 61, no. 4 (2002): 1163–1203.

Khazanov, Anatoli M. "Characteristic Features of Nomadic Communities in Eurasian Steppes." In *The Nomadic Alternative*, ed. Wolfgang Weissleder. The Hague: Mouton Publishers, 1978.

_____. *Nomads and the Outside World*. Cambridge: Cambridge University Press, 1984.

Kim, Dae-jung. "Is Culture Destiny? The Myth of Asia's Anti-Democratic Values." *Foreign Affairs* (November/December 1994).

Kim, Key-hiuk. *The Last Phase of the East Asian World Order*. Berkeley: University of California Press, 1980.

Kim, Seonmin. "Ginseng and Border Trespassing Between Qing China and Chosŏn Korea." Paper presented at the annual meeting of the Association for Asian Studies, San Diego, Calif., April 6–9, 2006.

Klein, Peter. "The China Seas and the World Economy Between the Sixteenth and Nineteenth Centuries: The Changing Structures of Trade." In *Interactions in the World Economy: Perspectives from International Economic History*, ed. Carl-Ludwig Holtfrerich. New York: New York University Press, 1989.

Kohli, Atul. "Where Do High-Growth Political Economies Come From? The Japanese Lineage in South Korean Development." *World Development* (September 1994): 1269–1293.

Krasner, Stephen. "Organized Hypocrisy in Nineteenth-Century East Asia." *International Relations of the Asia-Pacific* 1 (2001): 173–197.

_____. *Sovereignty: Organized Hypocrisy*. Princeton, N.J.: Princeton University Press, 1999.

Kwanten, Luc. *Imperial Nomads*. Philadelphia: University of Pennsylvania Press, 1979.

Lake, David A. "American Hegemony and the Future of East-West Relations." *International Studies Perspectives* 7 (2006): 23–30.

_____. "Escape from the State of Nature: Authority and Hierarchy in World Politics." *International Security* 32, no. 1 (2007): 47–79.

Lam, Truong Buu. "Intervention Versus Tribute in Sino-Vietnamese Relations, 1788–1790." In *The Chinese World Order*, ed. John K. Fairbank, 165–179. Cambridge, Mass.: Harvard University Press, 1968.

Larsen, Kirk. *Tradition, Treaties, and Trade: Qing Imperialism and Choson Korea, 1850–1910*. Cambridge, Mass.: Harvard University Press, 2008.

Layne, Christopher. "The Unipolar Illusion: Why New Great Powers Will Arise." *International Security* 17, no. 4 (Spring 1993): 5–51.

Lebow, Richard Ned. *A Cultural Theory of International Politics*. Cambridge: Cambridge University Press, 2008.

Ledyard, Gari. "Cartography in Korea." In *Cartography in the Traditional East and Southeast Asian Societies*, ed. J. B. Harley and David Woodward. Chicago: University of Chicago Press, 1994.

_____. "Confucianism and War: The Korean Security Crisis of 1598." *The Journal of Korean Studies* 6 (1988–1989): 81–119.

Lee, Chong-Sin. *Koryŏ sidaeui chŏngch'i pyŏndonggwa daeoejŏngch'aek* [Political Changes and Foreign Policy of Goryo]. Seoul: Gyongin Munwhasa, 2004.

Lee, Jang-Hee. *Imjin waeransa yŏngu* [Research on the History of the Imjin War]. Seoul: Asea Munwhasa, 1999.

Lee, John. "Trade and Economy in Preindustrial East Asia, c. 1500–1800: East Asia in the Age of Global Integration." *Journal of Asian Studies* 58, no. 1 (1999): 2–26.

Lee, Kenneth. *Korea and East Asia: The Story of a Phoenix.* Westport, Conn.: Praeger, 1997.

Lee, Ki-baek. *A New History of Korea.* Cambridge, Mass.: Harvard University Press, 1984.

Lee, Peter, ed. 1993. *Sourcebook of Korean Civilization.* Vol. 1: *From Early Times to the Sixteenth Century.* New York: Columbia University Press, 1993.

Lewis, James B. *Frontier Contact Between Chosŏn Korea and Tokugawa Japan.* New York: Routledge Courzon, 2003.

Lewis, Mark Edward. *The Early Chinese Empires: Qin and Han.* Cambridge, Mass.: Harvard University Press, 2007.

Lieber, Keir, and Gerard Alexander. "Waiting for Balancing: Why the World Is Not Pushing Back." *International Security* 30 (2003): 109–139.

Lieberman, Victor. "Local Integration and Eurasian Analogies: Structuring Southeast Asian History, c. 1350–c. 1830." *Modern Asian Studies* 27, no. 3 (1993): 475–572.

_____. 2003. *Strange Parallels: Southeast Asia in Global Context, c. 800–1830.* Vol. 1: *Integration on the Mainland.* Cambridge: Cambridge University Press, 2003.

Little, Richard. "The English School's Contribution to the Study of International Relations." *European Journal of International Relations* 6, no. 3 (2000): 395–422.

Lloyd, Martin. *The Passport: The History of Man's Most Travelled Document.* Stroud: Sutton Publishing, 1976.

Lo, Jung-Pang. "Maritime Commerce and Its Relations to the Sung Navy." *Journal of the Economic and Social History of the Orient* 12, no. 1 (January 1969): 57–101.

Lococo, Paul. "The Qing Empire." In *A Military History of China,* ed. D. Graff and R. Higham, 115–134. Boulder, Colo.: Westview Press, 2002.

Luc, Thuan. "An Early Trade Coin and the Commercial Trade Between Vietnam and Japan in the Seventeenth Century." May 1999. http://www.charm.ru/coins/vn/nagasaki.shtml.

Marr, David. *Vietnamese Tradition on Trial, 1920–1945.* Berkeley: University of California Press, 1981.

Mass, Jeffrey. "The Early Bakufu and Feudalism." In *Court and Bakufu in Japan: Essays in Kamakura History*, ed. Jeffrey Mass, 123–142. New Haven, Conn.: Yale University Press, 1982.

Mastanduno, Michael. "Hegemonic Order, September 11, and the Consequences of the Bush Revolution." *International Relations of the Asia Pacific* 5 (2005): 177–196.

_____. "Incomplete Hegemony: The United States and Security Order in Asia." In *Asian Security Order: Instrumental and Normative Features*, ed. Muthiah Alagappa, 141–170. Stanford, Calif.: Stanford University Press, 2003.

McCombs, Brady. "U.S.-Mexico Border Fence Comes at High Cost." *ScrippsNews* (January 30, 2009). http://www.scrippsnews.com/node/40521.

McGregor, James. *One Billion Customers*. New York: The Free Press, 2005.

McNeill, William. *The Pursuit of Power: Technology, Armed Force, and Society Since a.d. 1000*. Chicago: University of Chicago Press, 1992.

Mears, John. 2001. *Analyzing the Phenomenon of Borderlands from Comparative and Cross-Cultural Perspectives*. Manuscript. Southern Methodist University. http://www.historycooperative.org/proceedings/interactions/mears.html.

Mearsheimer, John. *The Tragedy of Great Power Politics*. New York: W. W. Norton, 2001.

Miller, Alice. "Some Things We Used to Know About China's Past and Present (But Now, Not So Much)." Paper presented at the Conference on History and China's Foreign Relations, U.S.-China Institute, University of Southern California, February 16, 2008.

Min, Duck-gi, et al. "Hanil-gan Pyoryuminae gwanhan yongu" [A Study on the Pyoryummin Between Korea and Japan]. In *Hanilkwangye-ui sahhakheo* [Aspects in the History of Korea-Japan Relations], ed. Min Duck-gi et al. Seoul: Gukhakjaryowon, 2000.

Mizuno, Norihito. "Japan and Its East Asian Neighbors: Japan's Perception of China and Korea and the Making of Foreign Policy from the Seventeenth to the Nineteenth Century." Ph.D. dissertation, Ohio State University, 2004.

Mote, Frederick W., ed. *The Cambridge History of China*. Vol. 7: *The Ming Dynasty, 1368–1644, Part 1*. Cambridge: Cambridge University Press, 1988.

_____. *Imperial China: 900–1800*. Cambridge, Mass.: Harvard University Press, 1999.

Naohiro, Asao. "The Sixteenth-Century Unification." In *The Cambridge History of Japan*, vol. 4: *Early Modern Japan*, trans. Bernard Susser, ed. John Hall, 40–91. Cambridge: Cambridge University Press, 1991.

Naval History and Heritage Command. "USS *Constitution*: Chronology." Department of the Navy. http://www.history.navy.mil/faqs/faq68-2.htm.

Nguyen, Khac Vien. *Viet Nam: A Long History*. Hanoi: The Gioi, 2004.

Nye, Joseph S. "Transformational Leadership and U.S. Grand Strategy." *Foreign Affairs* (July/August 2006): 139–149.

Obama, Barack. "Renewing American Leadership." *Foreign Affairs* 86, no. 4 (July/August 2007): 2–9.

Onuf, Nicholas. *World of Our Making: Rules and Rule in Social Theory and International Relations*. Columbia: University of South Carolina Press, 1989.

Osamu, Oba. *Sino-Japanese Relations in the Edo Period*. Trans. Joshua A. Fogel. Tokyo: Toho Shoten. 1980. http://chinajapan.org/archive.html.

Osiander, Andreas. "Sovereignty, International Relations, and the Westphalian Myth." *International Organization* 55, no. 2 (2001): 251–301.

Pape, Robert A. "Soft Balancing Against the United States." *International Security* 30 (2005): 7–45.

Park, Eugene Y. *Between Dreams and Reality: The Military Examination in Late Choson Korea, 1600–1894*. Cambridge, Mass.: Harvard University Press, 2007.

_____. "War and Peace in Premodern Korea: Institutional and Ideological Dimensions." In *The Military and Korean Society*, ed. Young-Key Kim-Renaud, Richard Grinker, and Kirk W. Larsen, 1–14. Washington, D.C.: George Washington University, 2006.

Park, Seo-hyun. "The Language of Sovereign-Nationalism in Japanese and Korean Security." Paper prepared for presentation at the annual convention of the International Studies Association, New York, February 15–18, 2009.

Paul, Darel E. 1999. "Sovereignty, Survival, and the Westphalian Blind Alley in International Relations." *Review of International Studies* 25 no. 2: 217–231.

People's Liberation Army. *Zhongguo lidai zhanzheng nianbiao* 《中国历代战争年表》 (중국 역대 전쟁 연 표) [Chronology of Wars in China Through Successive Dynasties]. 2 vols. Beijing: Jiefangjun chubanshe, 2003.

Perdue, Peter. *China Marches West: The Qing Conquest of Central Eurasia*. Cambridge, Mass.: Harvard University Press, 2005.

Perry, William. "U.S. Strategy: Engage China, Not Contain It." *Defense Issues* 10, no. 109 (October 30, 1995). http://www.defenselink.mil/speeches/1995/s19951030-kaminski.html.

Pollack, David. *The Fracture of Meaning: Japan's Synthesis of China from the Eighth Through the Eighteenth Centuries*. Princeton, N.J.: Princeton University Press, 1986.

Pombejra, Dhiravat na. "Ayutthaya at the End of the Seventeenth Century: Was There a Shift to Isolation?" In *Southeast Asia in the Early Modern Era*, ed. by Anthony Reid, 250–272. Ithaca, N.Y.: Cornell University Press, 1993.

_____. "Princes, Pretenders, and the Chinese Phrakhlang: An Analysis of the Dutch Evidence Concerning Siamese court politics, 1699–1734." In *On the*

Eighteenth Century as a Category of Asian History: Van Leur in Retrospect, ed. Leonard Blussé and Femme S. Gaastra, 107–130. Brookfield, Vt.: Ashgate, 1998.

Prak, Roderich. *China's Seaborne Trade with South and South-East Asia (1200–1750).* Aldershot: Ashgate, 1999.

Prestowitz, Clyde. *Trading Places: How We Are Giving Our Future to Japan and How to Reclaim It.* New York: Basic Books, 1993.

Pyle, Kenneth B. *Japan Rising: The Resurgence of Japanese Power and Purpose.* New York: Public Affairs, 2007.

Rafael, Vicente. *Contracting Colonialism: Translation and Christian Conversion in Tagalog Society Under Spanish Rule.* Ithaca, N.Y.: Cornell University Press, 1988.

Reid, Anthony. "An 'Age of Commerce' in Southeast Asian History." *Modern Asian Studies* 24, no. 1 (February 1990): 1–30.

———. *Southeast Asia in the Age of Commerce, 1450–1680.* Vol. 2: *Expansion and Crisis.* New Haven, Conn.: Yale University Press, 1993.

Reus-Smit, Christopher. "The Constitutional Structure of International Society and the Nature of Fundamental Institutions." *International Organization* 51, no. 4 (1997): 555–589.

Robinson, Kenneth. "Centering the King of Chosŏn: Aspects of Korean Maritime Diplomacy, 1392–1592." *Journal of Asian Studies* 59, no. 1 (February 2000): 109–125.

———. "From Raiders to Traders: Border Security and Border Control in Early Chosŏn, 1392–1450." *Korean Studies* 16 (1992): 94–115.

———. "Policies of Practicality: The Chosun Court's Regulation of Contact with the Japanese and Jurchens, 1392–1580." Ph.D. dissertation, University of Hawai'i, 1997.

Roh, Gye-Hyun. *Yŏmong oegyosa* [Diplomatic History of Koryŏ-Mongol Relations]. Seoul: Gapin Press, 1993.

Roland, Alex. "Review of Kenneth Chase, *Firearms: A Global History to 1700.*" *Journal of Interdisciplinary History* 35, no. 4 (2005): 617–619.

Rossabi, Morris, ed. *China Among Equals.* Berkeley: University of California Press, 1983.

Roy, Denny. *Taiwan: A Political History.* Ithaca, N.Y.: Cornell University Press, 2003.

Rudolph, Susanne. *State Formation in Asia: Prolegomenon to a Comparative Study.* Unpublished manuscript. 2007.

Ruggie, John. "Continuity and Transformation in the World Polity: Toward a Neorealist Synthesis." *World Politics* 35, no. 2 (1983): 261–285.

Ryan, N. J. *The Making of Modern Malaysia and Singapore: A History from Earliest Times to 1966.* Oxford: Oxford University Press, 1976.

Sakai, Robert. 1964. "The Satsuma-Ryukyu Trade and the Tokugawa Seclusion Policy." *Journal of Asian Studies* 23, No. 3: 391–403.

Samuels, Richard. *Machiavelli's Children: Leaders and Their Legacies in Italy and Japan*. Ithaca, N.Y.: Cornell University Press, 2003.

Sanderson, Stephen K. *Social Transformations: A General Theory of Historical Development*. Oxford: Blackwell, 1995.

Sarkees, Meredith, Frank Whelon Wayman, and J. David Singer. "Inter-State, Intra-State, and Extra-State Wars: A Comprehensive Look at Their Distribution Over Time, 1816–1997." *International Studies Quarterly* 47 (2003): 49–70.

Schmid, Andre. "Rediscovering Manchuria: Sin Ch'aeho and the Politics of Territorial History in Korea." *Journal of Asian Studies* 56, no. 1 (February 1997): 26–46.

Schottenhammer, Angela. "Japan: The Tiny Dwarf? Sino-Japanese Relations from the Kangxi to the Early Qianlong Reigns." Asia Research Institute, Working Paper Series, No. 106. Singapore: National University of Singapore, 2008.

Sechin, Jagchid, and Van Jay Symons. *Peace, War, and Trade Along the Great Wall: Nomadic-Chinese Interaction Through Two Millennia*. Bloomington: Indiana University Press, 1989.

Shively, Donald, et al. *The Cambridge History of Japan*. Vol. 2: *Heian Japan*. Cambridge: Cambridge University Press, 1999.

Shoji, Kawazoe. "Japan and East Asia." In *The Cambridge History of Japan*, vol. 3: *Medieval Japan*, ed. Kozo Yamamura. Cambridge: Cambridge University Press, 1990.

Shu, Immanuel. *The Rise of Modern China*. Oxford: Oxford University Press, 1995.

Simmons, Beth A. "Rules Over Real Estate: Trade, Territorial Conflict, and International Borders as Institutions." *Journal of Conflict Resolution* 49, no. 6 (2005): 823–848.

Smith, George Vinal. *The Dutch in Seventeenth-Century Thailand*. DeKalb: Northern Illinois Press, 1977.

Smith, P. J., and R. von Glahn, eds. *The Song-Yuan-Ming Transition in Chinese History*. Cambridge, Mass.: Harvard University Press, 2003.

Smits, Gregory. *Visions of Ryukyu: Identity and Ideology in Early Modern Thought and Politics*. Honolulu: University of Hawai'i Press, 1999.

Son, Seung-chol. *Chosŏn sidae hanil gwangywe yonku* [Korea-Japan Relations During the Chosun Period]. Seoul: Jisungui Sam, 1994.

Spence, Jonathan. *The Search for Modern China*. New York: W. W. Norton, 1991.

Steenstrup, Carl. "The Middle Ages Survey'd." *Monumenta Nipponica* 46, no. 2 (1991): 237–252.

Standen, Naomi. *Unbounded Loyalty: Frontier Crossings in Liao China*. Honolulu: University of Hawai'i Press, 2007.

Strange, Mark. "An Eleventh-Century View of Chinese Ethnic Policy: Sima Guang on the Fall of Western Jin." *Journal of Historical Sociology* 20, no. 3 (2007): 235–258.

Stuart-Fox, Martin. *A Short History of China and Southeast Asia: Tribute, Trade, and Influence*. Crows Nest: Allen and Unwin, 2003.

Suganami, Hidemi. "Japan's Entry Into International Society." In *The Expansion of International Society*, ed. Hedley Bull and Adam Watson, 185–199. Oxford: Clarendon Press, 1984.

Sutherland, Heather. "Believing Is Seeing: Perspectives on Political Power and Economic Activity in the Malay World, 1700–1940." *Journal of Southeast Asian Studies* 26, no. 1 (March 1995): 133–146.

Sutter, Robert G. "China's Rise: Implications for U.S. Leadership in Asia." *Policy Studies* 21. Washington, D.C.: East-West Center, 2006.

Suzuki, Shogo. *Civilization and Empire: China and Japan's Encounter with European International Society*. London: Routledge, 2009.

Swope, Kenneth M. "Crouching Tigers, Secret Weapons: Military Technology Employed During the Sino-Japanese-Korean War, 1592–1598." *Journal of Military History* 69 (January 2005): 11–42.

———. "Deceit, Disguise, and Dependence: China, Japan, and the Future of the Tributary System, 1592–1596." *International History Review* 24, no. 4 (2002): 757–782.

Tana, Li. *Nguyen Cochinchina: Southern Vietnam in the Seventeenth and Eighteenth Centuries*. Ithaca, N.Y.: Cornell University Press, 1998.

———. "A View from the Sea: Perspectives on the Northern and Central Vietnamese Coast." *Journal of Southeast Asian Studies* 37, no. 1 (February 2006): 83–102.

Taylor, Keith W. *The Birth of Vietnam*. Berkeley: University of California Press, 1983.

———. "China and Vietnam: Looking for a New Version of an Old Relationship." In *The Vietnam War: American and Vietnamese Perspectives*, ed. Jayne Werner and Luu Doanh Huynh. New York: M. E. Sharpe, 1993.

———. "The Early Kingdoms." In *The Cambridge History of Southeast Asia: From early times to c. 1500*, 2nd ed., ed. Nicholas Tarling, 137–182. Cambridge: Cambridge University Press, 1999.

———. "The Literati Revival in Seventeenth-Century Vietnam." *Journal of Southeast Asian Studies* 18, no. 1 (March 1987): 1–22.

Terada, Takashi. "Forming an East Asian Community: A Site for Japan-China Power Struggles." *Journal of Japanese Studies* 26, no. 1 (May 2006): 5–17.

Tilly, Charles, ed.. *The Formation of National States in Western Europe*. Princeton: Princeton University Press, 1975.

Thomson, James, et al. *Sentimental Imperialists: The American Experience in East Asia*. New York: Harper & Row, 1981.

Toby, Ronald. "Reopening the Question of Sakoku: Diplomacy in the Legitimation of the Tokugawa Bakufu." *Journal of Japanese Studies* 3, no. 2 (1977): 323–363.

———. "Rescuing the Nation from History: The State of the State in Early Modern Japan." *Monumenta Nipponica* 56, no. 2 (Summer 2001): 197–237.

_____. *State and Diplomacy in Early Modern Japan: Asia in the Development of the Tokugawa Bakufu*. Stanford, Calif.: Stanford University Press, 1984.

Turnbull, Stephen. *Pirates of the Far East, 811–1639*. Oxford: Osprey, 2007.

_____. *Samurai Invasion: Japan's Korean War, 1592–1598*. London: Cassell, 2002.

Van de Ven, Hans J. "War and the Making of Modern China." *Modern Asian Studies* 30, no. 4 (1996).

Van Leur, J. C. *Indonesian Trade and Society: Essays in Asian Social and Economic History*. The Hague: W. van Hoeve, 1955.

Viraphol, Sarasin. *Tribute and Profit: Sino-Siamese Trade, 1652–1853*. Cambridge, Mass.: Harvard University Press, 1977.

Vogel, Ezra. *Japan as Number One: Lessons for America*. Cambridge, Mass.: Harvard University Press, 1979.

Von Glahn, Richard. "Myth and Reality of China's Seventeenth-Century Monetary Crisis." *Journal of Economic History* 56, no. 2 (1996): 429–454.

Von Verschuer, Charlotte. "Looking from Within and Without: Ancient and Medieval External Relations." *Monumenta Nipponica* 55, no. 4 (Winter 2000): 537–566.

Vuving, Alexander. "The References of Vietnamese States and the Mechanism of World Formation." *Asien* 79 (2001): 62–86.

Wade, Robert. "States, Markets, and Industrial Policy." In *Governing the Market*, by Robert Wade, 8–33. Princeton, N.J.: Princeton University Press, 1990.

Waley-Cohen, Joanna. "Commemorating War in Eighteenth-Century China." *Modern Asian Studies* 30, no. 4 (October 1996): 869–899.

Waltz, Kenneth N. "The Emerging Structure of International Politics." *International Security* 18, no. 2 (Fall 1993): 44–79.

_____. *Theory of International Politics*. Reading, Mass.: Addison-Wesley, 1979.

Wang, Gungwu. *China and the Overseas Chinese*. Singapore: Times Academic Press, 1991.

Wang, Zhenping. *Ambassadors from the Islands of Immortals: China-Japan Relations in the Han-Tang Period*. Honolulu: University of Hawai'i Press, 2005.

Weber, Katja. *Hierarchy Amidst Anarchy: Transaction Costs and Institutional Choice*. Albany, N.Y.: SUNY Press, 2000.

Weber, Max. *Economy and Society*. Ed. Guenther Roth and Claus Wittich. Berkeley: University of California Press, 1978.

_____. "The Profession and Vocation of Politics." In *Weber: Political Writings*, ed. Peter Lassman and Ronald Spiers, 309–369. Cambridge: Cambridge University Press, 1994.

Wendt, Alexander. "Anarchy Is What States Make of It: The Social Construction of Power Politics." *International Organization* 46, no. 2 (1992): 391–425.

Wendt, Alexander, and Daniel Friedheim. "Hierarchy Under Anarchy: Informal Empires and the East German State." *International Organization* 49, no. 4 (1995): 689–721.

Wheeler, Charles. "Rethinking the Sea in Vietnamese History: Littoral Society in the Integration of Thuan-Quang, Seventeenth and Eighteenth Centuries." *Journal of Southeast Asian Studies* 37, no. 1 (February 2006): 123–153.

Whitmore, John K. "Cartography in Vietnam." In *Cartography in the Traditional East and Southeast Asian Societies*, ed. J. B. Harley and David Woodward. Chicago: University of Chicago Press, 1994.

_____. "China Policy in the New Age: Le Thang-tong (1460–1497) and Northern Relations." Paper presented at the annual meeting of the Association of Asian Studies. 2005.

_____. "Literati Culture and Integration in Dai Viet, c. 1430–c. 1840." *Modern Asian Studies* 31, no. 3 (1997): 665–687.

_____. "The Rise of the Coast: Trade, State, and Culture in Early Dai Viet." *Journal of Southeast Asian Studies* 37, no. 1 (February 2006): 103–122.

_____. *Vietnam, Ho Quy Ly, and the Ming (1371–1421)*. New Haven, Conn.: Yale University Press, 1985.

_____. "Vietnamese Embassies and Literati Contacts." Paper presented at the annual meeting of the Association of Asian Studies. 2001.

Wigan, Karen. "Culture, Power, and Place: The New Landscape of East Asian Regionalism." *American Historical Review* 104, no. 4 (October 1999): 1183–1201.

Wills, John E. *Embassies and Illusions: Dutch and Portuguese Envoys to Kang-shi, 1666–1687*. Cambridge, Mass.: Harvard University Press, 1984.

_____. "Great Qing and Its Southern Neighbors, 1760–1820: Secular Trends and Recovery from Crisis." Manuscript, University of Southern California. N.d. http://www.historycooperative.org/proceedings/interactions/wills.html.

_____. "South and Southeast Asia, Near East, Japan, and Korea." In *The Chinese Civilization from its Origins to Contemporary Times*, vol. 2, ed. Grandi Opere Einaudi and Maurizio Scapari. Forthcoming.

_____. "The South China Sea Is Not a Mediterranean: Implications for the History of Chinese Foreign Relations." M.s., University of Southern California, 2008.

_____. "Tribute, Defensiveness, and Dependency: Uses and Limits of Some Basic Ideas About Mid-Ch'ing Foreign Relations." *American Neptune* 48 (1988): 225–229.

Wohlforth, William. "The Stability of a Unipolar World." *International Security* 24, no. 1 (Summer 1999): 5–41.

_____. "Unipolarity, Status Competition, and Great-Power War." *World Politics* 61, no. 1 (2009): 28–57.

Wolferen, Karl Van. *The Enigma of Japanese Power*. New York: Knopf, 1989.

Wolters, O. W. "Le Van Huu's Treatment of Ly Than Ton's Reign (1127–1137)." In *Southeast Asian History and Historiography*, ed. C. D. Cowan and O. W. Wolters, 203–226. Ithaca, N.Y.: Cornell University Press, 1976.

———. *History, Culture, and Region in Southeast Asian Perspectives*. Singapore: Institute of Southeast Asian Studies, 1982.

———. *Two Essays on Dai-Viet in the Fourteenth Century*. New Haven, Conn.: Yale University Southeast Asia Studies, 1988.

Womack, Brantly. *China and Vietnam: The Politics of Asymmetry*. Cambridge: Cambridge University Press, 2006.

Wong, R. Bin.*China Transformed: Historical Change and the Limits of European Experience*. Ithaca, N.Y.: Cornell University Press, 1997.

Woodside, Alexander. *Lost Modernities: China, Vietnam, Korea, and the Hazards of World History*. Cambridge, Mass.: Harvard University Press, 2006.

———. "Territorial Order and Collective-Identity Tensions in Confucian Asia: China, Vietnam, Korea." *Daedalus* 127, no. 3 (Summer 1998): 191–221.

Wray, William. "The Seventeenth-Century Japanese Diaspora: Questions of Boundary and Policy." Manuscript, University of British Columbia. N.d.

Wright, David. "The Northern Frontier." In *A Military History of China*, ed. David A. Graff and Robin Higham, 57–80. Boulder, Colo.: Westview Press, 2002.

Wyatt, David. *Thailand: A Short History*. New Haven, Conn.: Yale University Press, 1984.

Yamamura, Kozo. "The Growth of Commerce in Medieval Japan." In *The Cambridge History of Japan*, vol. 3: *Medieval Japan*, 3rd ed., ed. Kozo Yamamura, 344–395. Cambridge: Cambridge University Press, 1990.

———. "Introduction." In *The Cambridge History of Japan*, vol. 3: *Medieval Japan*, ed. Kozo Yamamura, 1–45. Cambridge: Cambridge University Press, 1990.

Yoo, Geun-Ho. *Chosŏnjo taeoe sasangui hurum* [Flows of Ideologies on Foreign Relations During the Choson Period]. Seoul: Sungshin Women's University Press, 2004.

Yun, Peter I. "Rethinking the Tribute System: Korean States and Northeast Asian Interstate Relations, 600–1600," Ph.D. dissertation, University of California–Los Angeles, 1998.

Zakaria, Fareed. "A Conversation with Lee Kwan-yew." *Foreign Affairs* March/April (1994).

Zhao, Gang. "Shaping the Asian Trade Network: The Conception and Implementation of the Chinese Open Trade Policy, 1684–1840." Ph.D. dissertation, The Johns Hopkins University, 2006.

Zundorfer, Harriet T. "Ming China, the Imjin Waeran, and the Dynamics of Peace and War in East Asia, 1550–1600." Paper presented at the Korea Regional Seminar, Columbia University, 2004.

INDEX

alliance behavior, 70
Altan Khan, 148
anarchy, 3
anticolonial wars, 160
Ariwara No Narihira, 54
Ashikaga shoguns, 34, 41–42, 45–46,
　60–61, 67, 96, 118
Ashikaga Yoshimitsu, 67

balance-of-power politics, 3, 82–83
banner system, 151
barbarians: civilization vs., 29–30, 140;
　Manchurians and, 69. *See also*
　nomads
Beijing University, 162
Berkeley mafia, 163
Border Defense council, 94
borders: Burmese, 149; Chinese, 63–67,
　65, 144–49, 152–54; conflict along,
　85; fixed, 84, 157; frontiers vs.,
　139, 156–57; Japanese, 144, 154–56;
　Korean, 63–65, 65, 144–45, 154–56;
　mutually recognized, setting of, 23;

skirmishes at, 88–90, 92; Taiwanese,
　154–56; Vietnamese, 65–67, 66
Burma: borders of, 149; in status
　hierarchy, 59; tribute relations in, 67

Cambodia, 128–29
centralized territorial rule, history of, 25
Chieu Thong, 101
China: authority of, 56–57; borders
　of, 63–67, 65, 144–49, 152–54;
　bureaucratic administration in,
　32; civilization and idea of, 29–33;
　Confucian society in, 8–9, 25–26,
　43–46; dominance of, xiii, 2, 9–10,
　15, 54, 70, 83, 98, 107–8, 131, 161,
　166, 170; hegemony of, 167–71;
　Korea supported by, 1; leadership
　by, 167–71; linguistic traditions of,
　35; Manchu conquest of, 69, 83,
　103, 149–53; migration from, 130;
　military presence of, in Korea, 97–98;
　name of, 12–13; nomads threatening,
　9–11, 15, 90, 91; opponents of, 91;